Journal of Pentecostal Theology
Supplement Series
27

Editors
John Christopher Thomas
Rickie D. Moore
Steven J. Land .

T&T Clark International
A Continuum imprint

The Shepherding

Movement

Controversy and Charismatic

Ecclesiology

S. David Moore

T & T CLARK INTERNATIONAL
A Continuum imprint
LONDON • NEW YORK

Copyright © 2003 T&T Clark International
A Continuum imprint

Published by T&T Clark International
The Tower Building, 11 York Road, London SE1 7NX
15 East 26th Street, Suite 1703, New York, NY 10010

www.tandtclark.com

British Library Cataloguing-in-Publication Data
A catalogue record for this book is available from the British Library

Library of Congress Cataloging-in-Publication Data
A catalogue record for this book is available from the Library of Congress

Typeset by ISB Typesetting, Sheffield
Printed on acid-free paper in Great Britain by Cromwell Press, Trowbridge, Wiltshire

ISBN   0-8264-7159-5 (hardback)
       0-8264-7160-9 (paperback)

CONTENTS

Preface   vii
Acknowledgments   ix
Abbreviations   x

Chapter 1
PERSPECTIVES   1

Chapter 2
TURBULENT TIMES   16

Chapter 3
THE FORT LAUDERDALE FIVE   33

Chapter 4
A MOVEMENT IS BORN   46

Chapter 5
CHARISMATIC ECCLESIOLOGY   68

Chapter 6
CHARISMATIC CONTROVERSY   87

Chapter 7
THE DRAMA OF CONTROVERSY   99

Chapter 8
SUCCESS AND CONSOLIDATION   125

Chapter 9
STRUGGLE AND SEPARATION   154

Chapter 10
REFLECTIONS   179

Appendix 1   192
Appendix 2   194
Appendix 3   198

References and Sources   205
Index of Names   225

PREFACE

In February 1992, I was pursuing a practical ministry degree at Fuller Theological Seminary. Because I have a love for history, I decided to take an extension class on the history of the Pentecostal and Charismatic movements that was offered in Southern California by Oral Roberts University. Little did I realize how that decision would change my academic path. Dr Vinson Synan taught the modular class, and in a lunchtime conversation with a group of students, he learned of my pastoral participation with the Shepherding movement and he suggested that I think about writing a history. I liked the idea but I was unsure. I decided to take another class there, offered the next month, for which I wrote a final paper on the Shepherding movement. Dr Henry Lederle's comments on the paper were similar to Synan's. That was all I needed.

Ten years have now passed and this monograph is the culmination of my study of the Shepherding movement. Since 1995 I have given myself to extensive study of the movement's history and theology.

This work presents a complete history of the Shepherding movement. It is not, however, an exhaustive history. I have left out many events and details of the story. Nevertheless, given the limits of most readers' interest, I have yielded to good judgment and kept the narrative to a manageable size. I hope that it is an interesting and engaging chronicle.

I came to my research expecting a different end product. I had left the movement because of what I believed were its problems, and therefore I imagined I would write a more critical document. My commitment to proper historical method did not lead me there.

There were, no doubt, serious abuses of spiritual authority among the Shepherding movement's practitioners. I knew that going into my research. When I went beyond the polemical rhetoric, however, and studied the movement's leaders, constituents, critics, and documents, I found it was difficult to make categorical judgments.

I discovered that some of the issues attracting critics' charges, which initially seemed so black and white, became gray when I interviewed all sides. This went both ways. The defenses given for the movement's many casualties also proved inadequate. Still, I found no evidence that the Shepherding movement's principal leaders led a conspiracy to take over the Charismatic Renewal or had evil designs to exploit and dominate their followers. Quite the opposite was the case. The research suggested that the movement's five leaders were well-intentioned and well-motivated. This does not exonerate them for their mistakes, but it does argue for a different assessment of their legacy.

I have been surprised that books continue to be written and materials produced which purport to analyze the Shepherding movement based almost entirely on the charges of critics and disillusioned former members. One purpose for this history is to provide a more reasonably objective evidentiary perspective.

Those who want a thorough condemnation of the Shepherding movement will be disappointed with this study, and its proponents will perhaps feel that I have been too critical. Those judgments belong to the readers. However this work is considered, I have endeavored to provide a carefully researched, fair account.

It is significant that this account is more than the story of the Shepherding movement; it is a history of the Charismatic Renewal as well. For example, the narrative records the origins of the historic 1977 Conference on Charismatic Renewal in the Christian Churches in Kansas City, Missouri, and of the first meeting of the Charismatic Leaders Conference in Seattle, Washington, in 1971. Moreover, the controversy over the Shepherding movement's teachings reveals an unfortunate underside of the Renewal.

Indeed, the story of the controversy is both dramatic and saddening. Weaknesses and sins are apparent. While I never sought to needlessly expose individuals or groups to embarrassment, the narrative required an honest telling of the facts, which were occasionally painful to write. Nevertheless, my conscience was eased when I remembered how forthright and honest the Scriptures are in revealing humanity's failings. If anything, seeing the sins and weaknesses of David, Peter, and other biblical characters remind us of our own need for forgiveness. I trust this story will have that effect.

It has been said that the past is the greatest teacher we have. History tells stories that help those who listen decide their future course. I am convinced that the story of the Shepherding movement can indeed be of use to Charismatics, Pentecostals, and the whole body of Christ in developing an ecclesiology that is more closely correlated with discipleship.

ACKNOWLEDGMENTS

There are many special people who deserve to be thanked. This monograph was drawn largely from my doctoral dissertation at Regent University, Virginia Beach, VA, and I want to thank first my dissertation committee chair, Dr Vinson Synan, for his constant support and wise guidance in this project. To my other committee members, Dr J. Rodman Williams and Dr Russell West, thanks for being so available to me when I needed advice. Special thanks to Steven J. Land who not only served on my doctoral committee but served also as an editor to the monograph. His confidence in my scholarship was a great encouragement.

I am especially grateful for Jane McClish and Barbara Farfan, who not only worked to prepare the manuscript, but also gave helpful advice. Brutal honesty was essential. Thanks as well to Diane Heimer who read the manuscript and offered suggestions and corrections.

To the staff, elders, and congregation of New Hope Church in Monteca, CA, I am ever grateful. They were willing to give me away as I researched and wrote. Thank you.

To my children and wife, what can I say? I love them very much, and I realize they paid a great price along with me in the completion of this project. To my dear Patty, companion of over 30 years: you are a Godly woman whose example of faithfulness to God and family is a model for others to follow. You are the real hero in this endeavor, and I could not have finished without your support.

Finally, words are inadequate to express my thanks to the Lord Jesus, who met me so many times and guided me in this project. It was truly amazing. I am so privileged to be his servant.

ABBREVIATIONS

CBN	Christian Broadcasting Nework
CCRCC	Conference on Charismatic Renewal in the Christian Churches
CGM	Christian Growth Ministries
CRS	Charismatic Renewal Service
FCC	Federal Communications Commission
FGBMFI	Full Gospel Businessman's Fellowship International
HSTM	Holy Spirit Teaching Mission
IFA	Intercessors for America
LCRS	Lutheran Renewal Service
PCC	Presbyterian Charismatic Conference
World MAP	World Mission Assistance Plan

Chapter 1

PERSPECTIVES

Introduction

It hardly looked like a meeting of 30 of the best-known leaders of the burgeoning Charismatic Renewal. Tempers flared, accusations were exchanged, and tension filled the air.[1] The meeting in Minneapolis on 9–10 August 1975 came to be known as the 'Shoot-out at the Curtis Hotel'.[2] *Logos Journal* likened the meeting to 'the tradition of councils at Jerusalem in the book of Acts'.[3] While no doubt an overstatement, this was indeed a crucial meeting.

The leaders were gathered to deal with what, at the time, was being called 'the most controversial issue ever to hit the Charismatic movement'.[4] That issue was over the teachings and practice of discipleship and pastoral care as taught by five prominent leaders in the Charismatic Renewal: Don Basham, Ern Baxter, Bob Mumford, Derek Prince, and Charles Simpson. Together, their ministries had become associated with Christian Growth Ministries based in Fort Lauderdale, Florida. *New Wine Magazine*, published by Christian Growth Ministries, had become the most widely circulated periodical in the Charismatic movement.[5]

The five teachers were advocating the need for discipleship through personal pastoral care or, as they termed it, 'Shepherding' care. In Shepherding care a believer was to submit to a 'personal pastor' who would help the individual develop Christian maturity. This teaching was widely circulated

---

1. Don Basham, 'Toward Healing the Rift', *New Wine Magazine* (May 1976), 20-22.
2. Charles Simpson, *The Challenge to Care* (Ann Arbor, MI: Servant, 1986), 82.
3. 'Logos Report: What Really Happened at Minneapolis?', *Logos Journal* (November/December 1975), 58-62 (58).
4. 'What Really Happened at Minneapolis?', 58.
5. While *New Wine Magazine* is the full published title of the periodical, for brevity we shall refer to *New Wine* henceforth.

through articles in *New Wine* and through the five teachers' audiotapes. The five were popular and well traveled on the national Charismatic teaching circuit, and this added to the spread of the teachings on shepherding and discipleship.

By 1975, Basham, Baxter, Mumford, Prince, and Simpson were the *de facto* leaders of an emerging movement in the Charismatic Renewal that not only emphasized pastoral care but focused on a church structure of cell groups led by lay pastors. Each lay pastor was submitted to another pastor in a kind of chain of command, with a senior or presiding pastor overseeing a local church network of pastoral leaders. Each presiding congregational pastor was in turn submitted to one of the five teachers or his designate.

The movement also taught that any spiritual leader or pastor who exercised spiritual authority needed to be under spiritual authority. This, coupled with the movement's practice of translocal pastoral relationships with the five teachers, led some critics to think that the movement was trying to take over the Charismatic Renewal and form a new Charismatic denomination.[6] This allegation was one of the major points of argument at the Minneapolis meeting. Charismatic Catholic scholar Kilian McDonnell summarized the critics, charges and concerns:

> Rightly or wrongly, the Ft Lauderdale men were perceived as advocating a kind of individualism, empire building, constructing a highly personal following which bound together as a pyramid…an interlocking web of sheep and shepherds… At the top of the pyramid, doctrinally and financially stood the men from Ft Lauderdale… The dynamics of this conception was seen as leading to a new denomination, whether Christian Growth Ministries and *New Wine* wished it or not.[7]

6. The issue of becoming a denomination or not is inherent to the movement's history and an ongoing part of its controversy and tension. When the five leaders used the term they were referring to a formally and legally organized corporation of churches. Using this definition they never became a denomination. They were not using the term in its sense in modern sociological classification. The movement is hard to classify because of its curious mix of separatism and ecumenism and its Charismatic versus institutional tension. Sociologically, I believe the movement is best described as a religious sect. See Richard Quebedeaux, *The New Charismatics II* (San Francisco: Harper & Row, 2nd rev. edn, 1983), 175-79; Margaret Poloma, *The Charismatic Movement* (Boston, MA: Twayne, 1982), 193-95.

7. Kilian McDonnell, 'Seven Documents on the Discipleship Question', in *idem* (ed.), *Presence, Power, Praise: Documents on the Charismatic Renewal* (3 vols.; Collegeville, MN: Liturgical Press, 1980), II, 116-47 (120).

This controversial emerging group became known as the Shepherding movement[8] and ushered in what British Charismatic author and teacher Michael Harper, echoing the above *Logos Journal* statement, called, 'far and away the most disturbing controversy to hit the Charismatic Renewal'.[9] Writing in 1980, Kilian McDonnell observed:

> One of the characteristics of the Charismatic Renewal is its *de facto* ecumenical dimension; indeed, it has been called the most significant force on the ecumenical scene today. Given its unitive function, there was some surprise to find that the Renewal was itself torn by division over the discipleship question, which became the most divisive issue since the rise of the Charismatic Renewal in the historic churches.[10]

The Minneapolis meeting, attended by the five Shepherding movement leaders, along with Charismatic patriarchs Dennis Bennett, Harald Bredesen, Charismatic publisher Dan Malachuk, Charismatic broadcasting pioneer Pat Robertson and others, was an attempt to address this controversy and establish dialogue. Instead, according to participant Don Basham, the two-day meeting was a time 'of almost total frustration', with the strained atmosphere allowing 'little progress'.[11]

Unfortunately for the Charismatic Renewal, the struggle over Shepherding became a very public debate in 1975 and 1976. The controversy made the *New York Times* with the headline: 'Charismatic Movement is Facing Internal Discord Over a Teaching Called Discipling'.[12] The popular evangelical periodical *Christianity Today* carried a cover page headline: 'The Deepening Rift in the Charismatic Movement'.[13] Moreover, all the significant Charismatic publications carried articles on the struggle from the fall of 1975 and throughout 1976. The controversy was high drama among Pentecostals and Charismatics.

---

8.   The movement has sometimes been called the discipleship/Shepherding movement or just the discipleship movement. The term Shepherding movement used in this history is concise and more descriptive of the movement's emphasis on personal pastoral care. For Charles Simpson and those who continue the movement's heritage, the term Covenant movement is preferred.

9.   Michael Harper, *Three Sisters* (Wheaton, IL: Tyndale, 1979), 30.

10.   McDonnell, 'Seven Documents', II, 116.

11.   Basham, 'Toward Healing', 20.

12.   'Charismatic Movement is Facing Internal Discord Over a Teaching Called "Discipling"', *New York Times* (16 September 1975), sec. C31, col. 1.

13.   Edward E. Plowman, 'The Deepening Rift in the Charismatic Movement', *Christianity Today* (10 October 1975), 52-54.

   This monograph seeks to provide a contextualized history of the Shepherding movement with a particular emphasis on the years of controversy. The historical narrative will present the emergence and development of the movement's teachings, emphasizing its theological self-understanding with special focus on its distinctive ecclesiology and pastoral practices. Throughout, my aim is to convey the mindset of the five leaders.

Historiographic Issues

This history is important for several reasons. The story of the Shepherding movement provides the contemporary church, particularly Pentecostal-Charismatic churches, with a highly relevant chronicle of the challenges and problems that involve the renewal and revitalization of church structures.[14] The Shepherding movement was very focused on developing a practical ecclesiology and finding new ways of 'doing church'.[15] The movement was developing and practicing a cell church model in the early 1970s long before it had become a more popular trend. Some of its controversial practices in church life are now readily accepted as viable options for church structure.[16] Moreover, studying the Shepherding movement's successes and problems in its attempts to provide an environment for

---

   14. Church history reminds us that renewal is more than personal and theological revitalization. While George Whitefield's preaching was more popular in sheer numbers than John Wesley's, it was Wesley's insights into lay leaders and small groups that produced an enduring church renewal. See Howard A. Snyder, *The Radical Wesley and Patterns for Church Renewal* (Downers Grove, IL: InterVarsity Press, 1980).

   15. I write as a participant in the Pentecostal-Charismatic tradition. I would suggest that among Pentecostals and Charismatics a more thoroughgoing and intentional ecclesiology is sorely needed. Perhaps this historical account will stimulate further movement in this direction.

   16. The Shepherding movement used the terms 'house church' and 'cell group' synonymously. I shall follow its use of terms. In *Home Cell Groups and House Churches*, one of the few academic studies on the ecclesiology of house churches and cell churches, a distinction is made between the two terms. House churches are groups that 'embody all aspects of a New Testament Church' but meet in homes not church buildings. They are not subunits of an institutional church. Cell groups, on the other hand, meet in homes but are controlled by a host church of which they are a subunit. Given these definitions the Shepherding movement first began as a house church movement and became a cell church movement over time. C. Kirk Hadaway, Stuart A. Wright and Francis M. DuBose, *Home Cell Groups and House Churches* (Nashville, TN: Broadman, 1987), 13-14.

practical discipleship and spiritual formation may help today's church do a better job in producing devoted followers of Jesus.

Issues of the exercise of spiritual authority, methods for pastoral care and producing authentic Christian community continue to be debated and written about. The Shepherding movement's story can contribute significantly to this process since the above issues were a part of the movement's distinctive theology. While this work does not center on a theological analysis of the movement's teachings, it does present the movement's distinctive doctrines as the movement defined them, seeking to show the reasons for and influences upon its development. Further, as a part of the theological definition, brief discussion is occasionally given to the movement's biblical foundations for its teachings. This focus can provide other researchers with a starting point in analyzing the theology of the Shepherding movement.

The story of the controversy over the teachings on the Shepherding movement is an engaging narrative that warrants reflection. The contemporary church continues to debate doctrinal and practical differences. At this time of writing (2000), Pentecostals and Charismatics are struggling over the validity of revivals in Toronto and Pensacola and the unusual emotional and physical phenomena associated with them. It is my hope that the dramatic chronicle of Charismatic Renewal leaders' unsuccessful attempts to resolve controversy and dispute will be instructive to today's leaders in developing better systems that encourage dialogue and reconciliation.[17] The history of the Shepherding controversy illustrates how difficult it is to appropriately confront other leaders and how challenging it is for other leaders to hear and respond to critics' charges.

Understanding the Shepherding movement's emphasis on apostolic ministry and relational networks of pastors may help provide lessons for an emerging trend called the 'new apostolic' paradigm.[18] Championed by respected church leaders, the apostolic paradigm emphasizes the present-day ministry of apostles who lead networks of churches that are joined together by relationship as opposed to ecclesiastical structure. There are

---

17. It is obvious that there are no easy answers for handling disputes and differences within the Pentecostal and Charismatic movements. The incredible diversity and lack of any jointly recognized adjudicating structures present a seemingly insurmountable problem. Notwithstanding, it seems appropriate that more focused dialogue be given to addressing the challenge.

18. C. Peter Wagner, *The New Apostolic Churches* (Ventura, CA: Regal Books, 1998); *idem*, *Churchquake* (Ventura, CA: Regal Books, 1999).

some remarkable similarities of terms and approach to church structures. It is hoped that this narrative will provide some needed perspective for this growing movement.

Historiographically, the Shepherding movement deserves a detailed treatment. Significantly, the movement was the first identifiable, non-denominational church movement within the larger Charismatic Renewal in the United States.[19] Moreover, it gained broad influence and brought about the first major crisis in the Charismatic Renewal. According to Pentecostal historian Vinson Synan, 'The Shepherding movement was the first of its kind to spread in influence among both Charismatics and Pentecostals and also the first to divide them. It came as kind of a pan-Pentecostal/Charismatic movement.'[20]

While there is little question of the movement's broad influence, documenting its constituency is challenging. No official records of membership were kept, since the movement never saw itself as an official organization. Charles Simpson estimated that 50,000 adherents were directly related to the Shepherding movement at its peak in 1982 with 500 associated churches.[21] According to missiologist and church statistician David Barrett in the *World Christian Encyclopedia*, an estimated 100,000 people were affiliated with the movement.[22] Its influence, however, went far beyond these estimates. For example, *New Wine*, which became the movement's principal publication, had broad distribution with a monthly circulation of over 110,000[23] in 1976, and at its peak was distributed in 140 nations. Its circulation far surpassed, in the mid-1970s, the other popular Charismatic periodicals, *Logos Journal* and *Charisma*. What makes this even more significant is that more than 50 percent of *New Wine*'s readership were

19.   Some may suggest that Calvary Chapel, pastored by Chuck Smith, and its associated churches which predated the Shepherding movement, are a part of the Charismatic Renewal. From my perspective, Calvary Chapel churches are only remotely Charismatic. Their services are not Charismatic in practice. The charismata are discouraged in public worship services and put into ancillary services if practiced at all.

20.   Vinson Synan, telephone interview with author, 14 February 1996.

21.   Robert Digitale, 'An Idea Whose Time Is Gone?', *Christianity Today* (19 March 1990), 38-42 (40); Charles Simpson, personal interview with author, 3 August 1998.

22.   David Barrett, *World Christian Encyclopedia* (New York: Oxford University, 1982), 722.

23.   Don Basham, 'Forum: CGM and New Wine', *New Wine* (December 1976), 31. No complete year-by-year record of *New Wine* circulation was available. I did find one note in a letter of Charles Simpson's that said circulation was as high as 130,000 (Charles Simpson, letter to Carolyn Rodman, 18 September 1974, private holding, 2).

leaders.[24] In addition, the five teachers distributed their own newsletters, tapes, and books over the years of their association. Statistics for the five-year period from 1979–84 show a distribution of 4,500,000 magazines, 1,000,000 newsletters, 600,000 cassette tapes, and 250,000 books.[25]

Basham, Baxter, Mumford, Prince, and Simpson spoke often at large national teaching conferences and conventions in the broader Charismatic Renewal, impacting thousands on a regular basis. Perhaps the high-water mark for both the Charismatic Renewal and the Shepherding movement was the 1977 Kansas City Conference on Charismatic Renewal in the Christian Churches. After the Charismatic Catholics, the Shepherding movement had the largest representation with over 12,000 in attendance.[26]

Michael Harper observed that the considerable gifts of the five teachers, coupled with their committed and talented support group's 'skillful and sophisticated use of media', contributed to the movement's influence far beyond those directly linked through relationship to the five key leaders.[27] The movement was always a vanguard in using arts and media to creatively advance its teachers' messages. Through *New Wine*, audio and videotapes, music and books, the teachings that were distinctive to the movement were published far beyond its direct sphere of influence. This, along with the movement's own practice of these teachings, fueled the great controversy.

While the association of the five men ended by 1986, the movement's influence continues. As recently as 1993, esteemed evangelical theologian Alister McGrath said 'their influence is still considerable', referring to Charles Simpson's continuing leadership of the movement's remnant, along with others that were at one time in their association.[28]

In addition to the Shepherding movement's significant place in Charismatic Renewal history, other factors suggest the need for an objective and dispassionate history. First, in *The Modern Researcher*, Barzun and Graff have said that 'the value of a piece of testimony usually increases in proportion to the nearness in time and space between the witness and events

24. Fundraising case for *New Wine* Memorandum, 1984 (unpublished internal document; Mobile, AL: Integrity Communications), 6.

25. Don Basham *et al.*, *Integrity Update* (Mobile, AL: Integrity Communications, 1984), audiocassette.

26. Synan, Interview, 14 February 1996.

27. Harper, *Three Sisters*, 30.

28. Alister McGrath (ed.), *The Blackwell Encyclopedia of Modern Christian Thought* (Cambridge, MA: Basil Blackwell, 1993), 431-32.

about which he testifies'.[29] Considering this perspective, the movement needs to be studied while its participants, critics, and documents are readily accessible. Though the movement presents bibliographic challenges that will be discussed below, the accessibility of numerous primary sources serve as a rich resource for study.

Admittedly, some historiographers believe that one's familiarity with recent events invites 'personal involvement in the events that may be so great it is difficult to step back toward objective interpretation'.[30] Nevertheless, the need for accurate and exhaustive sources is compelling and necessitates this historical study.

The issue of objectivity is always a challenge in historical method. I am convinced that total objectivity is practically impossible because the historical process itself is subjective. For every historian 'the selection of facts is a judgment passed upon their importance. With selection and individual judgment comes partiality.'[31] What the historian must do is commit to a methodology of research that makes every effort to 'let the materials of history speak on their own terms...'[32] It is also important that the historian recognize the subjectivity factor and acknowledge personal bias.[33]

With this perspective in mind, let it be said that I am writing as a former insider of the Shepherding movement. This fact lends itself to an acquaintance with the unique jargon and terms of the movement, which is most important for accurate definition. Also, I left the movement in 1984 because of concerns over what I believed to be doctrinal and practical extremes. Fortunately I did not exit hurt or disillusioned. In fact, my overall experience with the movement was quite positive. Together, I hope these factors lend themselves to an ability to be somewhat objective. It is for the reader to decide if I have written fairly and dispassionately.

An additional historiographical concern is the issue of context. It is fair to say that Pentecostals, and to some degree Charismatics, given their restorationist tendencies, have neglected historical connections; and, in particular, they have neglected context. Seeking to avoid this tendency, I

29. Jacques Barzun and Henry F. Graff, *The Modern Researcher* (Boston, MA: Houghton Mifflin, 1995), 158.

30. James Bradley and Richard A. Muller, *Church History: An Introduction to Research, Reference Works, and Methods* (Grand Rapids: Eerdmans, 1995), 34.

31. Bradley and Muller, *Church History*, 48.

32. Bradley and Muller, *Church History*, 49.

33. Bradley and Muller, *Church History*, 51.

have sought to consider the Shepherding movement in its larger context. Primarily this project is a narrative history of the movement's development and defining events, but its context is a vital part of the story. According to Richard Marius, 'Good historians see things in context including people and events surrounding the event they seek to describe.'[34] This must always be considered so that one avoids an undue isolation of the people and events studied. With this in mind, I have made a deliberate effort to understand the unique environment from which the Shepherding movement emerged.[35]

Lastly, while the Shepherding movement is still relatively recent history, I believe enough time has passed to begin to see its place within the Charismatic Renewal and the larger religious history of North America. For the most part, the anger and dispute have now faded, as have the strident defenses.[36] It is hoped that this account will provide future researchers with an accurate record of what the movement taught and practiced against a chronology of the movement's history.[37]

34. Richard Marius, *A Short Guide to Writing about History* (New York: Harper-Collins, 1989), 41.

35. Historical origins are always complex and multidimensional. Sociologist Margaret Poloma, in her 1982 study on the Charismatic movement, discussed the challenge in understanding the rise of social movements and the tendency to oversimplify causation. Poloma said, 'One trap is to reduce all explanation to a single cause, be it psychological, historical, behavioral, or structural.' Because of this I have placed the Shepherding movement in the context of the larger Charismatic Renewal and against the backdrop of the North American religious and cultural scene at the time of its emergence. While this project is primarily a historical study, I have nevertheless made a distinct effort to present the historical record noting sociological, cultural, circumstantial, and even personal issues that were a part of the movement's origin and story. Still, I write as a historian first who agrees with Poloma's assessment that 'basic to understanding the rise of any social movement is an awareness of its history'. Poloma, *The Charismatic Movement*, 32, 37.

36. I was surprised to find so many of the movement's most vocal critics, including Pat Robertson, Ralph Mahoney, and Ralph Wilkerson, unwilling to be interviewed. Also, FGBMFI was uncooperative. For a few people, the Shepherding movement remains a most painful memory. I also encountered many former participants who continue to speak against the movement.

37. Students of church history are aware that movements perceived as heretical often had their documents destroyed leaving us with only the critics' voices to tell us their story. This document at least gives the historical record a guide to the movement and its materials with a reasonably objective perspective.

Bibliographic Sources

As a former insider to the Shepherding movement, I have had unique access to the personalities and documents associated with it. This access has provided 73 interviews, totaling over 200 hours. The movement's two most influential leaders, Bob Mumford and Charles Simpson, were fully cooperative and were interviewed extensively. The audiotaped interviews included not only the movement's participants, but also some critics and observers. In addition, the internal documents, correspondence, audio- and videotapes, and publications of the movement have been located, identified, and in most cases, copied.[38]

In considering sources for further study of the Shepherding movement, the very fact of its controversy has posed a challenge for study. In general, there are two very different kinds of sources available: those sources that propagated and defended the movement, largely its internal materials; and those sources highly critical of the movement's teachings. The lack of critical objectivity in these materials requires careful review.

Three exceptions stand out. First, is Kilian McDonnell's 'Seven Documents on the Discipleship Question' in his three-volume work *Presence, Power, Praise*. McDonnell provides a brief but objective survey of the controversy over the Shepherding movement in the 1970s.[39] He has collected, as the title suggests, seven historical documents from this controversy.[40]

The second helpful resource is *The Discipling Dilemma*, edited by Flavil Yeakley, Jr. While focusing on a discipling movement within the Churches of Christ, this book contains much helpful bibliographic data on materials written about the Shepherding movement. In Part III of the book, researcher Don Vinzant explores the historical roots of Crossroads Church of Christ's emphasis on authoritarian discipleship. In Vinzant's view, the five teachers from Ft Lauderdale indirectly had great influence on this church and a contemporary Shepherding-like movement that emerged from it. While more negative than McDonnell's material, *The Discipling Dilemma* reflects careful research.[41]

---

38. S. David Moore, 'The Shepherding Movement in Historical Perspective' (Unpublished MA thesis, Oral Roberts University, Tulsa, OK, 1996).

39. McDonnell, *Seven Documents*, II, 116-23.

40. McDonnell, *Seven Documents*, II, 123-47.

41. Flavil Yeakley (ed.), *The Discipling Dilemma* (Nashville, TN: Gospel Advocate, 1988), 123-67.

The third resource, *Home Cell Groups and House Churches*, explains the emergence of contemporary 'innovations in church structure'.[42] The book studies the origins, diversity, and potential of home cell groups and house churches worldwide, and among its case studies is the Houston Covenant Church, a part of the Shepherding movement.[43] The authors treat the movement favorably. It is the only written study that seriously explores the movement's innovative ecclesiology.

Another book deserving mention is Ron Burks and Vicki Burks's *Damaged Disciples*. The couple were long-time members of the movement. The book's subtitle, *Casualties of Authoritarian Churches and the Shepherding Movement*, reveals its focus on perceived abuses. The first one-half of the book gives a historical account of the movement with reasonable objectivity. As the book moves into theological analysis, however, it loses its objectivity, and the authors' personal disillusionment seems to affect their interpretation, in that their arguments become more strident and strained. Nevertheless, the book accurately depicts how many former members who left the Shepherding movement see its teachings and practices.[44]

Essential for an accurate history of the Shepherding movement is a complete collection of *New Wine*. The magazine, published from 1969 through 1986, was the principal publishing voice of the five teachers and the movement. I have been able to secure a complete collection that has provided an objective means to determine key dates and to observe the emergence of the distinctive teachings. *New Wine*, in many ways, is in itself a kind of mini-history of the Charismatic Renewal, reflecting the optimism and euphoria that characterized the early days of renewal. Later issues reveal a more pragmatic and realistic tone as Charismatics matured.

A few *New Wine* articles deserve special mention because of their historical importance. 'Birth of a Mission', written by Don Basham in the April 1970 issue, provides an excellent history of the founding and early years of the Holy Spirit Teaching Mission in Ft Lauderdale.[45] The Holy Spirit Teaching Mission and its founder, Eldon Purvis, indirectly brought the five Shepherding teachers together through its teaching conferences

42. Hadaway, Wright and DuBose, *Home Cell Groups*, 8.
43. Hadaway, Wright and DuBose, *Home Cell Groups*, 142-56.
44. Ron Burks and Vicki Burks, *Damaged Disciples: Casualties of Authoritarian Churches and the Shepherding Movement* (Grand Rapids: Zondervan, 1992).
45. Don Basham, 'Birth of a Mission', *New Wine* (April 1970), 12-16.

and its magazine, *New Wine*. The Holy Spirit Teaching Mission changed its name to Christian Growth Ministries in 1972.

'How It All Began', also written by Basham, in the June 1984 issue of *New Wine*, is a helpful survey of the movement's history up to 1984.[46] The June 1984 issue of *New Wine* carries 'An Open Letter to Our Readers and Christian Friends', written by Simpson, that has important historical information.[47] These articles and many more that could be listed demonstrate the importance of *New Wine* in documenting the movement's story.

I have reviewed the two other major Charismatic periodicals contemporary to the Shepherding movement, *Logos* and *Charisma*, and also the Catholic Charismatic publication, *New Covenant*. Much historical material for this project was found and is listed in the bibliography. Relevant articles from other Christian periodicals and newspapers, as well as secular publications, were also reviewed though not always cited.

The Shepherding movement blazed a trail in the use of audiotaped Bible teaching. Millions of tapes were distributed over the years. I was able to secure more than a thousand relevant tapes. This provided much insight into not only the movement's teachings, but its mood as well. Tapes significant to historical and theological study are listed in the bibliography.

Of great help in documenting the emergence of the movement are the tapes from the September 1975 National Men's Shepherds Conference held in Kansas City. These tapes are most helpful in revealing the mindset of the movement in the midst of the growing controversy. Tapes from the Shepherding movement's 1977 regional men's conferences are especially important in following the maturing theology and momentum as the movement grew.

I located and reviewed tapes from the first two Shepherds conferences held in 1973 and 1974. Though I was not able to locate tapes of all sessions, the ones I listened to provided a unique perspective on the movement's seminal teachings.

Finally, three documents have proven very significant in providing key dates. Glen Roachelle, an associate of Charles Simpson and pastor in the movement, wrote an unpublished document titled 'Chronology' that gives key dates and events for the movement into 1978.[48] The document was produced for a historical record. Charles Simpson's unpublished manu-

---

46. Don Basham, 'How It All Began', *New Wine* (June 1984), 10-15.

47. Charles Simpson, 'An Open Letter to Our Readers and Christian Friends', *New Wine* (June 1984), 17-21.

48. Glen Roachelle, 'Chronology' (unpublished paper, 1978).

scripts, 'Another Kind of Storm' and 'A Covenant', provide invaluable historical information, specifically of his church in Mobile, AL, and generally of the larger Shepherding movement.[49] 'A Covenant' is particularly valuable for its presentation of the movement's understanding of covenant with God and humanity.

To better understand the theology and ecclesiology of the Shepherding movement, several sources need mention. Simpson's two books, *The Challenge to Care* and *The Covenant and the Kingdom*, provide insight to the doctrinal self-understanding of the movement.[50] Simpson's Covenant Life Seminar on ten audiocassettes is especially important in that it was recorded in 1977 when the movement was experiencing momentum and growth.[51] It was designed for all those new to Simpson's part of the movement, but it was also circulated beyond Simpson's sphere of influence. Bob Mumford's *Focusing on Present Issues*,[52] written in 1979 as an apologetic document, defends Shepherding care and covenant.

As would be expected, critics have often been less than charitable and have frequently made false and undocumented accusations. Conversely, some pro-Shepherding material is reactive. What has helped the process of sorting out the truth has been the personal correspondence, newsletters, minutes, and other periodical literature. Bob Mumford provided me access to all his personal files on the movement. Also, Charles Simpson gave me full and unrestricted access to his rather exhaustive collection of correspondence and documentation. Both Mumford and Simpson kept the documents of their critics. In addition, each person interviewed supplied documentation whenever possible.

To refine and nuance my understanding of the Shepherding movement and to establish a more exhaustive foundation of sources, I traveled to Mumford's Raleigh, North Carolina offices and Simpson's Mobile, Alabama offices to review materials personally. I also traveled to the Holy Spirit Research Center at Oral Roberts University in Tulsa, Oklahoma. Besides being able to search their Pentecostal and Charismatic periodicals

49. Charles Simpson, 'Another Kind of Storm' (unpublished paper, 1979); *idem*, 'A Covenant' (unpublished paper, 1980).

50. Charles Simpson (ed.), *The Covenant and the Kingdom* (Tonbridge, Kent: Sovereign World, 1995); *idem*, *The Challenge to Care*.

51. Charles Simpson, *The Covenant Life Seminar* (10 tapes; Mobile, AL: Charles Simpson Ministries, 1977).

52. Bob Mumford, *Focusing on Present Issues* (Hollywood, FL: LifeChangers, 1979), 1-24.

collection, I found helpful files at the Research Center on the movement and its leaders.

At the David du Plessis Center at Fuller Theological Seminary in Pasadena, California, I found many historical documents. Additionally, I contacted the archives of the Assemblies of God and the Full Gospel Businessmen's Fellowship International, seeking specific documents.

Nearly four years of research have produced substantial documentation to provide for a fair, accurate, and thorough history of the Shepherding movement. This also explains the large and comprehensive bibliography. Since this project serves as a beginning place in understanding the movement, I have chosen to include sources beyond those cited in the text. In doing this I have provided a foundation for further research.

In summary, I believe that my commitment to a careful methodology of research, along with the coaching of my respected mentors, has guided me in the appraisal of materials and in the writing process. The end result is an informative contribution to historical study.

Overview

The following narrative is primarily focused on a 16-year period from 1970 to 1986 that covers the association of the movement's leaders. While their association began in 1970, it was not until 1974 that the Shepherding movement became a distinct expression of the Charismatic Renewal which would continue until 1986. The narrative follows this general chronology, but it is not seamless. The movement's story is unique, given its composition of five leaders, two centers, and interaction with the larger renewal. Some aspects of this history are developed to a logical endpoint, and the narrative then returns to follow another part of the story. The movement's ecclesiological development is always considered.

Although I have not ignored the other leaders, I have given more attention to Bob Mumford and Charles Simpson. I have done this for three reasons. First, the leadership of these two men was more critical than that of the other three to the development and maturation of the Shepherding movement. Second, I had more documentation on their stories. And third, to give equal attention to all five men would have made an already complex story more difficult to follow.

To guide the reader, I want to chart the course of the narrative. Chapter 2 provides an overall context for the rise of the Charismatic Renewal—from which the Shepherding movement developed—and explains the unique circumstances that drew the movement's leaders together. Chapter 3 then introduces the five men and presents their perspective on the times. Chapter 4 traces their early association, the emergence of their distinctive teachings, and the developments in Ft Lauderdale and Mobile. The distinctive ecclesiology of the movement is explored in Chapter 5. The heated controversy over the discipleship and Shepherding teachings is the subject of Chapters 6 and 7. Chapter 8 charts the Shepherding movement's growth and consolidation to 1986. Chapter 9 tells the story of the dissolution of the movement and follows each leader's journey thereafter. Finally, Chapter 10 offers a summary evaluation and lessons to be learned from the movement in the light of contemporary developments. All told, it is a history both ordinary and dramatic.

Chapter 2

TURBULENT TIMES

The Sixties and Beyond

Whatever one thinks of Richard Nixon, he brilliantly read the times in 1968 and adeptly maneuvered his way to being elected as the United States' thirty-seventh president. Addressing the concerns of 'the silent majority' of 'Middle America', Nixon recognized the conservative back-lash to the social upheaval that characterized the sixties. Nixon offered a vision of stability, law and order, and government retrenchment.[1] For many Americans, Nixon's election signaled hope as 1968 ended. It was a year they were glad to see end, and a year now infamous in United States history with the assassinations of Martin Luther King, Jr and Robert Kennedy, the Tet Offensive in Vietnam, the debacle of the 1968 Democratic convention in Chicago, and race riots. 1968 came to symbolize the turmoil of the times. The sixties, by all accounts, was a tumultuous decade in US history, a decade 'marked by moral revolution'.[2]

The 1960s were marked by both vision and disillusion. John Kennedy's campaign for a 'New Frontier' ended with his assassination in 1963. Lyndon Johnson's plan for a 'Great Society' had a momentous and lasting beginning but was overshadowed as the trauma and division over the Vietnam War forced Johnson to resign his presidency. The idealistic euphoria among the young counterculture that became so popularized in San Francisco's 1967 Summer of Love, and reached its apex with 1969's Wood-stock, was forever lost with the stabbings and beatings at the Rolling Stone's California Altamont Speedway concert in December 1969, an ironic end to a turbulent decade.

1.   David Farber (ed.), 'The Silent Majority and Talk About Revolution', in *idem* (ed.), *The Sixties... From Memory to History* (Chapel Hill, NC: University of North Carolina Press, 1994), 291-316.
2.   Mark Noll, *A History of the United States and Canada* (Grand Rapids: Eerdmans, 1993), 442.

The above portrayal of the 1960s is admittedly a stereotype of the times. Nevertheless, it reflects the popular perception that many religious conservatives had of the period and provides a larger contextual backdrop to the emergence of the Charismatic Renewal in the 1960s.[3] Beyond the popular cultural icons that people use to define the 1960s—rock music, The Beatles, the hippies, student protests—the deeper, more pervasive areas of social change that characterized the decade need to be recognized.

The affluence and optimism of the post World War II era were fertile ground for the continuing rise of liberal secularism.[4] By the 1960s, the power structures of the United States, the political and education institutions, the media, and system of commerce were, for the most part, entirely secularized. The practice of religion was a private matter not to affect 'modern man's' public and social pursuits. In 1965, secularization's effect on religion was illustrated with the *New York Times* and *New Yorker* columns featuring the 'God is Dead' theology.[5] Many believed that religious practice would continue to fade.[6]

The secularization had fostered a growing liberalism in North American culture that affected social conditions. The radicalization of many young university students came to symbolize the 'New Left'. The 1964 dispute over distribution of political materials at the University of California's Berkeley campus and free speech movement that followed, popularized growing student unrest over issues of social injustice and led the way toward the later protests against the Vietnam War.

The greatest expression of the liberalism of the 1960s was the Civil Rights movement, which so dramatically confronted the racial divide in the nation. Violence, protest, riots, and political reaction were center stage for much of the decade. In the end, significant victories were won by African Americans. Nevertheless, the Civil Rights movement served to illustrate not only the ills of the larger culture, but to manifest division in the

3. I am only seeking to describe this era in US history. The analysis made reflects a necessary perspective for the emergence of the Shepherding movement within the larger Charismatic Renewal. For a nuanced perspective of the sixties from several historians see Farber (ed.), *The Sixties*; Todd Gittlin, *The Sixties* (New York: Bantam Books, 1993).

4. Robert M. Collins, 'Growth of Liberalism in the Sixties', in Farber (ed.), *The Sixties*, 11-44.

5. See Thomas J.J. Altizer and William Hamilton, *Radical Theology and the Death of God* (New York: Bobb-Merrill, 1966); Harvey Cox, *The Secular City* (New York: Macmillan, 1965).

6. Quebedeaux, *The New Charismatics*, 1-2, 216-18.

Christian community. It was clear that most white, evangelical, conservative Christians had kept their distance or had openly opposed the battle for racial equality.

The feminist movement with its call for gender egalitarianism, Caesar Chavez and the United Farm Workers' strike in California, the rise of Black power, and the call for social justice for Native Americans were but a part of the overall public turmoil that characterized 1960s America. In addition, as historian Mark Noll has observed:

> Disorder in public life seemed also to be matched by disorder in private. Whether an actual sexual revolution occurred in the 1960s or there was simply a new frankness about practices already habitual in private, the public became ineluctably aware of shifting values. More and more people talked about a relaxation of sexual standards; less and less restraint hindered public discussion of sexual issues. The feminist movement, the increased participation of women in the job market, the rising divorce rate, the widespread availability of pornography, and the public advocacy of homosexuality were symptoms of upheaval in family and sexual ethics.[7]

The growing counterculture of hippies, students, and intellectuals who were experimenting with and normalizing the use of drugs, also reflected the shifting values within North American culture. Further, conservatives saw the counterculture's anti-authoritarianism and anti-institutionalism as a threat to the fabric of society.

Against this social revolution backdrop, a conservative backlash began to emerge, with Nixon's election leading the way. Underneath the public conservatism was a new religious conservatism as well.

The 1960s had marked a significant decline among North America's mainline denominations, as many of the mainline denominational clergy and leaders, already 'thoroughly secularized',[8] sought to accommodate the changing times. Increasingly, greater toleration was given to theological dissent.[9] The Roman Catholic Church in America began the 1960s with talk of a 'post-Protestant era', especially given previous decades of growth and the election of Catholic John F. Kennedy as president. But by the latter part of the decade, the Catholic Church was facing a vast exit of priests, monks, and nuns, as well as open challenges to many of its fundamental

---

7.   Noll, *History*, 442.

8.   Quebedeaux, *The New Charismatics*, 217.

9.   While many saw this as entirely negative, the new toleration would later prove positive for clergy embracing the belief of neo-Pentecostalism. See Quebedeaux, *The New Charismatics*, 215-16.

teachings. Both Catholics and Protestants began to talk of 'post-Christian America'.[10]

The religious liberalism that affected the mainline denominations also created a spiritual vacuum for many constituents who did not share their leaders' embrace of modernity. Troubled by the cultural revolution they were observing all around, many began to look for a return to a biblical certainty characteristic of conservative Christianity, believing the moral absolutes of the Bible provided meaning and order for their lives. A more biblically conservative view gave them a framework to interpret and make sense of the difficult times.[11] This, in part, explains the rise of conservative churches during the 1960s and also sets the stage for an openness to neo-Pentecostalism.[12] Richard Quebedeaux, in accounting for the success of the Charismatic Renewal, said:

> It is apparent, moreover, that with the ever more pervasive rationalization and routinization of life inherent in modernity, the nonrational, the ecstatic, have again become appealing. In secular society, it is quite understandable that an *experiential* religious tradition that also provides meaning and discipline—such as pentecostalism—has become widely attractive. Both classical pentecostalism and charismatic renewal owe their growth and spread, in large part, to a new enthusiasm for religious experience in Western culture today.[13]

Given the United States' deeply religious history, it was no surprise to see a new religious awakening in response to the secularization of culture.[14]

A significant and sometimes underappreciated part of the spiritual awakening of the late 1960s and early 1970s was the Jesus movement.[15]

---

10. Vinson Synan, *The Holiness-Pentecostal Tradition* (Grand Rapids: Eerdmans, 1997), 235. For a broad analysis of the religious climate of the 1960s, see Robert S. Ellwood, *The Sixties Spiritual Awakening* (New Brunswick, NJ: Rutgers University Press, 1994); Steven M. Tipton, *Getting Saved from the Sixties* (Berkeley: University of California Press, 1982).

11. The eschatological apocalyptic interpretations of history have characterized Evangelical Christians. See Ernest Sandeen, *The Roots of Fundamentalism* (Chicago: University of Chicago Press, 1970).

12. Quebedeaux, *The New Charismatics*, 217. See also Dean M. Kelly, *Why Conservative Churches Are Growing* (San Francisco: Harper & Row, 1977).

13. Quebedeaux, *The New Charismatics*, 217-18.

14. Sociologist Margaret Poloma explores the issue of secularization and the rise of the Charismatic movement in Poloma, *The Charismatic Movement*, 28-39.

15. There are few studies on the Jesus movement and no comprehensive history of this significant revival. See Edward Plowman, *The Jesus Movement in America* (Elgin,

Many countercultural youth became disillusioned with the ideals of the sexual revolution and the drug scene. Love, peace, and freedom had been confronted by the harsh realities of venereal disease, addiction, and survival. Into this malaise came the message of hope in Jesus Christ, and a 'Jesus revolution' resulted.[16] The Jesus movement became a unique generational revival. In San Francisco, Los Angeles, New York, and many US cities, hippies and students took part in 'Bible raps', proclaimed Jesus as the 'one way' to salvation, and opened coffee house outreaches. The Jesus movement was nontraditional and characterized by an emphasis on community, contemporary music, outreach activism, use of indigenous media, and parachurch structures.[17] Important to this study, the Jesus movement was Charismatic and nondenominational. Some consider the movement's high point to be the 1972 Dallas 'Explo '72', sponsored by Campus Crusade for Christ and attended by 50,000 young people. The Jesus movement's influence on the 1970s was substantial.

The 1970s have been described as the 'moral reaction' to the 'moral revolution' of the 1960s.[18] 'Born-again' Jimmy Carter's 1976 election heralded what pollster George Gallup, Jr would call the 'year of the evangelical'. The decade indeed saw a resurgence of conservative Christianity, and despite the failure of Richard Nixon with the Watergate scandal of 1973 and 1974, the conservative swing continued with Ronald Reagan's 1980 landslide election victory as president. It was a presidential election led, at least in part, by the new Christian political right wing. The powerlessness so keenly felt in the 1960s by religious conservatives was replaced by a new political enfranchisement that, though short-lived, fostered an almost revival-like conservative triumphalism in the early 1980s.

One additional cultural factor influenced the emergence of the Shepherding movement. By the 1960s, North America's growing industrialization and urbanization had altered the societal landscape. Sociologists were observing the depersonalization of human beings and the fragmenting of the social order. People were feeling increasingly isolated and threatened by aspects of modern life that had eclipsed community.[19] By 1973, one-

IL: David C. Cook, 1971); Robert S. Ellwood, *One Way: The Jesus Movement and Its Meaning* (Englewood Cliffs, NJ: Prentice–Hall, 1973); Duane Peterson, *Jesus People* (Glendale, CA: Regal Books, 1971).

16. Plowman, *Jesus Movement*, 13.
17. Plowman, *Jesus Movement*, 8.
18. Noll, *History*, 442.
19. Hadaway, Wright and DuBose, *Home Cell Groups*, 183-85.

third of all North Americans were consciously feeling an intense need for mutuality and community, and by 1980 nearly one-half of North Americans felt that way.[20] The Shepherding movement's emphasis on house church and cell groups tapped into this social trend. Widick Schroeder, Professor of Religion and Society at Chicago Theological Seminary, recognized the importance of the house church as an answer to the need for community. He wrote in 1976:

> Human beings cannot live exclusively in such secondary groups, for they have needs for intimacy, sharing, caring and wholistic and integrating relations. These needs are best met in primary groups, and it seems to me the House Church is exploring one means of fostering such groups.[21]

The Shepherding movement would become 'the most extensive expression of the house church movement in the United States'. This growth was not in consequence of a passing fad, but because the movement created ecclesiological structures that were 'a direct response to problems inherent in a complex mass society'.[22]

The Shepherding movement emerged in a unique and complex period of United States history as a response to the turbulent times of the 1960s and early 1970s. It was a part of the more general religious and conservative resurgence that gained momentum into the early 1980s. The movement also must be seen in its context as an expression of the Charismatic Renewal.

The Charismatic Renewal

As noted above, the modernism of the mainline denominations, which was most fully expressed in the 1960s, had created a nominalism that left many of its constituents hungering for spiritual reality. Neo-Pentecostalism, later to be termed the Charismatic Renewal, grew rapidly because it seemed to satisfy this need by means of its most defining characteristic: the dramatic spiritual experience of Spirit baptism.[23] This experience describes a person

20. Hadaway, Wright and DuBose, *Home Cell Groups*, 184.
21. Widick Schroeder, 'A Sociological and Theological Critique of the House Church Movement', in Arthur L. Foster (ed.), *The House Church Evolving* (Chicago: Exploration Press, 1976), 54, quoted in Hadaway, Wright and DuBose, *Home Cell Groups*, 184.
22. Hadaway, Wright and DuBose, *Home Cell Groups*, 30, 184.
23. Usually referred to as the baptism with (or 'in') the Holy Spirit by Pentecostals and Charismatics.

being filled or empowered by the Holy Spirit, the third person of the Trinity. The experience of Spirit baptism is usually accompanied by glossolalia or other spiritual gifts (1 Cor. 12.4-8 NIV). Spirit baptism brought a powerful provision of the spiritual reality for which many people were longing.

Since the movement began in the early days of the twentieth century, non-Pentecostals would experience Spirit baptism and leave their churches to start or join Pentecostal congregations. In the 1950s, there had been a few scattered incidents where clergy in mainline denominations experienced Spirit baptism and stayed in their denominations. In the 1960s, thousands of clergy and members of their historic churches were Spirit-baptized and purposely remained in the churches as a renewing force. This was the essential feature that distinguished neo-Pentecostalism from Classical Pentecostalism, where many left or were pushed out.

Episcopalian Dennis Bennett's experience of Spirit baptism and glossolalia marked the popular beginning of the neo-Pentecostal outbreak in mainline denominations. After the Van Nuys rector announced his experience to his church in April of 1960,[24] the news media caught wind of 'speaking in tongues among Episcopalians'. The publicity helped birth a new movement that during the decade spread throughout the historic denominations in the United States and parts of Western Europe.[25] The Charismatic Renewal's characteristics and constituency would be dynamic and complex, and its impact slowed the liberalization of the mainline denominations. By 1970, an estimated 10 percent of the clergy and 1 million lay people had received Spirit baptism and remained in their mainline churches.[26] The Catholic Charismatic Renewal, which began in 1967, had also mushroomed in its influence among Roman Catholics.[27]

While many Charismatics stayed in their historic churches, others left, some joining prayer groups and parachurch ministries. A large number of

24. Bennett resigned his pastorate and was assigned to a small parish in Seattle, Washington.

25. For a survey history of both Pentecostalism and the Charismatic Renewal, see Synan, *Holiness-Pentecostal Tradition*. For a concise history and analysis of the Charismatic Renewal, see Peter Hocken, 'The Charismatic Movement', in Stanley M. Burgess and Gary B. McGee (eds.), *The Dictionary of Pentecostal and Charismatic Movements* (Grand Rapids: Zondervan, 1986). Now dated but still the best survey of the Charismatic Renewal see Quebedeaux, *The New Charismatics*.

26. Vinson Synan, *In the Latter Days* (Ann Arbor, MI: Servant, 1991), 96.

27. See Edward O'Conner, *The Pentecostal Movement in the Catholic Church* (Notre Dame, IN: Ave Maria Press, 1971); Kevin Ranaghan, *Catholic Pentecostals* (New York: Paulist Press, 1969).

independent Charismatics simply went from teaching conference to teaching conference. As the Charismatic Renewal continued to grow, this independent Charismatic constituency became a large and significant part of the movement. By 1970 there were three distinct sectors of the Renewal: mainline Protestant Charismatics, Roman Catholic Charismatics, and the independent Charismatics. At the same time, the movement had no central leadership and few structures for unity and cohesion. According to historian David E. Harrell: 'Until the late 1960s, the only institutional cohesion in the Charismatic Renewal was the Full Gospel Businessmen's Fellowship International (FGBMFI) and its small magazine, *Voice*.'[28] The renewal was also changing.

In the early 1960s, the Charismatic Renewal was a 'testimony revival'[29] as 'thousands were spellbound by repeated tales of miraculous conversions, healings, and other spiritual wonders'.[30] As the movement grew, it began to change character and developed 'an urgent need for teachers'.[31] The renewal's continued growth into the Roman Catholic and mainline Protestant churches created a more intellectually and theologically astute constituency that was more critical and analytical of supernatural testimonies.[32] Adding to this was the revival among young people and hippies through the Jesus movement, many of whom became Charismatics. Richard Quebedeaux, author and ecumenical consultant, observed: 'In a word, there was a widespread felt need among new Charismatics for deeper teaching and more discipline for their lives of faith.'[33] The need for biblical teachers created an opportunity 'for new leaders to come forward'.[34]

It was in this changing context that various Charismatic Renewal teaching and media centers began to emerge around the nation; and by the early 1970s, there were several identifiable centers.[35] Melodyland Christian Center in Anaheim, California, led by Pastor Ralph Wilkerson, had become a teaching center hosting conferences with major speakers in the renewal.

28. David E. Harrell, Jr, *All Things Are Possible* (Bloomington: Indiana University Press, 1975), 181.
29. Derek Prince, quoted in Harrell, *All Things*, 180.
30. Harrell, *All Things*, 180.
31. Harrell, *All Things*, 181.
32. Harrell, *All Things*, 181.
33. Quebedeaux, *The New Charismatics*, 139.
34. Harrell, *All Things*, 181.
35. For a discussion on centers in the Charismatic Renewal, see Jack W. Hayford, 'Conciliation Without Compromise', *Logos* (November/December 1975), 26-32 (26-27).

Its Melodyland School of Theology, directed by Presbyterian Charismatic
J. Rodman Williams, was a training center for Charismatic leaders. In
Seattle, Charismatic patriarch Dennis Bennett at his St Luke's parish was a
center, particularly because a transdenominational presbytery had formed,
composed of large numbers of Charismatic pastors in the region. In Virginia
Beach, the Christian Broadcasting Network (CBN), founded and led by Pat
Robertson, had established itself as a significant influence in the renewal.[36]
The Charismatic Catholic ecumenical communities in Ann Arbor, MI and
South Bend, IN, led by Steve Clark, Ralph Martin, and Kevin Ranaghan,
were important centers of leadership, made even stronger in 1971 with the
publication of the Charismatic periodical *New Covenant*. Dan Malachuk's
New Jersey-based Logos Publications and its Charismatic periodical, *Logos
Journal*, represented another important center of influence, publishing Charismatic resources. Most important to the story of the Shepherding movement would be the emergence of the Holy Spirit Teaching Mission in Ft
Lauderdale, Florida; it was a teaching center, with large Charismatic
conferences, audiocassette and videotape ministry, television station, and a
teaching periodical, *New Wine*.[37]

Preceding and concurrent with the development of these Charismatic
centers was the multiplication of Charismatically themed conferences
fostered by various retreat centers and independent parachurch groups
around the United States.[38] These conferences and Charismatic centers,
together with the continuing activity of FGBMFI through its local chapters,
national, and international conventions, provided a platform for individual
Charismatic Bible teachers. It was through these meetings and conferences
that Don Basham, Bob Mumford, Derek Prince, Charles Simpson, and later
to a lesser degree, Ern Baxter, gained prominence as teachers in the Charismatic Renewal. They all met through their interaction on this teaching

36. In 1971 and 1972, CBN regularly taped and broadcast the Bible teaching of
Basham, Mumford, Prince, and Simpson. Simpson, telephone interview with author, 5
February 1996.

37. Some have called the proliferation of audiotaped teachings the 'audiocassette
revolution' as audiotape libraries sprung up all around the nation to distribute tapes.
David Selby, telephone interview with author, 17 November 1998.

38. For discussion on one such conference and retreat sponsor, Camps Farthest
Out, see Hocken, 'The Charismatic Movement', 131. Other camps and conference pro-
moters included Christian Books Unlimited, which held conferences in Montreat,
North Carolina, and in California the World Missionary Assistance Plan led by Ralph
Mahoney.

circuit and their close association with the Holy Spirit Teaching Mission in Ft Lauderdale.

Despite the turbulent social changes that surrounded the growing Charismatic Renewal, there was among its leaders and constituents great optimism. In their perspective, God was restoring his Church to New Testament vigor, and the renewal was heralding hope for the future.[39] For Charismatics, all of this made for exciting and interesting times.

In the summer of 1970, the Shepherding movement had not yet been conceived, but that was soon to change. The four early leaders of the movement were to be drawn together through a crisis surrounding the Holy Spirit Teaching Mission.

The Holy Spirit Teaching Mission

In the fall of 1964, Eldon Purvis, a Ft Lauderdale stockbroker and a nominal Episcopalian, was seeking a deeper spirituality.[40] Purvis had read about Episcopalians experiencing the Holy Spirit's power and realized it was what he was looking for. He called a Spirit-baptized priest who put him in touch with two Bible teachers. Purvis invited one of them, Grace Munsey, to teach a class in his home. There Purvis 'received Christ' and four months later experienced Spirit baptism at a FGBMFI meeting in Miami.[41]

39. In reviewing hundreds of cassette tapes and periodical articles from the late 1960s and 1970s, I was impressed by the euphoric optimism and the self-concept that the Charismatic Renewal was eschatologically significant. The following editorial quote from the initial issue of *New Wine* is an example: 'Man has amassed such knowledge and achieved such sophistication that outwardly he pretends to ignore spiritual truth and reality. And because of this spiritual neglect, the world teeters on the edge of disaster… We stand today where the children of Israel stood when the waters of the Red Sea stretched before them, and the horizon behind them was clouded with the dust from the chariots of the armies of Egypt, bent on their destruction. In the eyes of man, there was no way out. And so it is today. But Christians are meant to worship and serve a God who can make a way where there is no way! We worship and serve the same miracle-working God who rolled back the waters of the Red Sea and let the Israelites race across dryshod. The Bible clearly promises that signs and wonders are the marks of the Spirit-led life, and God's supernatural gifts the heritage of every Christian.' 'Editorial', *New Wine* (June 1969), 2.

40. Nancy Purvis, 'Hostess for a Home Prayer and Bible Study Meeting', *New Wine* (April 1970), 25.

41. A more detailed history of the Holy Spirit Teaching Mission is recorded in Basham, 'Birth of a Mission', 12-16. See also *HSTM Newsletters*: 12 July 1968; 20

After Purvis's Miami experience with the Holy Spirit, a Charismatic emphasis was introduced into the home Bible study, and it quickly began to grow, leading to the group's associating with and birthing other home meetings.[42] From these Charismatic meetings Purvis and others became increasingly aware that there was a need for 'some kind of teaching mission' to tell others about the Holy Spirit's power.[43] From this vision came the birth of the Holy Spirit Teaching Mission (HSTM). Purvis, along with a group of other laymen, mostly successful businessmen and professionals, started the 'Committee of Forty'.[44] This group, comprised of only ten or twelve men, sponsored the first HSTM conference in June 1965, and it was successful beyond their expectations. The conference, held in Ft Lauderdale, featured Episcopalian Dennis Bennett, Pentecostal David du Plessis, and author John Sherrill. Several hundred attended the teaching mission, including 70 local ministers. Many of those attending, including a few pastors, received Spirit baptism.[45]

This first teaching mission in Ft Lauderdale was a significant beginning for the HSTM, which soon incorporated in 1965.[46] Over the next few years, the HSTM held regular teaching conferences in Miami and Ft Lauderdale, inviting the top leaders of the Charismatic Renewal to speak. Purvis, a man of vision and administrative skill, wanted the HSTM to become a center for the Charismatic Renewal with multifaceted ministries. To fulfill his vision, Purvis established a number of Charismatic prayer and Bible study groups as a base of support in the Ft Lauderdale area.[47] He then invited Harald Bredesen to pastor the groups. Bredesen first agreed to come, but then changed his mind.[48] Bredesen's decision, however, did not discourage Purvis, who pressed forward to expand the influence of the mission. From 1966 to 1970, the HSTM sponsored teaching conferences not only in Florida but all over the United States, including Arizona, California, Penn-

September 1969; 15 November 1968; *New Wine Newsletter* (29 March 1969); Midsummer *Newsletter* (31 July 1969). All on file at the Holy Spirit Research Center, Oral Roberts University, Tulsa, OK.

    42. Neil Frank, telephone interview with author, 14 October 1998.

    43. Basham, 'Birth of a Mission', 12.

    44. According to Purvis the number 40 had no significance other than being a 'good Biblical number'. See Basham, 'Birth of a Mission', 12.

    45. Basham, 'Birth of a Mission', 13.

    46. Neil Frank, 'Editor's Letter', *New Wine* (November 1970), 2.

    47. Frank, interview, 14 October 1998.

    48. Harald Bredesen, telephone interview with author, 8 December 1998.

sylvania, Texas, Michigan, and Wisconsin. International tours were sponsored to Europe, Jamaica, and Israel.[49]

In 1968, the HSTM initiated steps toward beginning a Christian television station, and on 3 September 1969, the FCC granted a construction permit for the construction of WFCB, Channel 45, in Miami. In January 1970, successful automotive engineer Tom Monroe moved from Indiana to be the general manager of WFCB.[50] Don Bohl, who had directed the network shows *To Tell the Truth*, *Password*, and *The Price is Right* joined the station as its program director.[51] Florida Christian Broadcasting, a separate nonprofit corporation from the HSTM, was established as WFCB's parent company. Numerous financial problems hindered construction and the station did not go on the air until March 1975.[52]

Of greater significance, the HSTM started *New Wine* in the spring of 1969. Purvis invited Don Basham and Derek Prince, both living in Ft Lauderdale, to serve with him on the magazine's editorial board. The magazine's first issue was published in June 1969, with articles by Basham, Mumford and Prince. Neil Frank, a full-time meteorologist and director of the National Hurricane Center in Miami, was the magazine's managing editor and wrote in the June 1969 editorial: 'It is the supernatural brand of Christianity which the Lord is restoring in the world today. *New Wine* is dedicated to sharing the message of restoration.'[53] Beginning with the magazine's second issue, Charles Simpson wrote a monthly Bible study, 'Breaking Bread', and also joined the editorial board in early 1970 along with Bob Mumford. At Purvis's invitation, Mumford moved to Ft Lauderdale in August 1970, while Simpson continued to pastor Bayview Heights Baptist Church in Mobile, Alabama.

New Wine was distributed free, supported by contributions, and carried no advertising. Its circulation grew to 33,000 by October 1970.[54] Basham, Mumford, Prince, and Simpson supplied their personal ministry mailing lists to help the magazine's growth.[55]

49. Basham, 'Birth of a Mission', 15.
50. Tom Monroe, telephone interview with author, 23 February 1996.
51. Tom Monroe, 'Editorial', *New Wine* (January 1970), 2.
52. WFCB, Channel 45, was sold in July of 1976 to Lester Sumrall's television ministry. The station would later be purchased by Trinity Broadcasting Network. Monroe, interview, 23 February 1996.
53. Neil Frank, 'Editorial', *New Wine* (June 1969), 2.
54. Charles Simpson, Statement to Bayview Heights, October 1970, private holding.
55. Basham, *Integrity Update*, 82.

By summer 1970, the HSTM was a thriving ministry center. Purvis had proven adept at drawing people together to fulfill his vision. He had also helped set the stage for the association of the four teachers when the HSTM experienced major difficulties in September and October of 1970.

Crisis and Change at the Holy Spirit Teaching Mission

The vision and energy of Eldon Purvis made him the uncontested leader of the HSTM and also created a leadership crisis for the ministry when he was accused of serious misconduct in the late summer of 1970. As the problem surfaced, Purvis reluctantly admitted to the allegations. Over the next few weeks, Purvis admitted to further wrongdoing.[56] Also adding to the crisis, the HSTM and its ministries, including *New Wine*, had accumulated a debt of $36,000. Overwhelmed by the situation, the Committee of Forty and other HSTM ministry leaders asked Basham, Mumford, Prince, and Simpson, the *de facto* spiritual leaders of the HSTM, to assist in managing the crisis.[57] A previously scheduled conference, which convened on 5–9 October 1970, brought all four men to Ft Lauderdale to teach and provided an opportunity for them to get together regarding the crisis.

After midnight on 8 October 1970,[58] at the Galt Ocean Mile Hotel in Ft Lauderdale, Florida, the four teachers met in a hotel suite to discuss the situation with Purvis and the HSTM.[59] Since they were closely identified with the HSTM through its teaching publication, *New Wine*, and were serving with Purvis on *New Wine*'s editorial board, Basham, Mumford,

56. Frank, interview, 14 October 1998; Simpson, interview, 5 February 1996.
57. Basham, 'How It All Began', 12.
58. A bit of historical detective work gave me the date of 8 October. Neither Mumford or Simpson could remember on what day of the 5–11 October conference they met and committed themselves together. I was able to arrive at 8 October by deduction. All agree their meeting was early in the morning and all agree that at the meeting they decided to resign from the *New Wine* editorial board. Simpson said they notified *New Wine* that 'next day' referring to the same day after they had slept. The *New Wine* November 1970 'Editors Letter' says that the four resigned on 8 October 1970. Frank, 'Editor's Letter', 2.
59. The following narrative detailing the association of the four Bible teachers is drawn from personal interviews with Bob Mumford and Charles Simpson. Bob Mumford, telephone interview with author, 1 October 1994; Simpson, interview, 5 February 1996. See also Basham, 'How It All Began', 12-15; Simpson, 'An Open Letter', 17-21. A particularly vivid narrative of this event, written in 1972 just two years later is Don Basham, *Deliver Us From Evil* (Old Tappan, NJ: Chosen Books, 1972), 209-13.

Prince, and Simpson were concerned about possible scandal if the situation became widely known or was mishandled. They were concerned for Purvis, but also for their own reputations and ministries. Contrary to what many thought, none of the four was officially tied to the HSTM, except for involvement in *New Wine* and regular participation in the HSTM's conferences as teachers.

At the meeting, the four decided to resign from the editorial board of *New Wine* and to request that a letter be published in the magazine stating that their ministries were and always had been independent from the HSTM and the magazine.[60] Derek Prince remembers: 'We wanted out of it, our names were tied to it.'[61] Still, they agreed to help *New Wine* by joining a much larger and diverse team of contributing editors. The four also agreed to work unofficially behind the scenes, to advise and counsel the HSTM with its problems, and specifically to help Purvis.[62]

As the four men discussed and prayed regarding the problems surrounding the crisis and particularly the unfortunate situation with Purvis, they recognized their own weaknesses. Simpson asserted, 'It's not just for [Eldon's] sake the four of us are here. Not one of us is immune from the deception which trapped [Eldon.]'[63] The four men talked of the tendency toward isolation and independence among so many of the leaders and ministries in the Charismatic Renewal. When ministries are 'submitted to no one, answerable to no one, they too often stumble'.

One by one the men acknowledged their own vulnerability to misconduct and confessed their fears and temptations to one another. The four knew they needed accountability and protection. It became especially sobering as Prince listed several ministries all four were aware of that had failed because of 'greed, immorality, or some other lure'. Mumford then observed, 'Perhaps God is showing us right here, not only the danger but the

---

60. *New Wine Magazine* published this letter in the November 1970 issue. Neil Frank, 'An Open Letter to the Body of Christ', *New Wine* (November 1970), 3.

61. Bob Mumford and Derek Prince, *Change of Local Authority* (n.p.: n.p., 1976), audiocassette.

62. Before this early morning meeting in 1970, Basham, Mumford, Prince, and Simpson were only friends who shared a mutual respect for each other's ministry. Other than Basham and Prince who were close friends, having both lived in the Ft Lauderdale area for two years, the four as a group were not close. Basham had met Mumford only six months earlier. Basham, *Deliver Us*, 209.

63. Basham, *Deliver Us*, 209. To protect Purvis's privacy Basham used the pseudonym Frank in reference to Purvis in his account.

answer. For years I've longed to join my ministry to those of other men I could trust. I've come to trust you three.' Then, according to Basham:

> We suddenly knew the Holy Spirit had brought us together in that hotel room, not merely to pray for a beloved brother, but to show us His sovereign intent to join our ministries together—and that meant submitting to one another as well as to Him.[64]

In response, they knelt and prayed. As they knelt, Prince recounts, 'God did something very sovereign and supernatural. When we rose, everyone knew without speaking a word or asking a question that God had in some way united us together spiritually.'[65] This commitment, all have said, came without plan or intention. Prince emphasized: 'It was not something we asked [God] to do; it was not something we anticipated.'[66] According to Mumford: 'On a hotel room floor, Don, Charles, Derek, and I encountered God and encountered one another. It wasn't a choice—it was an assignment.'[67] When teaching at the 1975 Shepherds Conference in Kansas City, Bob Mumford remembered the reservations each had about being joined together:

> There, sitting in a hotel room, dealing with a problem, and I cannot tell you all that happened neither do I want to justify it. I'm just saying what happened is this…suddenly the Spirit of God came into that hotel room and we had a sense…that we belonged to each other. I didn't like that especially, neither did Derek, or Charles or Don… We had been friends, we had preached together, but we didn't especially want to be tied together… I didn't know where Derek was theologically. [Derek] said to me: 'Mumford, you scare me; you are so impulsive!' Me? I couldn't believe that. Derek and Don, they were demon chasers. Charles and I didn't know if we wanted that or not, but that comes with the package.[68]

Charles Simpson, youngest of the four, said of the meeting: 'I felt flattered and honored to be with these men, because I considered myself both in age and stature to be a junior partner.'[69] He recalled that the other three decided to include him as they each made verbal commitments to one

64. Basham, *Deliver Us*, 209-11.
65. Mumford and Prince, *Change*, audiocassette.
66. Mumford and Prince, *Change*, audiocassette.
67. Bob Mumford, *How to Bring Forth New Leadership* (West Coast Men's Conference; Ft Lauderdale: Christian Growth Ministries, 1977), audiocassette.
68. Bob Mumford, *God's Purpose with His People Today* (National Men's Shepherds Conference; Kansas City, MO: His Men Tapes, 1975), audiocassette.
69. Simpson, interview, 5 February 1996.

another. After the meeting, Simpson returned to his room and remarked to an associate, 'I think I've done something tonight that will affect my life.'[70] Little did he realize how true that statement would be. None of the men fully recognized that by their association a new movement was being conceived, a movement that would not be manifest clearly for another three years.

Over the next few days, they 'met to explore the implications of united ministry'. They discovered that their individual ministries complemented each other and that together they could present a 'whole Christ' and a 'whole gospel' in a way that none of them could alone. Simpson observed that the four 'could go to [a] city together and share as a *team* the ministries God has given us'.[71] This strategy would begin an extended season of the four teaching as often as possible as a team.

Despite the sense of providence the four were feeling, hard work was ahead. Over the next few weeks they tried to sort out the issues with HSTM. Simpson, still pastoring in Mobile, made three trips to Ft Lauderdale in October to help the HSTM through the crisis. Tom Monroe, WFCB general manager, assumed the administration of the HSTM and ran its ministries for the next year and a half.[72] Simpson and others met with Purvis and presented a course of action to help him work through his problems. Financial support was offered to him with the eventual possibility of his returning to lead the HSTM. Purvis was not agreeable to the arrangement and felt that Basham, Mumford, Prince, and Simpson were trying to take over the ministry.[73] Recognizing that the teachers had the support of the Committee of Forty and the HSTM staff, Purvis resigned effective 29 October 1970. His resignation was announced in the November issue of *New Wine*, along with an expression of thanks for his 'tireless leadership to HSTM'.[74] Purvis, unhappy with how he had been handled, contacted many national Charismatic leaders, including Dennis Bennett and David du Plessis, and told them about his concerns.[75] Purvis was especially troubled by a public

---

70. Charles Simpson, *A 30-Year History of the Covenant Movement: Part 1 and Part 2* (Mobile, AL: Charles Simpson Ministries, 1990), audiocassette. The associate was Glen Roachelle. Glen Roachelle, telephone interview with author, 12 January 1999.

71. Basham, *Deliver Us*, 212.

72. Monroe, interview, 23 February 1996.

73. Simpson, interview, 5 February 1996.

74. Frank, 'An Open Letter', 3.

75. Simpson, interview, 5 February 1996; S. David Moore, 'The Shepherding Movement: History, Controversy, Ecclesiology' (D.Min dissertation, Regent University, Virginia Beach, VA, 1999), 50-51.

believers meeting held in Ft Lauderdale to announce his disciplinary situation. The meeting announcement leaflet was signed by area Charismatic leaders, including Basham, Mumford, and Prince. Purvis sent a copy of this announcement to those he contacted, and on the back he made his own comments of protest to 'this unscriptural idea of bringing a brother to public trial…'[76]

For the next few months, the four teachers continued to provide practical and spiritual counsel to HSTM. Don Basham said that they expected the ministry to fold and had taken a lower profile in the magazine. To their surprise, within a few months the financial crisis passed, and the magazine's circulation and influence continued to rise. The four teachers saw this as an expression of God's providential blessing on the ministry, particularly on *New Wine*.[77]

The association of the four teachers was not without some question. Charles Simpson encountered FGBMFI founder Demos Shakarian in Nashville at the end of 1970, and Shakarian expressed reservations about the association. Charismatic leader Ralph Wilkerson warned Simpson about associating with Derek Prince and Don Basham because of their emphasis on deliverance from demonization.[78] David du Plessis expressed similar concerns to Bob Mumford.[79] Mumford and the other three, however, were convinced that God had providentially brought them together.

The Charismatic Renewal and later the Shepherding movement arose during cultural upheaval. Varied circumstances and crises brought the four principle teachers together—in what they confess was a providential response to the turbulent times.

76. 'Notice to Members of the Body of Christ in Pompano Beach, Hollywood, and Ft Lauderdale' (Holy Spirit Research Center; Tulsa, OK: Oral Roberts University, n.d.).

77. Basham, *Integrity Update*, 321.

78. Simpson, interview, 5 February 1996.

79. Bob Mumford, telephone interview with the author, 9 February 1996.

Chapter 3

THE FORT LAUDERDALE FIVE

The Five Teachers

The term 'Fort Lauderdale Five' was frequently used in reference to the five teachers by observers and especially by critics.[1] The term was never accurate, nor did the five teachers appreciate its use. Many were unaware that the five never lived in Ft Lauderdale at the same time.[2] *New Wine Magazine*, the periodical with which they were strongly identified, was based in Ft Lauderdale and so that was perceived as the movement's center.

Explaining the backgrounds of the five unquestioned leaders of the Shepherding movement is essential to understanding its history. Their diverse backgrounds, unique personalities, and individual ministries would challenge their ability to hold together the commitments they had made to each other.

Don Basham

Don Basham was a gifted and creative writer with a passion for the spread of the gospel through distribution of the printed page.[3] Basham was born on 17 September 1926 in Wichita Falls, Texas, and spent his childhood and school years there, meeting his wife, Alice, in a Disciples of Christ church. They married in 1949. He left a promising career in commercial art in

---

1.   E.g., Jamie Buckingham, 'Changing Attitudes Among Discipleship Leaders', *Buckingham Report* (20 March 1985), 1-5 (1); 'Where Are "The Fort Lauderdale Five?"' *Charisma* (September 1998), 15.

2.   Simpson, interview, 5 February 1996.

3.   Much of Basham's life story is told through his highly readable books on various themes in which he recounts many personal experiences. Especially helpful are: Don Basham, *Face Up with a Miracle* (Northridge, CA: Voice Christian Publications, 1967); *idem*, *Deliver Us*.

The five teachers in 1980. From the left: Ern Baxter, Derek Prince, Charles Simpson, Don Basham, Bob Mumford.

1952 to pursue Christian ministry. He received his BA and BD degrees respectively from Phillips University and its Graduate Seminary in Enid, Oklahoma.[4] In the summer of 1953, while on break from college, Basham personally experienced Spirit baptism through the ministry of pioneer Charismatic leader Harald Bredesen at a Camp Farthest Out retreat.[5] Basham would later pastor Disciples of Christ churches in Washington, DC; Toronto, Canada; and Sharon, Pennsylvania. With the blossoming of the Charismatic Renewal in the 1960s, Basham traveled extensively, ministering in various Charismatic meetings, particularly Full Gospel Businessmen's Fellowship International (FGBMFI). In the fall of 1967, while still in Sharon, Pennsylvania, Basham decided to leave the pastorate and begin a full-time teaching and writing ministry.[6] After discovering that much of

4. 'In Memoriam: Don W. Basham', *Don Basham's Insights* (March/April 1989), 2.
5. Basham, *Face Up with a Miracle*, 49-60.
6. Alice Basham, telephone interview with author, 14 February 1996.

his ministry support was coming from the South Florida area, he moved to Ft Lauderdale, in January 1968.[7]

Don Basham was a gentle, casual man who spoke and taught in a relaxed, conversational manner. His messages and prose were clear, strong, and laced with stories and humor. In some ways, Basham was always in the background of the Shepherding movement. His manner and leadership style never brought him the public recognition the other four received. Basham was deeply committed to his wife and five children and was considered to be a true family man.

Basham was the force behind *New Wine Magazine*. He served as editor for many years and was the chief editorial consultant until the magazine ceased publication in December 1986. His editorial skills were evident in the magazine.[8]

Basham's journalistic career began almost by accident. As he handled the normal pastoral responsibilities of writing church newsletters and other church communications, he soon discovered that writing was much more than a casual pursuit for him.[9] Soon he was writing for denominational publications. He would go on to publish 16 books. His first book, *Face Up with a Miracle*, had several hundred thousand copies in print. His 1972 book, *Deliver Us From Evil*, is still in print and has the longest successive print run of any book ever published by Chosen Books.[10]

Basham's ministry included a decided emphasis on deliverance from demonic power. His belief that Christians could harbor demons in their lives drew criticism. Basham and Derek Prince both taught extensively on demonic bondage and practiced public exorcisms. In the late 1960s, Basham also taught on Spirit baptism and displayed a unique ability to draw people into the experience.[11]

7.   Basham, *Deliver Us*, 78-89.

8.   Simpson and Mumford have repeatedly told me that Basham's editorial skills were the strength of *New Wine*. Despite his changing roles at the magazine, he remained an influence until it ceased publication. In gaining perspective on Basham's role in the publication I am indebted to Basham's son-in-law and former *New Wine* managing editor, Dick Leggatt, telephone interview with author, 1 March 1996; Dick Leggatt, telephone interview with author, 10 September 1998.

9.   'In Memoriam: Don W. Basham', 2.

10. A. Basham, interview, 14 February 1996.

11. Simpson, interview, 5 February 1996.

Ern Baxter

Ern Baxter, the oldest and most experienced of the five leaders, was known as a great preacher. Though without formal theological training, Baxter was the most theologically oriented of the five men, using his extensive library to root himself in the Reformed tradition, which along with his Classical Pentecostal background, produced a unique blend of what he called 'Word and Spirit'.[12]

Ern Baxter was born on 22 June 1914, in Saskatoon, Saskatchewan, Canada. After his parents were converted in a small Holiness church, they moved into Classical Pentecostalism. As a teenager, Baxter rebelled against the legalism and emotionalism of his childhood church experience. In 1932, after a serious illness, he committed his life to Christ. A gifted musician, he soon began to travel as the pianist for an evangelist and, on 2 July 1932, received the Pentecostal experience of Spirit baptism.[13]

This Pentecostal experience eventually led to a dilemma for Baxter. His doctrinal emphasis on a more rational, propositional, objective truth was unacceptable to Pentecostals, and his Pentecostal experience was unacceptable to Evangelicals. After a season of struggling with the tension, Baxter received an invitation to pastor a church of 60 people in Vancouver that was meeting in a rented facility.[14] The church, Evangelistic Tabernacle, grew quickly under Baxter's strong preaching and was at one time the largest church in Vancouver. Baxter pastored this church for 25 years.[15]

In 1949, while continuing to pastor, Baxter became the campaign manager and Bible teacher for healing evangelist William Branham, and for seven years traveled the world with the Charismatic evangelist. Pastoring and traveling at the same time left Baxter severely fatigued, and he also became concerned over imbalances he observed in Branham's ministry. Consequently, he ended his association with Branham and returned to his church full-time and but soon afterward resigned. After a season of rest, Baxter started a small storefront church, Open Bible Chapel, that grew to several hundred members.[16] Baxter's first wife, Margaret, died in 1961.

    12. Ern Baxter, *Conversations with Dr Ern Baxter*, Part 1 (New York: Laseredit East, 1992), videocassette.
    13. Ern Baxter, *The Chief Shepherd and His Sheep* (Spring Valley, CA: Timothy Distribution, 1987), 11-14.
    14. Baxter, *The Chief Shepherd*, 14-15.
    15. Ern Baxter, *Charles Simpson Interviews Ern Baxter* (Mobile, AL: Charles Simpson Ministries, 1988), videocassette.
    16. Ruth Baxter, telephone interview with author, 21 February 1996.

In February 1964, he married his second wife, Ruth, and for the next six years served in several churches in the United States as a Bible teacher, while continuing to travel to various speaking engagements. Moving back to Canada in 1970, Baxter continued to travel and preach worldwide in Charismatic/Pentecostal churches and conferences.[17] He became associated with Basham, Mumford, Prince, and Simpson at the 1974 National Men's Shepherds Conference held in Montreat, North Carolina, and moved to Ft Lauderdale, Florida, in early 1975.[18]

Ern Baxter was an orator, who, as Charles Simpson said, 'used words as artistic tools, and in the pulpit painted magnificent pictures'.[19] His great passion was the study of Scripture, and his 'friends' were his books. Baxter had an extensive library, where he would spend hours and often entire days in study.[20] During his years in ministry, Ern Baxter participated directly or indirectly in Classical Pentecostalism, the Healing Revival, the Latter Rain movement, and the Charismatic Renewal.

Bob Mumford

Bob Mumford was the catalyst and celebrity of the Shepherding movement. Animated and humorous when teaching the Bible,[21] Mumford was a speaker in great demand during the height of the Charismatic Renewal. Kilian McDonnell called Mumford, 'a biblical teacher of real genius'.[22] At the very least, Mumford was 'one of the most respected Bible teachers in the Charismatic Renewal'.[23]

Bob Mumford was born 29 December 1930, in Steubenville, Ohio. At age 12, he was converted to Christ in a Church of the Nazarene revival meeting in Roanoke, Virginia, but soon fell away and was, as he describes, 'in a backslidden state for twelve years'.[24] He then joined the navy and, while home on leave in 1954, recommitted his life to Christ at an Assem-

17. Dick Williams, personal interview with author, 28 February 1996.
18. Ern Baxter, *Conversations with Dr Ern Baxter*, Part 3 (New York: Laseredit East, 1992), videocassette.
19. Charles Simpson, 'A Life On Wings: In Memory of Ern Baxter', *Christian Challenge* (September/October 1993), 3-4.
20. R. Baxter, interview, 21 February 1996.
21. Bert Ghezzi, 'Bob Mumford After Discipleship', *Charisma* (August 1987), 20-27 (23).
22. McDonnell, 'Seven Documents', II, 116.
23. Ghezzi, 'Bob Mumford', 22.
24. Bob Mumford, personal interview with author, 2 October 1994.

blies of God church in Atlantic City. After returning from his leave, Mumford was water- and Spirit-baptized at Glad Tidings Tabernacle in San Francisco. He said of the experience, 'I came from the water praying in tongues…'[25]

After his discharge from the navy he attended a small Assemblies of God Bible college, Eastern Bible Institute, and graduated in 1959.[26] While in college, Mumford married Judith, and the Mumfords spent the year after graduation in the Medical Missionary Training Institute in Toronto, Canada. Ordained in 1960 as an Assemblies of God minister, Mumford briefly served as an evangelist, then pastored for two years in a small church in Kane, Pennsylvania. In 1963, he began teaching at the Elim Bible Institute in New York and, over the next three years, served as Academic Dean and Dean of Men. It was at Elim that Mumford felt a profound call to minister transdenominationally after hearing Pentecostal ecumenist David du Plessis speak at the college.[27]

In 1966, Mumford left Elim to attend Episcopal Reformed Seminary in Philadelphia. From 1967 to 1969, while attending seminary, Mumford pastored in Wilmington, Delaware, seeing a church of 40 grow to 400 in just over a year. During his years in seminary, Mumford began to travel widely, ministering for FGBMFI, World Missionary Assistance Plan (World MAP), the HSTM, and other camps and conferences around the nation. He graduated from seminary in 1969 and moved to Southern California, where he taught a weekly Bible class at Melodyland Christian Center that was regularly attended by 700 people. In 1970, at Eldon Purvis's invitation, Mumford moved to Ft Lauderdale,[28] where the Mumfords raised four children.[29]

Bob Mumford was the figurehead and spokesman of the Shepherding movement, and his energy and enthusiasm were key to its growth. His name became associated with the movement; and, more than any of the teachers, he was the target of much accusation and criticism. In reviewing periodicals and publications critical of Shepherding, Mumford's name is mentioned most often.[30] Vinson Synan said of Mumford: 'I think, had he not gotten

25. Ghezzi, 'Bob Mumford', 21.
26. Eastern Bible Institute is now called Valley Forge Christian College and is located in Greenlane, Pennsylvania.
27. Bob Mumford, personal interview with author, 1 October 1994.
28. Mumford, interview, 1 October 1994.
29. For a brief autobiographical sketch see Bob Mumford, *Forty Years in Ministry 1954–1994* (Raleigh, NC: LifeChangers, 1994), 1-28.
30. Ghezzi, 'Bob Mumford', 24; Steven Strang, 'The Discipleship Controversy

into that controversy, he would have been the most outstanding Charismatic speaker of all.'[31]

Derek Prince

Derek Prince was a Bible teacher of precision and skill. His reserved, logical, and unemotional manner was a unique mix with his Charismatic focus on the Holy Spirit's work and power that so characterized his teaching in the early days of the Charismatic Renewal. Prince was the teacher who most clearly articulated some of the Shepherding movement's distinctive doctrines. His book, *Discipleship, Shepherding, Commitment*, published in 1976, was a concise biblical statement of many of the movement's teachings.[32] Prince was quite popular in the renewal and like Mumford was the subject of much criticism because of his teaching on Shepherding. In David Harrell's opinion, Prince 'was a central figure among the emerging neo-Pentecostal ministries' and he 'had a long and respected record of service in the Pentecostal movement'.[33]

Prince was born to British parents on 14 August 1915 in Bangalore, India, living there until his mother returned him to Sussex, England, to live with his grandparents. He excelled academically throughout his secondary and college education, studying at Cambridge University. In 1940, he was elected to a Fellowship in Philosophy at Kings College, Cambridge. Prince was skilled in Hebrew, Latin, and Greek.

World War II interrupted Prince's academic career and, while serving in the army, he was converted to Christianity in July 1941. Stationed in Jerusalem, Prince met Lydia Christianson; and, after he left the army, they were married in February 1946. With the marriage, he became the father of her eight adopted daughters (they later adopted a ninth child). For the next two years, after Prince was discharged from the army, the family lived in Jerusalem, where he attended the Hebrew University. He returned to England in 1949 and for eight years pastored a small Pentecostal church in central London.[34] Prince then went to Kenya as a missionary with the Pentecostal Assemblies of Canada in 1957 to lead a teachers' training

Three Years Later', *Charisma* (September 1978), 14-24 (22).

31. Synan, interview, 14 February 1996.

32. Derek Prince, *Discipleship, Shepherding, Commitment* (Ft Lauderdale, FL: Derek Prince Ministries, 1976).

33. Harrell, *All Things*, 184.

34. Derek Prince with Ruth Prince, *God is a Matchmaker* (Grand Rapids, MI: Chosen Books, 1986), 23-33.

college. In 1962, he and his family immigrated to the United States, initially pastoring in Seattle, and then traveling and teaching widely during the 1960s.[35] He moved to Ft Lauderdale in early 1968 from the Chicago area.[36] His first wife, Lydia, died in October 1975; he married his second wife, Ruth, in 1978.[37]

Prince placed a strong emphasis on the ministry of deliverance from demonic spirits, and like Basham became the focus of controversy over his belief that Christians could 'have a demon'. He also taught on intercessory prayer, and his book *Shaping History Through Prayer and Fasting* was widely circulated.[38] Of the five teachers, Prince was the one most committed to a more Classical Pentecostal position of the necessity of glosso-lalia as the 'initial physical evidence' of Spirit baptism.[39]

Charles Simpson

While Bob Mumford was the driving personality of the movement, it was Charles Simpson who became its primary administrator and manager. Charles Simpson was, of the five, the most gifted pastoral leader. Though not as well known, he was, along with Mumford, the most influential shaper of the Shepherding movement. Simpson was a gifted Bible teacher known for his dry wit and warm manner.

Born in New Orleans on 6 April 1937, Simpson was the son of a Southern Baptist minister. In 1942, his family moved to the Mobile, Alabama area, where he was raised. Simpson's entire childhood experience was centered around the church, and he was converted in 1951. As a teenager, he responded to a call from God to pastoral ministry, and in 1957, at the age of 20, began his ministry at Bayview Heights Baptist Church in Mobile.

35. Selby, interview, 17 November 1998.

36. Derek Prince and Lydia Prince, A Personal Letter from Derek and Lydia Prince —Joska!, March 1968. Holy Spirit Research Center, Oral Roberts University, Tulsa, OK, 1-2; Derek Prince and Lydia Prince, A Personal Letter from Derek Prince and Lydia Prince, January 1969. Holy Spirit Research Center, Oral Roberts University, Tulsa, OK, 1-2.

37. For helpful brief biographical information on Prince see Linda Howard, 'A New Beginning', *Charisma* (April 1984), 38-43; Derek Prince, *Jubilee 1995 Celebration: 50th Year in Ministry* (Charlotte, NC: Derek Prince Ministries, 1995), 1-23.

38. Derek Prince, *Shaping History Through Prayer and Fasting* (New York: Fleming H. Revell, 1973).

39. Classical Pentecostals, drawing from texts in the Acts of the Apostles, argue that glossolalia is the essential sign or initial, physical evidence that one has been filled with the Spirit. See Acts 2.1-4; 10; 19.1-6 NIV.

While pastoring, he commuted weekly to William Carey College in Hatties-burg, Mississippi, and after graduating, attended New Orleans Baptist Semi-nary for two years.[40] In 1960, Simpson married his wife, Carolyn, with whom he had three children.

The widely distributed tape *A Southern Baptist Looks at Pentecost*, recounts Simpson's experience of Spirit baptism in 1964. Ken Sumrall, a fellow Southern Baptist pastor and friend of Simpson, was instrumental in introducing him to a Charismatic understanding of the Holy Spirit.[41] Within a year, Simpson's church became Charismatic, and for the next sev-eral years, it struggled to stay in the Southern Baptist Convention, enduring much scrutiny from the denomination.[42] In the late 1960s, like the other teachers, Simpson traveled extensively, teaching in Charismatic conferences and meetings, particularly for FGBMFI and HSTM.[43]

The distinctive teachings of the Shepherding movement were shaped more by Charles Simpson than by any of the other teachers. It was Simpson who practiced them before the others—though without the same terminol-ogy—and who continues leading the movement today (2003). As the move-ment matured and developed, Simpson became the *de facto* leader of the other four teachers.

These five very different men were drawn together because they were like-minded in their concern for the spiritual maturity of the Charismatic believers. They had respected one another's ministries and appreciated the natural unpretentious manner with which each taught the Bible, but they were an unlikely mix: Basham, a Charismatic Disciple of Christ teacher and journalist; Baxter, a unique blend of the Pentecostal and Reformed traditions; Mumford, a Pentecostal trained at an Episcopal seminary; Prince, the scholarly Classical Pentecostal; and Simpson, a Charismatic Southern Baptist pastor. This team of leaders, not without struggle, sought to work

40. Simpson, *The Challenge to Care*, 3-7.

41. Charles Simpson, *A Southern Baptist Looks At Pentecost* (Spring Lake Park, MN: Springs of Living Water Tape Library, n.d.), audiocassette; Simpson, *The Chal-lenge to Care*, 9-13.

42. Simpson, *The Challenge to Care*, 15-20; C. Simpson, 'A Covenant' (unpub-lished paper, 1980), 18. I have more than 30 letters Simpson wrote from 1964 to 1970 dealing with the strains of being a Charismatic church in the Southern Baptist associ-ation.

43. For biographical information see Simpson, interview, 5 February 1996; Charles Simpson, *My Personal Testimony* (Mobile, AL: Charles Simpson Ministries, n.d.), audiocassette. C. Simpson, 'Another Kind of Storm' (unpublished paper, 1979), 1-74.

together in what they later called 'covenant relationship' and began a journey that led to the development of a distinct renewal ecclesiology.[44]

Knowing the Times

The problems with Purvis and HSTM cannot be underestimated in their
impact on the four teachers. The crisis at the HSTM reinforced concerns
they had for problems in the Charismatic Renewal. According to Basham,
'I found myself sharing leadership in conferences with men who had powerful public ministries, but whose private lives were a blatant contradiction
to their public teaching.'[45] Basham said that too often these 'Dr Jekyll/Mr
Hyde'[46] types were left free to minister because of the extreme independence among many Charismatic leaders. In addition, they looked at their
new association as a model that might help other leaders avoid the same
fate as Purvis. They believed 'that submission to spiritual authority provides the greatest spiritual protection anywhere available for Christian
ministers and teachers'.[47]

Their concerns were not only for leaders. According to Prince: 'We saw
a lack of spiritual growth in many Christians... Thousands of people were
coming into the Charismatic Renewal, but most had little or no knowledge
of Scripture, or how to live in the Spirit.'[48]

The teachers of the Shepherding movement were deeply troubled by
other weaknesses they saw. They believed that there had been male abdi-
cation of spiritual leadership in the home and a general dissolution of the
biblically modeled family unit. They were concerned over the lack of discernment regarding the exercise of spiritual gifts and a disregard for the
need of personal character.[49] In the Charismatic movement, there was a
kind of 'charismania', in which believers were caught up in an 'experi-
ence-based mentality' regarding their faith.[50]

---

44. One ongoing struggle was between Prince and Baxter. Prince, strongly dispensational and oriented toward present-day Israel's significance to God's plan, often
clashed with Baxter's view of the church as the replacement for natural Israel.

45. Don Basham, *True and False Prophets* (Grand Rapids: Chosen Books, 1986), 31.

46. Don Basham, *True and False Prophets*, 37.

47. Don Basham, *True and False Prophets*, 100.

48. Mary Ann Jahr, 'Christian Growth Ministries: Teaching for the Body of Christ',
New Covenant (March 1976), 22-24 (22).

49. Simpson, 'A Covenant', 30-32.

50. Bob Mumford, telephone interview with author, 7 April 1992.

Since the Charismatic Renewal in part was a reaction to a lack of spiritual experience in the historic churches, many Charismatics responded not only by leaving their churches, but also by casting off any sense of ecclesiastical polity, tradition, or restraint, making themselves vulnerable to confusion and deception.[51] It is not surprising then that the four believed this mass of independent Charismatics suffered from 'the lack of vital pastoral leadership'. In their view, many of the leaders of Charismatic prayer groups and parachurch ministries were theologically ill-equipped to provide adequate leadership.[52]

The 1960s cultural upheaval, with its anti-institutional orientation, had been carried into the Jesus movement revival and left many young people 'leaderless'. Also coming out of the 1960s was, in Mumford's words, 'a desperate cry for spiritual reality'.[53] The Jesus movement fostered a generation of energetic and idealistic young Christians in need of spiritual accountability and discipline.[54] Significantly, many of the young people and leaders that first attached themselves to the Shepherding movement were in some manner a part of the Jesus movement.[55]

It was not just the Charismatic Renewal and Jesus movement that concerned the teachers. They saw what they felt was the bankruptcy of modernity. Simpson believed 'man's self-assurance has decreased in virtually direct proportion to his technological discoveries. Society is now like an unstable adolescent with a big weapon.'[56] In a 1970 *New Wine* editorial, Bob Mumford wrote that, 'Everyone is searching for answers in this complex society.'[57] They believed the cultural convulsions of change were eschatological signs that God was shaking all things in the earth to manifest his 'unshakable Kingdom'.[58] The problems and confusion within modern society were providing great opportunity for Christ's church to

51. Mumford, interview, 7 April 1992.
52. Simpson, 'A Covenant', 31.
53. Mumford, interview, 7 April 1992.
54. Quebedeaux, *The New Charismatics*, 139.
55. 'New Wine Forum', *New Wine* (July/August 1973), 30.
56. Simpson, 'A Covenant', 6.
57. Bob Mumford, 'Editorial', *New Wine* (August 1970), 2.
58. Heb. 12.26, 27 NIV; Bob Mumford's 1972–73 tape series *Shepherd of a Dark and Cloudy Day* emphasized that as the society disintegrates, people will be forced to see the reality of the kingdom of God. Bob Mumford, *Shepherd of a Dark and Cloudy Day* (5 tapes; Ft Lauderdale: LifeChangers, n.d.).

be the 'hope of the world'.[59] They saw society crumbling economically, politically, morally, and spiritually, allowing for a proclamation of 'the message of the eternal triumph of God's glorious Kingdom'.[60]

Their analysis of the condition of the Charismatic Renewal and broader Christianity is especially important to understanding the Shepherding movement's self-concept. They saw themselves seeking to be 'men of Issachar, who understood the times and knew what Israel should do' (1 Chron. 12.30 NIV). They felt they were perceiving the issues facing the church and giving leadership in response to prophetic insight. Bob Mumford often referred to what he called a 'now word' or a 'preceding word'. His idea was that God was speaking contemporaneously to his people to give them guidance by emphasizing certain essential truths or teachings. The teachings that were to become their trademark on authority, submission, discipleship, Shepherding care, and the kingdom of God were seen as 'living-edge truths' to confront and guide their generation.[61] This perception began more and more to drive their association as they sought more effectively to teach Charismatics how to mature in their relationship with Christ. They sought to use conferences, video, audiotapes, television, books, and *New Wine Magazine* to bring healthy teaching to Charismatics.

One cannot understand the growing ecclesiological orientation of the four without recognition of their perception of the times. This perception fostered their emphasis on the need for biblical structures to assist in spiritual formation. The quest to find the means for maturing the Charismatic constituency led them down the road toward renewal ecclesiology. Their goal was in the beginning to renew existing churches through their teaching.[62] As time passed, however, this would prove more and more difficult. In the end, they would decide to create their own churches. The story of their journey reveals the tensions and contradictions that resulted as they attempted to stay broadly influential as teachers to the larger Charismatic Renewal, and also to develop church structures under their more direct control.

59. Mumford, 'Editorial', 2.

60. Bob Mumford, 'A Personal Word from Bob Mumford', personal newsletter, 1974, Ft Lauderdale, 1.

61. Mumford, *Shepherd of a Dark and Cloudy Day*. Mumford explains the 'now' word in Mumford, *Focusing on Present Issues*, 2-4.

62. Simpson, 'A Covenant', 36.

At the end of summer 1970, this journey was just beginning for the four teachers (Basham, Mumford, Prince, and Simpson). Despite their differences, they were convinced God had providentially brought them together (and later with Baxter) to bring a mutual accountability and protection, as well as to form a teaching team. They were soon to believe that God had an even larger plan for their association.

Chapter 4

A MOVEMENT IS BORN

Teaching Themes Emerge

As 1971 began, the four teachers were doing much more than sorting out the problems with HSTM. Besides continuing their individual ministries and, as often as possible, teaching together, they were experimenting with videotape ministry, seeing it as a new opportunity. Because Tom Monroe's leadership was needed to manage HSTM, work toward the television station WFCB had slowed. Consequently, Video Ministries Inc., an associate ministry of HSTM, was center stage and became a reality in early 1971 after an investment of nearly $100,000 had purchased cameras, lights, and a fully equipped mobile van for videotaping. The van would follow the teachers around the nation to record their teachings.[1] Videotapes would then be distributed for a rental fee from 'some twenty strategic locations across the United States…'[2] Teachings would not be restricted by the teachers' schedules, and even small Charismatic prayer groups could be regularly impacted by their ministries.

They scheduled a six-week teaching engagement at three churches in the Washington, DC area, in April and May 1971, in which all teaching meetings were to be videotaped.[3] Importantly, at a planning session with Simpson absent, the other three assigned to Simpson his teaching subjects for these meetings: discipleship, fellowship, and worship. Simpson had never

1.   'Enter a New Era in Bible Teaching', *New Wine* (January 1972), 7, 12-13; Don Widmark, 'A Concept Whose Time Has Come', *New Wine* (January 1972), 24-25. Charles Simpson saw video production as especially important as revealed in his 1971 correspondence, e.g., Charles Simpson, letter to John Duke, 7 February 1971, private holding; Charles Simpson, letter to Harold Alexander, 7 February 1971, private holding. 'Video Ministry News', *New Wine* (February 1972), 15.
2.   'Enter a New Era', 7.
3.   Burks and Burks, *Damaged Disciples*, 42.

given a specific message on any of these topics.[4] The message he developed on discipleship for these meetings became one of the Shepherding movement's seminal teachings. The meetings in Washington, DC, included concepts on the need for spiritual maturity, obedience, life transformation, and submission to God and human authority.[5] These were foundational to later teachings.

This new teaching emphasis was a direct response to the situation with HSTM that had brought them together and was also a reflection of other concerns for the Charismatic Renewal. Concepts on discipleship, authority, and submission seemed to address directly the 'individualism and lack of spiritual discipline' among the segment of the renewal they 'were ministering to most often'. These teachings on authority and submission were new to the four and to independent Charismatics, since they all, according to Simpson, 'were skeptical of authority because we associated [authority] with dead churches and abuse'.[6] Nevertheless, they believed the individualism and lack of maturity in the renewal necessitated the teachings despite their seminal and untested form. Throughout 1971, the four men, while still teaching on other themes, became more focused on these new truths which they deemed essential. Many of these teachings were videotaped and distributed through video ministries.[7]

'Florida Boys'

Perhaps, in part, because Purvis had written many important Charismatic leaders suggesting the four had taken over the HSTM and put it 'under strict doctrinal control',[8] questions over the association of the 'big four', or 'Florida Boys', continued.[9] While some of the focus was on Mumford and Simpson joining with the 'demon chasers', Basham and Prince, the concerns went beyond that issue.[10] Charles Simpson's friend and spiritual confidant, Ken Sumrall, had questioned Simpson's decision to make such

4. Simpson, interview, 5 February 1996.
5. Mumford, interview, 2 October 1994.
6. Simpson, 'A Covenant', 21.
7. I was able to secure approximately 20 of these early videotapes from the Holy Spirit Research Center at Oral Roberts University in Tulsa, Oklahoma.
8. Moore, 'Shepherding' (1999), 76.
9. Simpson, 'A Covenant', 34; Simpson says these were among the 'legendary' names they were called.
10. Harper, *Three Sisters*, 30; Quebedeaux, *The New Charismatics*, 141. Simpson, interview, 5 February 1996; Simpson, 'A Covenant', 34.

a substantial and life-changing commitment to the other three men without any consultation.[11] Additionally, a variety of stories began to circulate about their association. Some suspected that there might be 'ulterior or clandestine motives'.[12] Others questioned how long four independent leaders with popular ministries could hold together.[13]

All of this made them realize that the larger Charismatic community found it easier to receive their ministries individually than collectively. This was troubling to them since they, without question, considered themselves to be teachers to the broader renewal, with their new association providing personal accountability and protection as they carried out their ministries.

As a consequence of the suspicions regarding their association and other issues that challenged the Charismatic Renewal's unity,[14] Basham, Mumford, Prince, and Simpson were instrumental, along with Dennis Bennett, Harald Bredesen, and David du Plessis, in starting an annual 'Charismatic Leaders Conference'.[15] The first conference was held in June 1971 in Seattle, Washington, with 25 leaders of the renewal in attendance. The leaders' meeting became an annual event, eventually becoming known as the 'Glencoe meetings'.[16] Each spring Charismatic leaders would convene for several days of dialogue and interaction. The group met in Tulsa in 1972, and in St Louis in 1973 and 1974.[17]

The 1971 Seattle leaders' meeting was an important step in establishing Charismatic unity, because it served as an example of the ecumenical commitment that Basham, Mumford, Prince, and Simpson were attempting to show. Basham wrote of that first meeting:

11. Simpson, interview, 5 February 1996.
12. Simpson, 'A Covenant', 27.
13. Simpson, 'A Covenant', 34.
14. Other issues included views regarding deliverance from demons, mode of baptism, and infant baptism versus believer's baptism. Dennis Bennett, *St Luke's Newsletter* (13 July 1973). See also Harper, *Three Sisters*, 85-90. Quebedeaux, *The New Charismatics*, 141, 159-60.
15. Charles Simpson, letter to John Duke, 29 March 1971, private holding, 1; Charles Simpson, letter to John Duke, 15 June 1971, private holding, 1, 2; Basham, 'Toward Healing', 20.
16. Hocken, 'The Charismatic Movement', 138; Vinson Synan, *Launching the Decade of Evangelization* (South Bend, IN: North American Renewal Service Committee, 1990), 105-106. So named because many of the meetings were held in Glencoe, MO, near St Louis.
17. Basham, 'Toward Healing', 20.

I remember clearly the guarded, suspicious way we looked at each other that first morning. Most of that day was spent in slowly lowering our defenses, and summoning enough courage to speak openly and honestly with one another.

The next three days passed in earnest and sometimes heated discussion about water baptism and demonology. The subject of demons and deliverance was so controversial that at times tempers flared sharply. Ministers who for years had held strong convictions that a Christian could not have a demon or need deliverance, felt that those of us involved in the deliverance ministry were not only in error, but were creating real division in the body of Christ. After one of the sessions, an elderly Pentecostal minister sought me out privately.[18]

That 'elderly Pentecostal' was David du Plessis, who told Basham that he was deeply concerned that his emphasis on deliverance might ruin his ministry, because it was proving to be so divisive. Basham then reminded du Plessis of how much controversy had surrounded du Plessis's own ministry in taking the Pentecostal message to non-Pentecostals.[19] The discussion and the several days of meetings helped du Plessis and other leaders to 'tolerate' Basham and Prince's demonology and build mutual respect.[20]

Recognizing a need for guidelines to help mediate future disputes within the renewal, a 'code of ethics' was drawn up at the 1971 Seattle meeting. The 'document, entitled "Ethics for Christian Leaders", was drafted and solemnly agreed upon, although there was no formal signing of the document'.[21] The document called for criticisms and complaints against any fellow leader or his ministry to be handled according to the Matthew 18 guidelines, by first going privately to the person 'to establish the true facts'. Then, if the problem was not resolved, 'at least two other ministers' should be involved; and finally, if nothing was resolved, the matter should be brought to a 'larger group of fellow ministers'. All of these steps were to be taken before issues were to be made public.[22] It would prove significant that two key players in the dramatic 1975 controversy over Shepherding, Pat Robertson and Demos Shakarian, were not present in 1971, nor were

---

18. Basham, *True and False Prophets*, 189.

19. David du Plessis was asked to surrender his ministerial credentials with the Assemblies of God in 1962 because his ecumenical activities, especially with the World Council of Churches, were an embarrassment to his denomination. Russell P. Spittler, 'Du Plessis, David Johannes', in Burgess and McGee (eds.), *Dictionary*, 250-54.

20. Basham, *True and False Prophets*, 189.

21. Basham, *True and False Prophets*, 189-90.

22. Basham, *True and False Prophets*, 191.

they to be regular participants in the annual Charismatic leaders' conferences.

Fort Lauderdale

Despite their resignation from the *New Wine* editorial board, the four men continued to be viewed as the leaders of HSTM, and many believed *New Wine* was their magazine.[23] For a time, this proved personally frustrating to them, since they each maintained independent ministries completely separate from the HSTM. They were not receiving their salaries from the Ft Lauderdale organization and never did (except for Basham when he later served the magazine editorially).[24] It is understandable, however, that this perception grew even stronger. Circumstances by the end of 1971 were setting a course for their even closer linkage to *New Wine* and the Ft Lauderdale area.

In the summer of 1971, Bob Mumford invited several young men, most of whom were in successful youth ministries in the Jesus movement, to move to Ft Lauderdale to be discipled by him as a kind of discipleship experiment.[25] By fall of 1971, the men had moved to Ft Lauderdale and soon were meeting early each morning with Mumford for prayer, worship, and training.[26] The discipleship plan was well-intentioned, but did not work because the principles were not developed sufficiently to provide a clear purpose and direction for the group.[27] After six months, the group dissolved with several men moving from Ft Lauderdale to pursue other ministry opportunities.[28] From this original discipleship group, however, came three men—Robert Grant, Dick Key, and Paul Petrie—who would

23. Basham makes it clear that before October 1970 they never viewed HSTM as their responsibility and were perplexed at how they were 'tied' to the organization and *New Wine*. They came to believe that this perception 'was established by the Holy Spirit'. Eventually it would become their magazine. Basham, 'How It All Began', 10-12.

24. Ghezzi, 'Bob Mumford', 23.

25. Bob Mumford, letter to Lonnie Frisbee, Bob Grant, Dick Key, Mario Murillo, Duane Peterson, Mike Reed, Ray Rempt, Bob Swindoll, 21 July 1971, private holding, 1. The letter invites these men to an August 15 meeting. Six of these men, excluding Murillo and Peterson, moved to Ft Lauderdale. Key moved from San Francisco's Haight Ashbury area.

26. Gerrit Gustafson, telephone interview with author, 25 January 1996.

27. Dick Key, personal interview with author, 27 November 1995.

28. Mike Reed, telephone interview with author, 27 March 1996.

Bob Mumford's 1971 discipleship 'experiment' group. Standing from the left: Dick Key, Mike Reed, Paul Petrie, Robert Grant, Bob Swindoll, Ray Rempt, Lonnie Frisbee. Seated: Bob Mumford.

later work closely with Mumford. In addition, relationships among the men were established and continued for years.

Another part of the Ft Lauderdale story is the Charismatic ecumenism that had developed around the HSTM and its ministries. The leaders of the Charismatic prayer groups in the area joined with the four teachers and other pastors with a vision to work together as one church in the city. Charismatic Hap Arnold, who pastored Memorial Church, a former Southern Baptist congregation, hosted a Sunday evening 'believers' meeting', beginning in 1969. This interdenominational meeting encouraged the exercise of the gifts of prophecy, glossolalia and its interpretation, and the practice of prayer for physical healing. Basham, Mumford, Prince, and Simpson often were the Bible teachers at these meetings, whenever they were in town.[29]

In August 1971, Bob Mumford started teaching a Thursday night Bible class at Memorial Church in Ft Lauderdale. This class grew steadily and by early 1973 had outgrown the church. The class moved to the Governor's Club Hotel, meeting on Monday night, often with hundreds in attendance.[30]

29. Eldon Purvis, 'The Co-ordinator's Report', *New Wine* (October 1970), 3.
30. Hap Arnold, telephone interview with author, 26 February 1996. It was not

This Bible study became a source for many of the taped presentations of the movement's distinctive teachings.[31]

Charles Simpson, after pastoring Bayview Heights Baptist Church in Mobile for 14 years, decided to resign and move to Ft Lauderdale in December 1971 to work more closely with the other three men and to work with Video Ministries.[32] Simpson invited Sam Phillips, a Charismatic Southern Baptist from Lubbock, Texas, to pastor the church in Mobile. Phillips was a longtime friend, and the church initially received him well.

At the time of his resignation, Simpson was convinced Bayview Heights was ready for his departure, since he had trained the men serving as elders and leaders of the church. When the Mobile church had become fully Charismatic after Simpson's experience of Spirit baptism, the entire deacon board resigned. Seeing the need to restructure the church, Simpson re-studied biblical ecclesiology. Some time later he also ran across a small pamphlet, *The Lost Secret of the Early Church*,[33] which emphasized the need for small 'house church' groups to train and equip Christians to be devoted and committed followers of Christ. Soon Simpson began training lay leaders, though never calling it discipleship. The training of leaders was driven by need after losing so many of them. Several men who participated in the lay leadership training eventually became elders, and some went into pastoral ministry.[34]

The Lost Secret of the Early Church also reinforced Simpson's growing realization that the church was 'simply and constitutionally the people of God in community'. Simpson believed 'the most vital question facing Western civilization is: what is the Church?'[35] Along with Basham, Mumford,

---

uncommon for people to drive two or three hundred miles to be a part of Bible study meetings in the heyday of the renewal.

31. Ed Raitt, telephone interview with author, 26 February 1996. Raitt ran the book and tape library for the HSTM.

32. Charles Simpson, personal newsletter, 1972, private holding, 1; Charles Simpson, letter to John Duke, 3 November 1971, private holding, 1.

33. This pamphlet, *The Lost Secret of the Early Church*, would also influence Bob Mumford. It was written by W.J. Pethybridge and published by Bethany House from 1962–74. This remarkable little tract discussed the relative ineffectiveness of contemporary Christianity, and emphasized the essential need of the Holy Spirit's ministry. Its major focus was on the need for small groups in church structure in order to recover vital New Testament Christianity. The pamphlet was never copyrighted. W.J. Pethybridge, 'The Lost Secret of the Early Church', *New Wine* (April 1970), 1, 5-8.

34. Simpson, personal newsletter, 1972; Simpson, interview, 5 February 1996.

35. Simpson, 'A Covenant', 37.

and Prince, Simpson became more convinced that house churches were central to New Testament ecclesiology and were the missing dimension in contemporary church practice.

After Simpson arrived in Ft Lauderdale, he formed a home meeting with a number of men and their families, feeling the need for a circle of close friends.[36] Like Mumford's earlier attempt, his home meeting became an experiment in discipleship and house church ministry. The five or six couples with a few singles would gather for dinner once a week to share their lives openly and honestly with one another. Though Simpson led this small group he still attended a local Southern Baptist church with his family.

A young musician and member of the small group, Gerrit Gustafson, moved to the area to be trained by Simpson. A Californian, Bruce Longstreth, whom Simpson had met at a conference in California, moved to Florida as well. These men became some of Simpson's first formal disciples. Both would eventually lead churches in the movement.[37]

Through 1971 and into early 1972, the four teachers took an increasing role in leading the HSTM. In late 1971, they began serving on the board of directors for the nonprofit corporation and becoming more directive in advising the ministry's staff.[38] By early 1972, the teachers had again taken a more visible part in *New Wine* through teaching articles and participation in question and answer forums. In 1972, the teaching itineraries of the four were being regularly printed in the magazine.[39] Despite their growing involvement at the HSTM, each continued to maintain his own teaching ministries.

The March 1972 issue of *New Wine* announced the change in name of the HSTM to Christian Growth Ministries (CGM). The new HSTM board, which now included the four men, decided early in 1972 that CGM better reflected the ministry's purpose in bringing spiritual growth to believers through Bible teaching and also served to distance them from any negative association with HSTM. The editorial that announced the name change stated CGM's focus and vision:

> As most of our readers know, the Charismatic outpouring increases daily and so the teaching need expands.

36. Simpson, 'A Covenant', 37.

37. Gerrit Gustafson, interview, 25 January 1996. Bruce Longstreth, telephone interview with author, 29 December 1995; Simpson, *The Challenge to Care*, 21-22.

38. See 'Contents', *New Wine* (January 1972), 2.

39. 'Itineraries 1972', *New Wine* (February 1972), 31.

The magnitude of the demand for teaching, however, has made it necessary to use electronic means of teaching: i.e. audio cassette or reel tape, video tape, as well as literature, this magazine and bi-annual Christian Growth Conferences. God has sovereignly brought the men, ministries and equipment together here in Ft Lauderdale to establish a 'spiritual kitchen' from which He can provide for the needs of His people.[40]

At about this same time, Bob Mumford invited Dick Key, still living in Ft Lauderdale, to serve as the CGM administrator. New Zealander Bill Haythorne-Thwaite had succeeded Neil Frank as *New Wine* editor with the January 1972 issue, but would be replaced just five months later by Key.[41] Under Key's leadership, CGM and the magazine leased new office and production space, and by the September 1972 issue, had a monthly circulation of more than 60,000.[42] Over the next two years, *New Wine* would continue to feature most of the prominent leaders of the Charismatic Renewal, along with Basham, Mumford, Prince, and Simpson.

Through 1972, the emphasis on spiritual authority and submission was increased among the teachers. The spring 1972 CGM conference in Miami focused on the developing theme of spiritual authority:

Setting the tone for this spring's Christian Growth Conference was a series of messages by the noted conference speaker and teacher Bob Mumford. As Bob taught on 'Authority and Submission' God began to unfold before the eyes of the believers gathered in Miami, Florida, a new glimpse of what He is going to do throughout His body in these last days.

In past years God has laid the emphasis of teaching on the Baptism in the Holy Spirit, Water Baptism, The Gifts of the Spirit, and other topics usually associated with the Charismatic movement. This year the message came through loud and clear on a new area: AUTHORITY. God is beginning to place in His Church the authority that has been truly lacking for so many years. Along with this came a new understanding of the home and family relationship, divine order in the church, and a believer's personal relationship of submission to God.[43]

The September issue of *New Wine* presented the first in a significant series of seven articles by Mumford.[44] These articles focused on the need

---

40. 'Editorial', *New Wine* (March 1972), 3.
41. Bob Sutton, telephone interview with author, 19 January 1996.
42. 'Christian Growth Ministries Report', *New Wine* (September 1972), 22.
43. 'New Adventure in the Spirit', *New Wine* (July 1972), 20-21.
44. Bob Mumford, 'Lawlessness', *New Wine* (September 1972), 4-9. The whole series of articles was later published in book form as: Bob Mumford, *The Problem of Doing Your Own Thing* (Ft Lauderdale, FL: CGM, 1973).

for practical obedience to God and submission to his delegated authority in all spheres of life. On the back page of the May 1972 *New Wine*, Mumford recommended Watchman Nee's book *Spiritual Authority* with the comment: 'Spiritual authority...is what the Master is saying to his Body of Christ across this nation.'[45]

Another significant article in *New Wine* was Charles Simpson's 'Covering of the Lord' in the October 1972 issue.[46] This article was a direct result of the HSTM leadership crisis in 1970 and focused on the 'covering' or protection provided by submitting oneself to God's delegated authority in the home, church, and civil government.

By 1973, an ecclesiological emphasis by Mumford and the others was reflected in their articles in *New Wine* and in their teaching focus at conferences. In 1972 and 1973, all four men taught frequently on the fivefold ministry gifts of Eph. 4.11-12: apostles, prophets, evangelists, pastors (shepherds), and teachers. In January 1973, Prince started a series of articles in *New Wine* drawn from what he was teaching in conferences on the subject of the body of Christ.[47] Specifically, he emphasized the roles of apostles and prophets as present-day ministries.[48] Prince also presented an idealistic view of a 'one city, one church' concept in which Christians should congregate not by any one denomination, but by geographical groupings of 'cells' or house churches, in which leaders emerge. Those leaders would then join together to form the church government of the city.[49] Prince believed the 'Church needs a divine revolution, and it's on its way'.[50]

That divine revolution came in the development of the concept of the pastoral ministry they termed the shepherd–sheep relationship. At Mumford's Monday night meeting at the Governor's Club, he taught a series of messages, entitled 'Sheep and Shepherds', and he told everyone present:

> You need to find a shepherd... You make a commitment to him, he makes a commitment to you... If you don't have someone to whom you can go and

45. Bob Mumford, 'A Most Timely Book', *New Wine* (May 1972), back page.
46. Charles Simpson, 'Covering of the Lord', *New Wine* (October 1972), 24-27.
47. Derek Prince, 'Can These Dry Bones Live?' *New Wine* (January 1973), 4-10.
48. Derek Prince, 'The Apostle—God's Master Builder', *New Wine* (February 1972), 18-23; Derek Prince, 'God's Man on the Move', *New Wine* (March 1973), 11-15.
49. Derek Prince, 'The Local Church: God's View Vs Man's View', *New Wine* (May 1973), 14-18.
50. Derek Prince, 'The Local Church', 18.

say brother I want you to shepherd me...you better find one in God and find him soon.[51]

For Mumford and Simpson, the key to making pastoral care work was the formation of a definite, one-to-one, personal relationship between each person and a shepherd leader.[52]

The four teachers now began teaching widely on the need for a personal relationship to a shepherd. They saw shepherds as the most important of God's delegated authorities in mediating his government on the earth.[53] Jesus as the Great Shepherd delegated to 'undershepherds' the care for his sheep.[54]

This concept of Shepherding was a logical next step in implementing the ecclesiologically oriented principles of authority and submission, covering, and fivefold ministry offices. Moreover, their already developing concepts of discipleship and house church dovetailed nicely with the Shepherding emphasis. Discipleship emphasized the need for mentoring by a more mature leader, and house groups provided the venue for building the accountability and community the four teachers believed so essential. This led to a fusion in which a shepherd would care for a small group of people in a house church or cell group. This concept became the most basic ecclesiological structure in the Shepherding movement.

Bob Mumford was convinced that God was directing the innovations in church structure. In 1973, he said: 'I believe right now that the Lord himself by the Holy Spirit is presently dividing the whole body into cells. The move of God in cell groups is about ten years old.'[55] Mumford saw the cell group as 8 to 12 people meeting together under a shepherd or elder. He emphatically stated in his Ft Lauderdale Bible class: 'these cells are the key to what God is doing in the earth'.[56]

51. Bob Mumford, *Sheep and Shepherds* (Sheep and Shepherds Series; Leesburg, FL: Westside Tape Ministry, n.d.), audiocassette.

52. Charles Simpson, *The Shepherd Principle* (Mobile, AL: Charles Simpson Ministries, 1973), audiocassette.

53. Mumford, *Sheep and Shepherds* (audio); Prince, *Discipleship*, 26-27; Simpson, *The Shepherd Principle* (audio).

54. Bob Mumford, *Religious Politics* (Shepherd of a Dark and Cloudy Day Series; Ft Lauderdale, FL: LifeChangers, 1973), audiocassette.

55. Bob Mumford, *Christ's Victory in the Human Situation* (Shepherd of a Dark and Cloudy Day Series; Ft Lauderdale, FL: LifeChangers, 1973), audiocassette.

56. Mumford, *Christ's Victory* (audio).

Mumford and the teachers thought that finding a shepherd was the crucial step of finding one's 'placement' in Christ's Body.[57] Believers were not to be casual church participants who simply attended meetings. Each believer was a vital participant in the church.[58] Relationship was the key word. To be involved in church meant to have a vital relationship, first with a shepherd, and then with other believers. The goal was for the development of committed relationships in which believers found 'identity and function' in the Body.[59]

The focus on committed relationships and community fostered a new teaching emphasis, the concept of 'covenant relationship'. In 1972, Simpson had taught on the 'Anatomy of a Covenant' in Ft Lauderdale.[60] Thereafter, Simpson and the other three leaders began to discuss openly the term 'covenant relationship', as descriptive of their association together. They came to believe that 'Christianity in the biblical sense is a covenant relationship to God through Jesus Christ'.[61] As a consequence of that initial covenant relationship with God, all believers were brought into relationship with one another. They believed covenant relationships were one more answer to the problem of independence among Charismatics. It was not a biblical option to walk alone; believers were to be vitally connected to shepherds and fellow Christians and to learn to demonstrate commitment, loyalty, accountability, and service within community life.

Generally these teachings were well received in conferences and camps at which the four men spoke. Their teachings seemed to be another dimension of the revitalization of New Testament truth which Charismatics had experienced for over a decade. The early 1970s were exciting and exhausting times for Basham, Mumford, Prince, and Simpson, who were in as much demand as ever. The teachers remained committed to the practice of their concepts of shepherding, covenant relationship, and house church with people whom they were directly associated. In Ft Lauderdale, by spring 1973, several house church/cell groups were being led by shepherds. Basham, Mumford, and Prince were each leading groups, as was Simpson, who was preparing to move back to Mobile. These small groups

57. 'Forum: Discipleship', *New Wine* (March 1974), 27-31 (27).
58. Bob Mumford, *Christ in Session* (Ft Lauderdale, FL: Bob Mumford Ministries, 1973), 82-83. This small book reveals the developing ecclesiology in an early form.
59. Charles Simpson, *How Shepherds Relate to Other Shepherds* (Mobile, AL: Charles Simpson Ministries, 1973), audiocassette.
60. Simpson, 'A Covenant', 54.
61. Simpson, 'A Covenant', 54.

were not formally structured or organized churches, but were relationally focused around meals, prayer, worship, Bible teaching, and recreation.[62]

An important influence on the developing concepts of discipleship and Shepherding was the ministry of Argentinean pastor Juan Carlos Ortiz. Basham, Mumford, and Prince heard Ortiz speak in the fall of 1973 and invited him to Ft Lauderdale in October. Ortiz's teaching centered on principles of small group discipleship which he and other leaders were practicing in Buenos Aires. Orville Swindol and Keith Bentson, also from Buenos Aires, taught discipling principles at a November 1973 conference in Cherry Hill, New Jersey, which the three teachers, without Simpson, attended. According to Simpson, Ortiz had little influence on his discipling approach, and he never attended any of Ortiz's meetings.[63] Mumford acknowledges, however, that Ortiz was a strong influence on his own thinking regarding discipleship and Shepherding.[64] Watchman Nee's book *Spiritual Authority* was also a continuing conceptual influence for Mumford.

On Thanksgiving weekend in 1973, CGM held its last general teaching conference,[65] a decision that disturbed some CGM supporters. Nevertheless, the four teachers felt that while they were

> declaring the need for the Body of Christ in each area to come together under God-given leadership…[the] seminars were in fact hindering this very thing from happening by perpetuating the tendency for people to receive teaching apart from the leadership of the local church.[66]

Also contributing to this decision to stop the conferences was their emphasis on the role of male leadership. The conferences, especially daytime sessions, were attended mostly by women. They believed this was counterproductive to establishing male leadership in the home, since they were making wives more spiritual than their husbands.

By the end of 1973, Mumford, Prince, and Basham, and their house church shepherds continued their efforts at understanding how to structure

62. Key, interview, 27 November 1995; Sutton, interview, 19 January 1996.

63. Charles Simpson, telephone interview with author, 8 February 1996. Simpson does reference Ortiz and his discipleship methods in *The Shepherd Principle* (audio).

64. Mumford, interview, 9 February 1996.

65. At this conference the ministry Intercessors for America (IFA) was established. Although this prayer ministry became a separate organization under the leadership of Ohio businessman John Beckett, it has maintained close ties to CGM, and Beckett submitted to Basham as his pastor. IFA continues its ministries today. 'Forum', *New Wine* (December 1976), 27-31 (28).

66. 'Forum' (December 1976), 28.

the informal house churches.[67] Though uncertainty remained as to how much they should organize, they decided, nevertheless, to form a new organization called 'Good News Fellowship' as a corporate covering for the house churches in the Ft Lauderdale area.[68]

Mobile, Alabama

While Ft Lauderdale was increasingly seen as the operational base of the four teachers, another center was developing in the Mobile area. In July 1973, Charles Simpson moved from Ft Lauderdale to Gautier, Mississippi, near Pascagoula, which is about 40 miles from Mobile, Alabama. Weary from extensive travel and itinerant ministry, Simpson wanted to spend more time with his family and be closer to his roots. He also moved because of the growing number of pastors in the Mobile area who were looking to him for leadership.[69] Several of these pastors were trained by Simpson while he pastored in Mobile.

In the fall of 1972, some of these leaders had formed the Gulf Coast Fellowship as an association of house churches, and with his move, Simpson became the senior pastor of this organization.[70] Over the next three years, Simpson used his pastoral and structural acumen to build a growing house church fellowship. Their first joint meeting in August 1973 was attended by 100 committed members under the care of several shepherds.

At Simpson's request, his disciple, Gerrit Gustafson, was sent to pastor in Colorado in mid-1972.[71] Within weeks, Gustafson wrote and asked Simpson to continue pastoring him 'as Paul continued to care for Timothy and Titus'.[72] This became the first of many defined translocal pastoral relationships for Simpson.

In the fall of 1973, Simpson was pastoring some 20 leaders and working with three key associates, John Duke, Terry Parker, and Glen Roachelle, all of whom were pastoring other leaders as well. Simpson and these men were seeking to practice the principles of church life that recognized the

67. Key, interview, 27 November 1995.

68. Sutton, interview, 19 January 1996; Articles of Incorporation and Bylaws of the Good News Fellowship Church, Inc., July 1974, private holding, 1-16. They incorporated in July 1974.

69. Simpson, interview, 8 February 1996.

70. Simpson, 'Another Kind of Storm', 6.

71. Charles Simpson, letter to friends, 29 May 1972, private holding.

72. Simpson, *The Challenge to Care*, 22.

need for 'a committed constituency, a personal and not professional relationship between pastor and people, the church in the home, [and] the
family as the basic unit of church structure'.[73]

For a time some people in the house churches, including Simpson and
his family, attended traditional churches on Sunday.[74] The practice, which
continued until the end of 1975, eventually proved unworkable as Gulf
Coast Fellowship continued to become a functional but non-traditional
church. Indeed, it was much different than most churches in the area. House
church meetings were not announced and were closed to all but those committed to the fellowship.[75] The small house churches met weekly under the
shepherd's leadership, and once a month each small group joined together
with the other groups in a larger gathering for worship and teaching. These
larger meetings were open to the public. Structurally, each house church
leader was submitted to a leader, who in turn submitted to another, until all
reported to an associate who was directly submitted to Simpson. Simpson
preferred this chain of command not be viewed as a pyramid, but more of
a kind of 'unfolding genealogy'.[76]

After Simpson's return to the Mobile area, tensions surfaced with his
previous pastorate, Bayview Heights Baptist Church. Pastor Sam Phillips
had been disturbed over the exit of several leaders after Simpson left,
believing that they were having an ongoing relationship with him. Simpson had notified Phillips in 1973 that he was returning to the area with
Phillips initially offering no objection. Nevertheless, Phillips and his leaders soon issued a formal public statement against discipleship principles
and those who believed in them.[77] The February 1974 statement led to some
80 people leaving Bayview Heights Baptist Church, with most joining one

73. Simpson, 'Another Kind of Storm', 10.

74. Simpson would seek to maintain his role in Gulf Coast Fellowship and continue
attending a Southern Baptist church into late 1975. At that time he decided to give
himself solely to leadership of the pastors and churches associated with his leadership.
Charles Simpson, letter to Dick Coleman, 25 September 1975, private holding.

75. Closed meetings were seen by critics as an indication of exclusivism. The Ft
Lauderdale cell groups were also closed to those not in a committed relationship to a
shepherd.

76. Charles Simpson, letter to Merton L. Jannusch, 24 November 1975, private
holding, 1.

77. 'Statement Made to Fellowship BVHBC February 3, 1974', 3 February 1974,
private holding, 1.

of Simpson's house churches. Over the coming years, Phillips would strongly oppose Simpson and the movement.[78]

Shepherds Conferences

From 1972 and into early 1974, the four teachers continued to travel widely, ministering to the broader Charismatic Renewal. They hoped their teachings on submission to a shepherd and the importance of Christian community would help Charismatic leaders draw independent Charismatics into practical, committed church participation. Mumford and the other three men were not expecting leaders outside their direct spheres of influence to submit to their leadership; rather, they supposed their teachings would be applied in existing churches and prayer groups as a force for renewal. There was no conscious plan to start a movement or to take over leadership of the Charismatic Renewal.[79] Though not without some controversy, the teachings of the four men had always been appreciated by other Charismatic leaders and, perhaps naively, they saw no reason to think differently about the discipleship and Shepherding emphasis. They were also leading house churches in the Ft Lauderdale and Mobile areas and had established personal pastoral relationships with a few men translocally. Still, there was no Shepherding movement as yet. Two conferences, held in 1973 and 1974, would mark the birth of a distinct new movement within the Charismatic Renewal.

Leesburg, Florida

Dick Coleman, pastor of Westside Baptist Church in Leesburg, Florida, contacted Charles Simpson in mid-1972 about the possibility of gathering a group of pastors and elders together for a conference.[80] The idea was to

78. Much of the above narrative is from Simpson's unpublished historical paper 'Another Kind of Storm'.

79. I have never found any documents that suggest the teachers intended to start a movement or take over the renewal. To the contrary, tapes and documents suggest the opposite. Bob Mumford's message on authority and submission delivered in 1973 to a Charismatic gathering in Spokane affirmed the local pastors who were in attendance and encouraged his listeners, those present, to show them the proper honor and respect they deserved. Bob Mumford, *Knowing Authority and Submission* (Spring Lake Park, MN: Springs of Living Water Tape Library, n.d.), audiocassette. Simpson's correspondence reflects a belief that the discipleship teachings were to benefit the church at large. Charles Simpson, letter to Gary Browning, 2 October 1973, private holding, 1.

80. Charles Simpson, letter to Dick Coleman, 20 July 1972, private holding, 1-2.

provide leadership training not just for those in full-time ministry, but also for lay leaders who were becoming shepherds. Simpson liked the idea and, together with Coleman, promoted the conference by word of mouth.[81] When the conference was held, 1–4 March 1973, the response shocked them. They expected 75 leaders to attend, and more than 450 showed up, filling Westside Baptist Church. Chairs had to be set up outside the doors of the auditorium to accommodate everyone.[82]

This elders conference, later known as the first 'Shepherds conference', was an overwhelming success. According to participants, the meetings were powerful, with strong worship, much interaction among conferees, and important messages by the speakers. Derek Prince was the opening speaker and said emphatically, 'This is a history making conference'.[83] Prince's message defined the need for shepherds, and he discussed their qualifications and functions. Prince argued in his message that the term 'pastor' should be replaced by the term 'shepherd', because it is the more accurate translation of the Greek word *poimen*, and he pointed out that there was only one instance in most translations where the word was translated 'pastor' (Eph. 4.11). He forcefully argued that the New Testament terms 'shepherd', 'bishop', and 'elder' were used interchangeably. Prince also said that many Charismatics were not being properly shepherded by their leaders, if they even had a leader. Drawing on Mt. 9.35-38, he argued that the need in their day, as in Jesus' day, was for faithful shepherds. Prince did not realize how prophetic his words were when he declared:

> Now I want to warn you and be fair to you. This one truth I am propagating tonight, is far more revolutionary in its outworking than speaking in tongues. This…is going to turn things upside down. The one truth has got in it the dynamic power to revolutionize the entire Church of Jesus Christ and there are lots of people in the Church who don't want to hear it… I've discovered many revolutionary things in the last ten years. I've discovered about demons…demons are not one fraction as revolutionary as this. This is going to blow things sky high.[84]

For Prince and the other three men, the Shepherding role was not reserved only for professionally trained clergy. In Prince's second message at the

81. Simpson, interview, 8 February 1996.
82. Simpson, interview, 8 February 1996; Mumford, interview, 9 February 1996.
83. Derek Prince, *What Are Shepherds? Qualifications, Function* (n.p.: n.p., 1973), audiocassette.
84. Prince, *What Are Shepherds?* (audio).

Leesburg Shepherds conference, he stated that he did not recommend that people go to seminary, but instead advocated a mentoring model for ministry training, referring to the example in the New Testament of Paul discipling Timothy.[85] In this same message, Prince talked about the relationship of modern-day apostles to local churches. He taught that the elders of the local church are ultimately the final authority in local church affairs and that apostolic ministry must be invited in by the local presbytery of elders.

Simpson joined Prince with his teachings on the process of making disciples, and Mumford, not originally scheduled to speak, taught on 'Making Men of God'.[86] Together these teaching themes, along with the attendance of so many leaders, made the Leesburg conference a catalytic meeting. During 1973, more definition was given to pastoral relationships developed with the four teachers and the men they were leading. More translocal pastoral relationships were also established. Simpson wrote in October 1973: 'Now that we've seen how commitments and relationships are established, I believe we're going to see good healthy, normal bodies...' (referring to churches).[87] The surprising success of the conference was seen as God's confirmation to the teaching emphases on discipleship, Shepherding, submission, and authority. Plans were made for another conference in 1974.

Montreat, North Carolina
From the ecumenical involvement at the Charismatic leaders' conferences and through other contacts, the Shepherding teachers began a growing relationship with Charismatic Catholic leaders Steve Clark and Ralph Martin from the Word of God Community in Ann Arbor, Michigan. Charles Simpson joined with Steve Clark to plan a national follow-up conference to Leesburg.[88] It was from these planning sessions that Simpson remembers coining the term 'Shepherds conference'. 'We wanted to find a name that would be acceptable to Catholics and non-Catholics, Steve suggested "shepherd".'[89] As with Leesburg, the conference was promoted by word of mouth and was exclusively for male leaders.[90]

85. Derek Prince, *Relationship of Apostles and Elders to the Local Church* (n.p.: n.p., 1973), audiocassette.
86. Roachelle, 'Chronology', 2.
87. Charles Simpson, letter to Gary Brower, 2 October 1973, private holding, 1.
88. Charles Simpson, letter to Steve Clark, 17 August 1973, private holding, 1-2.
89. Simpson, interview, 8 February 1996.
90. The 1973, 1974, and 1975 Shepherds conferences were for male leaders only,

The follow-up conference was held in Montreat, North Carolina, 27 May–1 June 1974. The July/August 1974 issue of *New Wine* reported 'over 2100 pastors, leaders, elders, and shepherds gathered...for one of the most significant and powerful weeks the body of Christ has ever experienced. Leaders from around the nation and around the world gathered.'[91]

The four teachers, joined by Ern Baxter, John Poole, and Catholics Steve Clark, Ralph Martin, and Francis MacNutt, were the plenary session speakers. The *New Wine* report on the conference said:

> It was clear the Spirit was speaking one message to his people: become rightly related to each other! All over the Montreat campus men did just that. Little groups huddled here and there, sharing what had been happening in their lives or seeking out each other and straightening out their injured relationships, or seeking to establish new ones.[92]

The conference included teachings on authority and submission, but also emphasized unity in the church and the need for leaders to work together 'to build the house of the Lord'. Those attending the conference 'came away with a sense of awe at the power that had broken men into tears, convicted them of their need for one another and formed new and tight joints throughout the body of Christ'.[93]

According to Charles Simpson, he and the other teachers were afraid to walk out of their rooms because so many men were seeking to submit to them. Simpson remembered, 'At least twenty men sought to lay their lives down to me.'[94]

At the Montreat conference, for the first time, the four teachers held a joint meeting with those committed to their leadership. This meeting was a significant beginning point for the Shepherding movement. It was in this smaller meeting at the conference that Ern Baxter joined the other four teachers. Baxter had been invited to the private meeting as an observer and, as soon as he entered the meeting, he began to weep. The other four addressed the group and told of their 1970 association at the hotel room meeting. Baxter rose and walked to the front, and in tears, expressed his

reflecting the movement's emphasis, shared by the Charismatic Catholics and Lutherans, on male leadership.

91. 'Echoes of the Spirit', *New Wine* (July/August 1974), 23.
92. 'Echoes of the Spirit' (1974), 23.
93. 'Echoes of the Spirit' (1974), 23.
94. Simpson, interview, 8 February 1996.

desire for accountability and relationship, 'This is what I've been looking for in all my years of ministry.'[95]

At Montreat, a Philadelphia pastor, John Poole, joined the five teachers and for two years served with them in prominent leadership. Marital problems would later cause Poole to step away from association with the movement and leave the ministry. While some refer to the 'Ft Lauderdale six' by including Poole, he never received the same level of recognition gained by the other five during his association with them.

The world-renowned evangelist Billy Graham, who lived nearby in Black Mountain, North Carolina, attended one of the conference sessions and brought a greeting to conferees. This added to the sense of God's blessing.[96]

Summary

As had the Leesburg conference a year earlier, the great success of the Montreat Shepherds conference further convinced Mumford, Simpson, and the others that what they were teaching was addressing a deep need in the Charismatic Renewal. It also demonstrated, in their view, that God's approval was on what they were doing. At the Montreat conference, the Shepherding movement was born. From this time on, they recognized that they were riding a growing wave of momentum centered around their teachings on discipleship, shepherding care, and translocal relationships.

Also significant in 1974 were two issues of *New Wine*. The March 1974 issue's cover theme was: 'Discipleship—Being Made Ready for the Master's Use', and carried an important foundational article by Simpson, 'Making Disciples'.[97] This was followed by the May 1974 issue and its cover theme, 'The Ministry of the Shepherd', containing many articles on the subject.[98] *New Wine*'s wide national circulation, along with the five teachers' association with the magazine, gave them a stronger joint identification with these teachings than ever before. The Shepherds conferences had given them a sense of affirmation for their emphases and the

95. Ern Baxter, *Conversations with Dr Ern Baxter*, Part 3 (New York: Laseredit East, 1992), videocassette.

96. 'Renewal Leaders Move Toward Unity', *New Covenant* (August 1974), 26; Charles Simpson, personal newsletter, 1975, private holding, 1.

97. Charles Simpson, 'Making Disciples', *New Wine* (March 1974), 4-8.

98. *New Wine* (May 1974), 1-31.

realization that there was a growing number of pastors and leaders wanting to directly commit to their leadership.

In the beginning, the five taught the concepts of discipleship and Shepherding to the broader renewal in hopes of bringing about more effective leadership in existing groups and churches. They had not foreseen, however, how great a leadership vacuum existed within the Charismatic movement. Many church pastors and prayer group leaders felt themselves unpastored and undiscipled, and they saw Basham, Baxter, Mumford, Prince, and Simpson as men to whom they could submit. The five men had underestimated both the need and their influence. Moreover, pastors and leaders not only felt the need for personal pastoral care, but were frustrated with the people they were leading. Church members lacked commitment, vital involvement, and often went from church to church. Many leaders were longing for permanence, order, and respect from their constituents. The teachings on authority and submission, church life, and Shepherding struck a chord with many. Simpson later wrote:

> We operated on the conviction that a basic commitment to obey Jesus Christ and relate to fellow Christians was essential to the nature of a church. Non-involvement makes void the church. Someone has characterized American Christianity as 'the world's largest indoor spectator sport'.
>
> We determined not to become involved with people who had to be constantly motivated in order to accomplish the bare minimum Christian exercises. Pastorally, I had wearied of being involved with uninvolved people. In our sessions we talked about relationships, authority, commitment, character, service, honor, loyalty, and the nature of pastoral care. We took for granted that every Christian was a disciple being prepared for a ministry in Christ's body. Those were exciting and rewarding days. The people responded.
>
> Derek, Bob, and Don were experiencing similar developments. All around us we saw multitudes of 'homeless people' disenfranchised for one reason or another. They, like us, were searching for a permanent spiritual family with eternal values and a reason for life.
>
> The more we saw discipleship and dedication as anecdotes [*sic*: antidotes] to a disintegrating humanism, the more people came, called, wrote, and begged to lay down their lives with us for the Lord.[99]

Whether the five teachers were ready for it or even wanted it, all of these factors had created, by the fall of 1974, a distinct new movement within the Charismatic Renewal. Also by fall 1974, two centers had developed. In the Mobile area, Simpson and others were leading a growing

99. Simpson, 'A Covenant', 37-38.

fellowship of house churches, all practicing discipleship and shepherding principles. The more publicly identified center was Ft Lauderdale, with CGM headquarters and *New Wine*. Over the next two years, the Shepherding movement became the focus of national attention and controversy and nearly split asunder the Charismatic Renewal.

Chapter 5

CHARISMATIC ECCLESIOLOGY

Distinctives

The controversy of 1975 and 1976 was centered on the Shepherding movement's distinctive teachings, particularly on discipleship and Shepherding.[1] To help readers understand the controversy, this chapter provides a
descriptive summary of what the movement was teaching at that time.[2] It
is important to recognize that the distinctive doctrines were never static
and developed and adjusted over the years. The description in this chapter
is a picture of what they taught, drawn from materials in 1974 through
1976 as the emerging movement was still trying to both understand and
define itself. It must also be remembered that the movement's ecclesiology
was being driven by what the leaders thought was a God-directed response
to the times and, consequently, was not systematic. Its public ecclesiological
teachings were sometimes a commentary on its actual developing practice
with church structures. At other times, it seems its ecclesiological practices
resulted from concepts the teachers taught. Further, the five teachers were
not always united in the way they taught or practiced discipleship, shepherding, and translocal relationships.[3] Over the years from 1971 to 1974,

1. Chapter 7 discusses other factors that complicated the controversy.
2. The movement's teachings are complex and are a worthy topic for future study.
The five leaders developed a complicated, dynamic, and nuanced theological and
ecclesiological stance uncharacteristic of the theologically shallow stereotype often
ascribed to Pentecostals and Charismatics. These descriptions are as accurate as I could
make, given the need for brevity since I am not attempting to make any detailed theological analysis. In addition, I chose to define the movement's distinctives before they
became more moderated over time.
3. Basham and Prince were less directive and structured in their approach to pastoral care with Baxter and Mumford somewhere in between the more directive and structured style of Simpson. John Beckett, telephone interview with author, 14 March 1996;
Jim Croft, telephone interview with author, 3 January 1996.

they had already adjusted some of their teachings.[4] Notwithstanding these factors, by 1975 there were several developing distinctives clearly shaping the movement's ethos, and these distinctives would remain over the years.[5]

The Kingdom of God

The movement's ecclesiology was founded upon its view of the kingdom of God.[6] Though shepherding and covenant were the most visible distinctives, the kingdom of God was its central motif.[7] The five teachers shared a 'conviction that the Lord is doing something new—not new biblically, but a new emphasis in restoration of the concepts of the Kingdom of God, which will result in the maturity of the believer'.[8] They believed this new emphasis on the kingdom of God was to take the Charismatic Renewal beyond the emphasis on Spirit baptism and spiritual gifts to a more fundamental dimension in which God established 'His love and authority in the individual believer, and then through that believer to the nations of the world (Matt. 28.19)'.[9]

In their view, the kingdom of God spoke of the reign and rule of God. They believed that the message of the kingdom of God was the primary theme of the Bible and of Jesus' ministry. This message of God's rule necessarily raised the issue of authority. The message of the kingdom was about God's 'authority coming into a time, space, world and bringing man into a willing obedience to the order of God'.[10] Baxter, speaking for the

---

4.   E.g., early on they all seem to have emphasized a plurality of elders/shepherds. By 1975, while still teaching plurality, they emphasized the principle of headship in which one shepherd in a local congregation has final authority. Prince, 'The Local Church', 14-18.

5.   For a picture of its more developed theology and ecclesiology, see Mumford, *Focusing on Present Issues*, 1-24; Simpson, *Christian Life Seminar*; Simpson, *The Covenant and the Kingdom*.

6.   Charles Simpson, 'What Is the Gospel?' *New Wine* (June 1974), 4-7. This was the first of a series of articles on the kingdom of God and the church by Simpson. They were published later as a book. Charles Simpson, *A New Way to Live* (Greensburg, PA: Manna Christian Outreach, 1975).

7.   The movement was influenced by E. Stanley Jones's *The Unshakeable Kingdom and the Unchanging Person* (Nashville, TN: Abingdon Press, 1972), often recommended in *New Wine*.

8.   Bob Mumford, *LifeChangers Newsletter* (Holy Spirit Research Center, Oral Roberts University, Tulsa, OK, November 1975), 1-8 (2).

9.   Mumford, *LifeChangers Newsletter*, 2.

10.   Ern Baxter, Transcript of 'Thy Kingdom Come' message delivered at the

movement, said: 'God has always been absolute sovereign; there was never a time when God was not in total charge… God is the King of the cosmos.'[11]

Jesus' earthly ministry expressed God's breaking into the human situation to restore a new dimension of God's rule that had been lost by Adam's fall. After defeating Satan through his death and resurrection, Christ ascended and was seated at his father's right hand and given full authority over all creation (Mt. 28.18). At Christ's ascension and enthronement, he gave gifts to humanity, that is, the fivefold office ministries of apostle, prophet, evangelist, shepherd, and teacher, as delegated authorities for his kingdom rule (Eph. 4.9-12).

Drawing from Psalm 110, the movement taught that Christ was to remain seated in heaven until his enemies in the earth were subdued by the activity of the 'redeemed community…whereby he would establish God's sovereign right to reign in his own redeemed earth'.[12] The church, therefore, was the key to the establishment of God's kingdom. In a 1975 message, reflecting an eschatological hope, Baxter declared:

> This visitation of the Holy Spirit is not just to give us goose bumps and teach us to play tambourines and sing new choruses. That's all part of the package, but there is something much more important than all of that. It is God's almighty purpose being revealed, that at the end of this age He is going to manifest His glory in the redeemed community, and this outpouring of the Holy Spirit is not only an outpouring of blessing, but is also an outpouring of authority and He is establishing spiritual authority in the earth that He may in this hour bring into existence his Kingdom in power and answer the prayers of multiplied thousands through the centuries who have interceded by saying, 'Thy Kingdom come.'[13]

The expression of God's rule through the church made the movement's leaders address practical issues of spiritual authority. Mumford wrote:

> The message of God's Rule and the impact of the whole New Testament speaks to us about God's reign over His Church through those whom He delegates (see Ephesians 4.11-13) to implement that authority. When we speak of authority, we mean simply God's order, not authoritarianism. Submission, authority, and discipleship, as I understand and teach them, are the

National Men's Shepherds Conference, 1975, Holy Spirit Research Center, Oral Roberts University, Tulsa, OK, 2.
11. Ern Baxter, 'Thy Kingdom Come'.
12. Baxter, 'Thy Kingdom Come', 13.
13. Baxter, 'Thy Kingdom Come', 15.

uncomplicated and basic ingredients necessary for the practical outworking
of the Lordship of Christ in the life of every believer.[14]

The delegated authorities in the church serve to mediate God's rule
through their exercise of spiritual authority. By submitting to delegated
authority, believers were submitting to Christ. It becomes plain that this
concept drove their developing ecclesiology. They were convinced that
'within the concepts of divine authority, discipleship, and Shepherding, lie
the eventual health and well-being of the body of Christ'.[15] Since the church
was the center and vehicle of God's kingdom expression in the earth,
nothing could be of greater importance than its restoration to the biblical
ideal.

The term kingdom of God was frequently replaced by what was believed
to be a synonymous term, the 'government of God'. God was the ultimate ruler of all creation, and he was establishing his government in earth
through the church.

Ecclesiology

In the Shepherding movement's developing ecclesiology, the local church
was the people of God, and not buildings or institutions. In the historical
tradition of the Believers' Church, the Shepherding movement emphasized
the church as 'the covenanted and disciplined community of those walking
in the way of Jesus Christ...the believing people'.[16] They acknowledged
the invisible, universal Church, but stressed the visible and local nature of
the church as its essential character.[17] As with critics of the Free Church
position, the Shepherding movement was accused of being opposed to the
historic and institutional churches. This is part of the movement's para-
doxical story. Basham, Baxter, Mumford, Prince, and Simpson worked hard
at maintaining their commitment to the revitalization of the historic, institutional churches. Before, during, and after the heated controversy, they were
major speakers in denominational Charismatic conferences.[18] The controversy and their emphasis on developing their own churches did slow their

14. Mumford, *LifeChangers Newsletter*, 3.
15. 'Forum: God's Government', *New Wine* (June 1974), 30.
16. Donald Durnbaugh, *The Believers' Church* (New York: Macmillan, 1964), 33.
17. Bob Mumford, 'The Vision of the Local Church', *New Wine* (July/August
1975), 4-8.
18. Bob Mumford, 'Disciple Position Paper' (unpublished paper, 1976), private
holding, 11.

conference activity, but it never ceased.[19] They did believe, however, that the current church structures were inadequate to manifest fully the church in its role of demonstrating the kingdom of God.[20] This quest for building local churches that visibly manifest the kingdom became the main priority.

The church was to be a visible 'alternate society which sets forth un-equivocal norms for behavior and community life [that will] produce the kind and quality of people capable of influencing our society'.[21] They believed 'the ultimate of evangelism in this age...is to be the manifestation of God's power to the total of life of the redeemed community...'[22]

Discipleship and Shepherding

These convictions necessitated practical spiritual authority to provide lead-ership to believers. Convinced that God was working to take the renewal beyond its focus on 'spiritual blessings' to corporate maturity, they em-phasized the restoration of the fivefold ministries of apostles, prophets, evangelists, shepherds, and teachers. The concept of delegated authority undergirded discipleship and shepherding practices. It was through these ministry offices that God 'would bring into existence a community of men and women...who would resemble Christ...'[23] Of these five offices, the shepherd was the most vital to the realization of their ideal of an alternate society. It was the shepherds who were 'in charge of the redeemed com-munity...to develop it to maturity...and attract the world to an alternate society and counter-culture'.[24]

The movement's teachers had worked from 1970 discovering biblical foundations to introduce 'the concept of divine authority into our decadent and rebellious society'.[25] Discipleship and shepherding were the essential components they felt they had found in the Scriptures.

19. After 1975 they were no longer welcome at many independent Charismatic conferences but continued to speak for Catholics, Lutherans, and other denominational Charismatic conferences.

20. Mumford, 'Disciple Position Paper', 5.

21. Mumford, 'Disciple Position Paper', 5.

22. Baxter, 'Thy Kingdom Come', 14.

23. Baxter, 'Thy Kingdom Come', 16.

24. Baxter, 'Thy Kingdom Come', 23.

25. Mumford, *LifeChangers Newsletter*, 2.

Discipleship
Drawing from the relationship of Jesus to the Twelve as a pattern for the discipling relationship,[26] a shepherd/leader was to disciple a small group of men, spending time not only teaching them, but also training them by example and assignment. They believed it had been Jesus' method, and it was to be theirs as well.[27] Mumford believed discipleship

> was a very fundamental and vital ongoing relationship which brings maturity to the believer in every phase of his life. The Christian life is not simply knowledge to be learned, classes to be attended, etc., but rather a life-style which is primarily imparted and passed on by sharing closely with others who know the Way. This is the relationship that the 'youngest brother' Timothy had with Paul. We believe the Lord is leading us to 'grow up' or mature some disciples so that they will be capable of discipling and bringing others to a similar degree of maturity. As the older Christian teaches the younger, he is able to watch over his life, and often to prescribe what is needed for his continued growth and maturity. These prescriptions may come in the form of books to read, tapes to listen to, teachers to sit under, and various other input into one's life. It also involves feedback, oversight concerning his life-style, where he goes and what he does. It is my conviction that discipleship should be an ongoing part of every Christian's experience. The circumstances may vary, but what we want to transmit is not information or procedures, but a way of life. The life of Christ flowing between two persons is a manifestation of discipleship.[28]

While initially a distinction was made between discipleship (a more intense and focused relationship) and shepherding care (a less intense nurturing relationship), in practice, the distinction was blurred, with discipleship and shepherding being nearly synonymous. As the movement matured, there was little reference made to discipleship; the sheep–shepherd relationship was more the focus.[29]

Shepherding
Nothing more distinguished the movement than its teaching on shepherding care. Every believer was to have a personal, definite, committed relationship

26. Charles Simpson, letter to Chuck Farah, 8 May 1975, 12. Jesus as a pattern for Christian life was often stressed by Simpson.
27. Simpson, 'Making Disciples', 5.
28. Mumford, *LifeChangers Newsletter*, 2.
29. The concepts of discipleship were, in the view of the five teachers, affirmed by the practices of Dawson Trotman of the Navigators. Robert E. Coleman's *The Master Plan of Evangelism* (New York: Fleming H. Revell, 1964) not only recommended but sent to the movement's critics a kind of apologetic to their practices.

with a shepherd. The need was for 'personal pastoral care' as it was later termed. This was the cornerstone of the movement's ecclesiological practice. As noted before, a person was joined to the church through his or her relationship with a shepherd who was willing to lay his life down for his sheep. Contrary to charges of critics, the shepherd–sheep relationship never carried any soteriological dimension. The movement's leaders never questioned that salvation and entry into the universal, invisible church was through anything but faith in Christ, who alone was 'the Door'. They did believe that participation in local church necessitated a personal commitment to a shepherd who served as 'a door', caring for the sheep on Jesus' behalf. Mumford defended this controversial view and explained:

> In Spokane, Washington, under the oversight of some twenty pastors, I taught on John 10 concerning the shepherding concept and the requirements of a true shepherd to lay down his life for his sheep. In that teaching I made a statement concerning The Door which is Jesus Christ, and the fact that Jesus is *The Door*, and that a man, as a shepherd, one whom God has called, becomes *a door*. That is, he picks up his position as an under-shepherd to the Lord Jesus, '...to shepherd the church (that is, tend and feed and guide the church) of the Lord...' (Acts 20.28, Amplified), and begins to function in the calling which the Lord has given him. This function in no way affects another man's salvation or redemptive relationship with his Lord. It has nothing to do with a man putting himself between the Lord and the individual believer as a substitute for the Lord in his life. This teaching on John 10 was intended to show that a true shepherd must not be a hireling, but rather that he embrace *the standard of conduct* taught and exemplified by the Lord Jesus Christ as The Door and the Chief Shepherd.[30]

The movement taught that submission to a shepherd provided spiritual 'covering' by being in right relationship to God's delegated authority in the church. The shepherd assumed responsibility for the well-being of his sheep. This responsibility included not just their spiritual well-being, but for their full development emotionally, educationally, financially, vocationally, and socially.[31] Submitting to a shepherd necessarily involved a thoughtful recognition of 'those whom God has placed over us and required a deeper level of transparency and openness' than many in the Charismatic Renewal were accustomed to.[32] Mumford wrote:

30. Mumford, *LifeChangers Newsletter*, 3-4; Mumford's italics.

31. Ern Baxter and Bob Mumford, *Elders' Meeting: Part 1* (Ft Lauderdale: Audio Publications Service, 16 November 1975), audiocassette; Mumford, 'Disciple Position Paper', 5.

32. Mumford, *LifeChangers Newsletter*, 5.

Submission means that we intend to share our lives and decisions as openly as possible. This means that major decisions, such as occupational changes, large financial expenditures, schedule changes, and other matters that affect us personally, as well as the group to which we are related, will be open to the group before they are finalized.

Categorically, let me say: The group or the shepherd does not make any ultimate determination as to whether the individual can or cannot make the decision, but they give feedback, guidance, and counsel which is expected to be seriously considered before action is taken… [There] is a need to embrace true Biblical and balanced authority if the Lordship of Christ is to become practical and applicable in this critical hour of world history.[33]

Many of the movement's early followers were young people who wanted and needed the discipline the Shepherding relationship brought with its concept of authority and submission. Shepherds were to lead their sheep and provide practical guidance in etiquette, personal dress, management, budgeting, and basic home, yard, and automobile care. Moreover, shepherds were to assist 'people in their financial difficulties, family complications, or similar intricate personal problems. To do so effectively requires an adequate degree of biblical authority', Mumford wrote.[34]

Key to understanding how this worked was the recognition that followers were voluntarily to make a definite commitment to a shepherd that included an invitation to be discipled and pastored in all areas of life.[35] Thus, the shepherd had permission to speak into his sheeps' lives. The movement's leaders believed this approach prevented the exercise of unwanted spiritual authority, since individuals had asked for it. Functionally, for a person to be a committed part of one of their churches required this definite commitment to a shepherd. Consequently, one was either 'in or out', based on one's willingness to be pastored personally. The movement's leaders failed to realize fully the strong desire people have to belong and that many of their followers committed to the system without recognizing how it would work practically. Many of them became uncooperative or disillusioned by the degree of authority exercised. Many of these people left to tell of their negative experiences. Others submitted willingly and believed they were a part of a kind of spiritual vanguard preparing the way of the Lord.

33. Mumford, *LifeChangers Newsletter*, 5.
34. Mumford, *LifeChangers Newsletter*, 3.
35. Don Basham, 'Leadership, A Biblical Look', *New Wine* (March 1974), 14-17 (16-17).

Covenant Relationship

The Shepherding movement taught that relationship to God was established through God's covenants. The Bible recorded God's past covenantal dealings with Abraham, Moses, David, Israel, and, finally, through the work of Jesus Christ. They taught that God was a covenant-making and covenant-keeping God, and that he established reconciliation with humankind through Christ's death on the cross.[36] Those who repent and turn in faith to Christ, and therefore meet the conditions of God's unilateral declaration of sovereign mercy, are reconciled to God.[37] Reconciliation brings the believer into relationship, not only with God, but with God's people through participation in the redeemed community.

This theology of 'covenant', with its distinct ecclesiological dimension in the movement's self-concept, became the truly identifying theme. The concept of covenant was very focused on lateral, person-to-person relationships. They saw covenant relationship as the solid ground for permanence and stability within a disintegrating culture. A believer's relationship to God was firmly rooted in God's covenant love, demonstrated by Christ's sacrificial death. Consequently, believers were to commit themselves with the same kind of self-sacrificial love and loyalty to their leaders and fellow believers. Covenant was the 'cohesive substance of kingdom life as given by Jesus Christ'.[38] Christ and his relationship with the Twelve, Mumford wrote, was an example for today's church:

> It was this foundation of a covenant relationship between Christ and His disciples which was a foundation poured for a whole new society. It is the nature of covenant and our loyalty to that covenant that gives Christ's work permanency in a fluctuating and impermanent world. Thus I began to understand that the covenant and the covenant relationship is the ark of safety in our degenerate society.[39]

The relational emphasis of covenant is evident in the movement's use of the term 'joints'. With a restorationist perspective, the leaders believed God was bringing together the dry bones of Ezekiel 37 in their day.[40] Derek Prince developed this perspective in his book *Discipleship,*

---

36. Charles Simpson, 'The Salt of the Covenant: Loyalty', *New Wine* (February 1975), 15-18 (15).

37. Charles Simpson, 'What Must We Do?' *New Wine* (July/August 1974), 18.

38. Mumford, 'Disciple Position Paper', 23.

39. Bob Mumford, 'Principles of Relationship' (unpublished paper, 1975), private holding, 5.

40. Prince, *Discipleship*, 40-42.

Shepherding, Commitment:

> In Colossians 2.19 Paul speaks not only of 'joints', but also of 'ligaments'.
> In the natural body ligaments are the bands of tissue, which hold bones
> together at the point where they are joined. Thus the strength of any joint is
> never greater than that of the ligament which holds it together. In the Body
> of Christ, 'joints' are the interpersonal relationships between believers whom
> God joins together. But what is the 'ligament' needed to keep each joint
> strong and secure? The answer, I believe, is: *covenant commitment*.[41]

Prince illustrated the depth of these covenant commitments by compar-
ing them to the marriage covenant. Many in the movement saw covenant
relationship as a commitment to lifelong relationship.[42] Practically, covenant meant 'abandoning the option to quit' in relationships. It meant one
assumed 'unlimited liability' in relationships by helping a brother or sister
at one's own expense if necessary.[43] The importance of covenant relationship accentuated their quest for authentic Christian community and fostered
their attempts to develop practical church structures. So much of what was
believed and practiced flowed out of this relational emphasis. The movement regularly used the biblical metaphors for the church, particularly ones
that emphasized relationships. The church was the Body of Christ, a spiritual family, an army, and a nation.

As has been seen, small groups were the fundamental building blocks of
church structure under the leadership of shepherds and also the leadership
of apostles, prophets, evangelists, and teachers. House church and cell
groups were not auxiliary, but the very center of church life. The house
church structure was validated both by the New Testament example and
by the Old Testament pattern (Exod. 18) of captains of tens, fifties, hundreds, and thousands. This ecclesiological structure created a need for
many small group shepherds/leaders. The shepherds were seldom professionally trained, but were products of the discipleship and shepherding
system. Most shepherds were lay people serving only part-time in their
roles. Many, however, did move into vocational salaried Christian service.

The Shepherding movement saw itself as developing a kind of spiritual
army. It emphasized the need for discipline, rank, and commitment.[44] It

41. Prince, *Discipleship*, 46; Prince's italics.
42. Derek Prince, *Ligaments* (n.p.: n.p., n.d.), audiocassette. Ern Baxter said, 'covenant loyalty is so strong it can only be broken by death'. Ern Baxter, *Covenant Relationships Part 1* (n.p.: n.p., 1976), audiocassette.
43. Simpson, 'The Salt', 17.
44. Mumford, *God's Purpose with His People Today*, audiocassette.

used the term 'spiritual fatherhood' to stress the goal of establishing nurturing relationships that carried true spiritual authority. A believer was encouraged to find fatherhood in his or her shepherd.[45] It taught that other lateral relationships with fellow believers in the house church or cell group resulted from the relationship a disciple made with the shepherd or spiritual father. In other words, the primary connection with the group was first to the shepherd, and spiritual family was a by-product.[46] Jesus had called together a diverse group of disciples who had then to learn to love each other, and so it was for the sheep who submitted to a shepherd.

Leaders taught that the pathway into ministry was through a submitted relationship to a shepherd. It was in this context that a man could learn to manage his personal and family life in order to qualify for spiritual leadership and ministry. It was often said, 'First the natural then the spiritual.'[47] Under a shepherd, a man was to prove responsible in the natural affairs of life: family, job, finance, and property stewardship. Thus he prepared himself for spiritual leadership.[48]

The Shepherding movement stressed the importance of serving one's shepherd as foundational to development for ministry. Believers were to prove faithful in serving another man's ministry before receiving their own.[49] Essentially, the concept was that, as followers served their shepherds, it helped shepherds serve the followers with more effective pastoral care.[50] This service involved practical labor such as yard work and housecleaning.

The movement held high expectations for participation and involvement. Members were expected to verbally commit themselves, to tithe their income, be fully involved in all aspects of church life, and submit all areas of their personal lives to their shepherd's counsel. Members were confronted by their shepherd if they failed to live up to those commitments.

45. Mumford, 'Disciple Position Paper', 18.
46. Mumford, 'Disciple Position Paper', 18-21.
47. A common phrase in the movement from 1 Cor. 15.46 NIV.
48. Charles Simpson, 'Faithful in the Natural Things', *New Wine* (September 1975), 24-29.
49. Mumford, 'Disciple Position Paper', 21.
50. Serving pastoral leadership became the focus of criticism by antagonists and some former members of the movement.

Emphasis on Male Leadership

The movement stressed the need for male leadership, with strong fathers and husbands in the home. It was understood that women were not to have governmental leadership in the church, and emphasis was placed on the very different roles in the Scriptures for men and women.[51] The movement's leaders believed that many churches suffered from men abdicating their rightful place of church leadership. Women had assumed roles that properly belonged to men. They were also concerned over the weak, effeminate stereotypes often ascribed to ministers and pastors.

Family Relationships

The movement's teachers viewed the home as the most basic unit in church life. They emphasized biblical order for husband–wife relationships and parenting.[52] Men were to be the heads of their households, and women were to submit to their husbands. It was stressed that healthy families made a healthy church.

Submission for All Spiritual Leaders

Mumford and the other four men regularly taught that for one to exercise spiritual authority or leadership one must be submitted to spiritual authority.[53] They believed their mutual submission and accountability served to model what all leaders needed. They emphasized that leaders needed to find someone who could provide spiritual authority and covering for them. These submitted relationships would protect not only the leader from the vulnerability of being alone, but protect the sheep from exploitation by 'Lone Ranger' leaders.

Translocal Spiritual Authority

The five teachers pastored other leaders around the nation, and in a few instances, pastored men internationally. This networking was not, in their perception, an ecclesiastical structure; rather, it was an 'organic' network based on relationship and true spiritual authority. Most of the men Mumford and the others pastored were independent Charismatics. A few relationships were established with men in denominational settings. These denominational relationships were justified, as Kilian McDonnell has observed, by

51. Basham, 'Leadership', 16.

52. *New Wine* regularly featured articles on the biblical family. Several entire issues were dedicated to the themes. See *New Wine*: October 1974; May 1975; October 1975.

53. Basham, 'Leadership', 15.

'the perceived distinction [by the five] between ecclesiastical authority and spiritual authority'.[54] The five teachers believed ecclesiastical authority was all too often external and without spiritual reality, where true spiritual authority was relational and life-changing. They saw the Apostle Paul and his translocal relationships with Timothy, Titus, and the churches at Corinth and Ephesus as illustrations of their translocal relationships.[55]

Personal Tithing

The movement taught that tithes were to be given to shepherds personally. The concept was that ten tithing households could support a full-time shepherd with a reasonable income and allow for the close pastoral care that was emphasized. It was stressed that the tithe was given to one's shepherd and not the church. They taught that as the sheep prospered under the shepherd's leadership, the shepherd would prosper as well. In actual church practice, the tithes were given to the shepherd, then collected into a general fund for establishing salaries based on a shepherd's productivity. The productivity was predicated on the number of sheep he shepherded and the amount of their tithes. Additionally, distribution of funds took into consideration the shepherds' needs. All of these decisions were made by the elders of the church. Tithes were reserved to support ministry activities with offerings given beyond one's tithe for church facility costs, and benevolence needs.[56] This financial approach made possible a very high ratio of full-time leaders to followers.

The practice of personal tithing meant not only that sheep tithed to their shepherd, but also that shepherds tithed to their shepherd. This led to the perception that all tithes were sent to Ft Lauderdale. This was not the case. Basham, Baxter, Mumford, Prince, and Simpson did receive tithes, but only from the men they directly pastored, usually three to ten men.[57]

54. McDonnell, 'Seven Documents', II, 117.

55. Don Basham, transcript of 'How Ministries Relate Beyond the Local Church', message delivered at the National Men's Shepherds Conference, September 1975, Holy Spirit Research Center, Oral Roberts University, Tulsa, OK, 5-8.

56. Prince, *Discipleship*, 32-35.

57. I have the personal teaching notes belonging to former Shepherding leader Scott Ross from a March 1975 meeting in Atlanta where Bob Mumford taught in detail on kingdom finances and the principles described above. Scott Ross, personal conference notes, 2–4 March 1996, private holding, 1-12.

Evangelism

The teachers defined the evangelization process as more than a personal decision to trust in Jesus Christ. From their perspective, evangelism was a disciple-making process in which a person, through faith and repentance, surrendered to Christ's lordship, then submitted to a shepherd, and integrated into the church community. Evangelism, simply for decisions, was discouraged in favor of evangelism that produced mature disciples.[58]

The essential evangelistic character of the Shepherding movement was clearly centered in its belief that Christian community authenticated and demonstrated the reality of the message of the kingdom of God. The formation of local churches into an alternate society and counterculture was necessary 'to successfully challenge our present society, so thoroughly influenced with secular and religious humanism, with the Good News of the Kingdom of God'.[59]

Eschatology

Basham, Baxter, Mumford, Prince, and Simpson stressed the present nature of the kingdom, or government of God, and the totality of Christ's lordship in all areas of life. They sought to avoid a distinction between the secular and the sacred.[60] They resisted the dispensational orientation of many Pentecostals and Charismatics. While the movement never fully embraced a postmillennial view, this orientation would grow over the years as Baxter influenced the others. They regularly taught against the pre-tribulation rapture view, believing it created an escapist mentality that surrendered the earth to Satan. Their collective position probably came closest to representing the historical premillennial position of G. Eldon Ladd, which stresses the 'already but not yet' dimension of the presence of the kingdom.[61] They were convinced that what they were teaching was eschatologically significant to God's plan for the last days that began at Pentecost.

A particularly revealing glimpse of their unique eschatology is seen in Bob Mumford's teaching from Isa. 60.1-3. Mumford told a group of leaders:

58. Charles Simpson, letter to Wayne Myers, 25 August 1975, private holding, 3-4.
59. Mumford, 'Disciple Position Paper', 12.
60. Charles Simpson, 'Establishing the Kingdom', *New Wine* (October 1974), 24-27.
61. Their eschatological position was always somewhat confused by the tension between Prince's dispensational orientation and Baxter's post-millennial views— Mumford once said he was an amillennialist.

> Light is coming to the church, darkness coming on the world. Now these
> two things I think are proceeding in some proportionate way, and I think
> what we can see here does not mean that we believe things are going to get
> better and better and all of a sudden the Kingdom of God is going to be on
> the earth. It doesn't mean that. It means that darkness is coming on the
> people and light is coming on God's people.[62]

In this kind of victorious eschatology, Christ would rule through his
church in the midst of a disintegrating world as a mighty witness for God's
kingdom. God would prepare in the last days a victorious church ready for
the second coming of Jesus Christ to consummate the age.

Restorationist and Eschatological Impulses

The movement's self-concept was linked to restorationist and eschatological
impulses which are far from unique in North American religious history.
Like the Pentecostal and Charismatic movements and general North American Protestantism from which the Shepherding movement emerged, there
was a deep restorationist influence.[63] Especially characteristic of the five's
1971–77 teachings, were their repeated references to a restoration of the
New Testament church order and practice. As already stated, they were
convinced their teachings were a part of God's ongoing renewal process.
Typical of the restorationist impulse, the five teachers believed that after
the death of the Apostles and more fully after Constantine, the church suffered a great loss of spiritual reality that gave rise to dead institutionalism.
While there had always remained a faithful remnant, it was Martin Luther's
95 Theses that ushered in the beginning of God's restoring work, which
had continued with the English and North American awakenings under
John Wesley and Jonathan Edwards. The Pentecostal and Charismatic
movements, with their emphasis on the person and work of the Holy Spirit,
were also a part of this renewal continuum. The teachers believed that, in
their day, God was restoring the ecclesiological dimensions of New Testament life. This restoration focused on the fivefold office gifts of biblical

62. Ern Baxter and Bob Mumford, transcript of Elders' Meeting, 16 November
1975, 1.

63. I am using the word 'restorationism' to refer to a quest to restore the primitive
New Testament church experience. Restorationism, sometimes used interchangeably
with the term 'primitivism', is the subject of a collection of essays edited by Richard
Hughes. See Richard Hughes (ed.), *The American Quest for the Primitive Church* (Chicago: University of Illinois Press, 1988).

government, with special emphasis on the role of shepherd and on covenant relationships.[64] In a 1975 message to a group of Charismatic Lutherans, Bob Mumford made a declaration to conferees that illustrates what he and the other five men believed:

> I believe with all my heart, God is going to restore to himself a New Testament church with apostles, prophets, evangelists, pastors and teachers and the nine gifts of the Spirit and the fruit of the Spirit. They will move and flow together as one. This is the next thing on God's agenda.[65]

Derek Prince was especially given to the restorationist ideal of a return to the primitive church's power and vitality. He saw this restoration as a difficult, but necessary process:

> Also, we must recognize that in many respects the contemporary church is functioning—by New Testament standards—on a gravely subnormal plane. While we cannot forever tolerate such subnormality, it is foolish to suppose that we can immediately make all the changes that are needed. To raise the church from its current subnormality up to the New Testament standard will require—for all of us—much time, labor, faith, and forbearance.[66]

It is evident that a strong eschatological impulse motivated the movement's identity. They were convinced that the restoration God was doing was a part of his end-time activity on the earth. In the message to Lutheran Charismatics in 1975, and again reflective of the other Shepherding leaders, Bob Mumford proclaimed: 'We are moving toward the end of the age' and he challenged his audience to 'embrace all that God is doing'.[67]

These restorationist and eschatological motifs were pervasive in the Shepherding movement's developing ecclesiology. This helps one to understand a striking dichotomy present in the movement, and one that became more apparent as the movement matured. On the one hand, their restorationism made them inherently anti-institutional, and the leaders seemed repulsed by the idea of becoming a denomination. Yet, on the other hand, as they were forced to organize themselves as a result of growth and controversy, they became functionally and increasingly institutional. The

64. This concept of restoration was more fully elaborated in a 1979 message by Mumford to a group of his leaders. The title itself is revealing. Bob Mumford, *Decline/ Dark Ages/Restoration of the Church, Part 1* (Oklahoma City: n.p., 1977), audiocassette.

65. Bob Mumford, *God's Will for the Body of Christ* (Ft Lauderdale, FL: Life-Changers, 1975), audiocassette.

66. Prince, *Discipleship*, 36; Prince elaborates his views in this small book, see 37-45.

67. Prince, *Discipleship*.

tension and struggle to sort out this dilemma is a most interesting part of the movement's story, and similar to the journeys of other religious sects.[68] In 1975, Mumford, Prince, and Simpson, in particular, were anticreedal, resisted the idea of church buildings, and, although sensitive to their denominational Charismatic friends, displayed a general anti-institutional rhetoric. By 1984, however, they went on to develop doctrinal statements, purchase buildings, and exhibit many other institutional characteristics.

Howard Snyder observed that renewal or restorationist movements are 'typically naive concerning institutional and sociological realities and blind to the institutional dimensions of their own movement'. This was true for the Shepherding movement.[69] Over the years, the leaders continued to emphasize the organic and relational nature of their association of churches, and they regularly sought to decentralize and dismantle what they saw as ecclesiastical structures. Just as certainly, they maintained clear institutional features. Although it was regularly denied, the Shepherding movement had a functional headquarters in Mobile from at least 1978. There was a functional, if not formal, leadership structure that acted in a chain of command. There were central unifying doctrines, and the movement held regional and national conferences for its leaders and members. Moreover, *New Wine* served as a corporate voice for the movement.

Nevertheless, the movement's leaders did not believe they were a denominational organization. It is noteworthy that the movement never formally organized itself into a legal corporation of churches. It was always a voluntary association of churches that never kept or maintained a formal roster of affiliated churches. Each associated church or cluster of churches incorporated independently. The leaders were correct in saying that the movement was held together by a network of personal relationships.

Other Developmental Factors

The unusual confluence created by the varied backgrounds and theological pedigrees of the five teachers also affected the growing movement's ecclesiological development and practice. Significantly, only Simpson was a true pastoral leader. Baxter pastored for a long period, but he did so as a pulpiteer more than a pastor. Mumford and Prince were primarily Bible

68. Margaret Poloma explores these tensions between 'Charisma and Institutional Dilemmas' from a sociological perspective in her *The Assemblies of God at the Crossroads* (Knoxville, TN: University of Tennessee Press, 1989), xv, 122-23.
69. Howard A. Snyder, *Signs of the Spirit* (Grand Rapids: Zondervan, 1989), 273.

teachers, and Basham, while also a Bible teacher, was most comfortable as a journalist. The challenge was that their united ministries and distinctive teachings had thrust them into pastoral and governmental roles as leaders of a movement of churches. As men submitted to them, they had to adjust to roles they had not anticipated, defined fully, or been equipped for. The new roles had created high expectations among their followers. While the five men never referred to themselves as apostles,[70] many of their constituents saw them as such. Whatever title one would use, they found themselves in the unique place of leading pastors around the nation, while at the same time, leading the establishment of new local church structures. The job would prove difficult over the years, and, in many cases, they were not able to meet the demands of the task.

An additional consideration in the movement's development was the discussion on ecclesiological renewal from voices outside the Charismatic Renewal. Missionary and author Howard Snyder's paper, 'The Church as God's Agent in Evangelism', read at the 1974 Lausanne Congress on World Evangelism and later published in the book *Let the Whole Earth Hear His Voice*, had caught the attention of Mumford.[71] *The Problem of Wineskins*, which further developed Snyder's Lausanne paper, was enormously influential on Mumford and Baxter in Ft Lauderdale.[72] Baxter called *The Problem of Wineskins* 'a manual for what we are doing'.[73] In the book and in his Lausanne paper, Snyder argued for radical change in church structures in order for Christ's church to fulfill its mission on the earth. Snyder believed that small groups were a part of the biblical pattern for church life. It is not surprising that Baxter and Mumford felt Snyder affirmed their emphases. Juan Carlos Ortiz's book *Call to Discipleship* was also released in 1975.[74] These and other books addressed concepts similar to the Shepherding movement's teachings and were a part of a growing emphasis in the early 1970s on the need for ecclesiological renewal and adjustment.[75]

70. Simpson, letter to Farah, 2.

71. Howard A. Snyder, 'The Church as God's Agent in Evangelism', in J.D. Douglas (ed.), *Let the Whole Earth Hear His Voice* (Minneapolis, MN: World Wide Publications, 1975), 327-60.

72. Howard A. Snyder, *The Problem of Wineskins* (Downers Grove, IL: InterVarsity Press, 1975).

73. Ern Baxter and Bob Mumford, *Elders' Meeting* (Ft Lauderdale: Audio Publications Service, 9 November 1975), audiocassette.

74. Juan Carlos Ortiz, *Call to Discipleship* (Plainfield, NJ: Logos, 1975).

75. Lawrence O. Richards, *A New Face for the Church* (Grand Rapids: Zondervan,

Ecclesiological renewal was converging with concepts of spiritual authority and family life as well. The early 1970s saw Bill Gothard's Institute of Basic Youth Conflicts impact tens of thousands of Christians around the United States. Gothard stressed the importance of a believer's submission to God's 'chain of command' in the family, church, workplace, and civil society. Charismatic Larry Christenson's 1970 book *The Christian Family* was a bestseller for years with its teachings of God's order and submission in the husband–wife relationship.[76] This environment reinforced the Shepherding movement's sense of being in season with what it believed God was doing in its day.

The Shepherding movement's leaders were self-consciously restorationist and eschatological in their teachings. They expected these truths to create a negative response from the contemporary culture. Mumford expected reaction to the introduction of 'divine authority into our decadent and rebellious society' because 'authority is not what our generation wants to hear'.[77] What they did not expect was the severity of the criticism that arose from within the Charismatic Renewal. The movement's leaders were forced to defend these teachings and grapple with the realities of leading a new church movement within the renewal. Days of bitter debate and controversy lay ahead.

1970); David Mains, *Full Circle* (Waco, TX: Word Books, 1971); Gene A. Getz, *Sharpening the Focus on the Church* (Chicago: Moody Press, 1974); Donald G. Bloech, *The Reform of the Church* (Grand Rapids: Eerdmans, 1970); Robert C. Girard, *Brethren Hang Loose* (Grand Rapids: Zondervan, 1972); Ray Stedman, *Body Life* (Glendale, CA: Regal Books, 1972); W. Graham Pulkington, *Gathered for Power* (New York: Morehouse–Barlow, 1972).

76. Larry Christenson, *The Christian Family* (Minneapolis, MN: Bethany Fellowship, 1970).

77. Mumford, *LifeChangers Newsletter*, 2.

Chapter 6

CHARISMATIC CONTROVERSY

The Calm Before the Storm

When Ern Baxter moved to Ft Lauderdale in early 1975, he joined Basham, Mumford, and Prince as a fellow elder of Good News Fellowship, with Mumford serving as the senior leader. The association of house churches was primarily focused on developing sheep and shepherd relationships and held only occasional public meetings. The priority in 1975 was to build a model for what they were teaching. In the fall, Baxter and Mumford began teaching weekly leadership training meetings. Mumford told the leaders there was a need for a 'base of operations out of which the redeemed community can attack a degenerating world'. Reflecting their restorationism, he said, 'The Lord is moving and it's important for me to say that we feel God is speaking to prepare us as an alternate society.'[1] This perspective motivated their efforts to mature their constituents. The Ft Lauderdale church was also being influenced by Charles Simpson's Gulf Coast Fellowship in the Pascagoula, Mississippi and Mobile, Alabama areas, which was more fully developed and functional.[2]

Simpson had visited Ft Lauderdale and was impressed with their progress. In a February 1975 letter to men he pastored, Simpson wrote:

> Relationship in Ft Lauderdale the best I've seen. God is doing a beautiful thing. Ern is moving there now. 'Good News Fellowship' is the church. Bob is pastor, Derek, Don, Ern are all in leadership—all are responsible for disciples. Tithing to shepherds being practiced—shepherds bring into General Fund and salaries are paid out.[3]

1. Baxter and Mumford, Transcript, 1.
2. Baxter and Mumford, Transcript, 2-4.
3. Charles Simpson, letter to Glen Roachelle (*et al.*), 17 February 1975, private holding, 1.

In the Pascagoula and Mobile area Simpson and the leaders of Gulf Coast Fellowship were holding periodic public teaching sessions. Now numbering several hundred committed members, they were continuing their focus on building house churches, holding men's meetings, and developing sheep–shepherd relationships.

Simpson and his leaders were focused on new developments as well. Their view of the totality of Christ's Lordship led them to believe that demonstration of the kingdom of God was more than teaching people about spiritual things. For the church to be the light of the world meant training their people to manifest excellence in all areas of life. In arts, crafts, business, labor, education, economics, marriage, and parenting, Christians needed to model principles of the life of the kingdom.[4] In a day in which eternal values were being eroded and culture was declining, people who practiced integrity, hard work, and excellence would stand out and serve as witnesses to the reality of the kingdom of God.

To facilitate this, businesses had been started to employ some members of the house churches. Shepherds and leaders were encouraged to disciple people toward excellence in their lives.[5] There was a recognition that the goal was not that everyone would become a shepherd, but rather that each person would be developed fully in his or her own unique gifting. An excellent craftsman was as important as an excellent shepherd.

This new focus had started after Simpson and his leaders met and received prophecies directing them to move in this direction.[6] This reveals the importance the Shepherding movement placed on the gift of prophecy. Frequently, their emphases would be influenced or confirmed by prophetic words which they believed were given by God.[7]

While Simpson's leadership team was primarily focused on building churches, they were also seeking reconciliation with Sam Phillips and Bayview Heights Baptist Church, Simpson's former pastorate.[8] Phillips had contacted a number of Charismatic leaders, alleging that Simpson and his associates were dominating their followers and getting rich off their

---

4.   Simpson, letter to Roachelle, 7.
5.   Simpson, letter to Coleman, 25 September 1975, 1.
6.   Roachelle, 'Chronology', 7.
7.   The gift of prophecy in the Pentecostal-Charismatic tradition is a gift of the Holy Spirit (see 1 Cor. 12.4-8). This prophetic gift is not primarily predictive or fore-telling but 'forth' telling whereby God speaks his will or promise for the immediate time.
8.   Charles Simpson, letter to Oliver Heath and Mary Louise Heath, 28 May 1974, 1.

tithes.[9] In response, Simpson carefully answered inquiries about his discipling practices from Ralph Wilkerson, Dan Malachuk, and Harald Bredesen.[10]

Despite signs of developing opposition to its teachings, the new movement was growing. Typical of young leaders joining the movement was Scott Ross, a former popular New York disc jockey, who had recommitted his life to Christ in the late 1960s. In 1975, he was a nationally recognized leader in the Jesus movement and Charismatic Renewal and had been a participant in the Charismatic leaders conferences. Ross was pastoring the Love Inn, a Charismatic church of mostly Jesus people in Freeville, New York, and hosting a nationally syndicated Christian radio talk show. In February 1975, he submitted himself to Bob Mumford, who began to pastor Ross translocally.[11] Ross is an example of one of the well-known leaders who were joining the Shepherding movement. Significantly, Ross had a close relationship with CBN president Pat Robertson, the significance of which would only become apparent later.

In March 1975, the five teachers brought together the men they pastored for a conference in Atlanta, Georgia. At this meeting, the five teachers presented more fully developed concepts of shepherding and covenant relationships. The Atlanta meeting was a milestone for the Shepherding movement. At one of the evening sessions, after Derek Prince had challenged the men, most of the 60 present made life or death 'military-type' commitments to the leaders.[12] Simpson wrote of the meeting in an April 1975 letter: 'Monday night the Holy Spirit fell and caused men to start weeping, reaffirming and making new commitments. We stood in the House of God.'[13] Mumford disciple Dick Key and other men signed written covenants to be committed to their pastor and fellow leaders.[14]

Scott Ross, who had only been with the movement a month, was one of the few men who did not make a commitment. He stood and said he needed

9.   Moore, 'Shepherding' (1999), 142-43.

10.   Charles Simpson, letter to Dan Malachuk, 22 May 1974, private holding, 1-5; Charles Simpson, letter to Dan Malachuk, 8 January 1975, 1-2; Charles Simpson, letter to Harald Bredesen, 10 January 1975, 1-2.

11.   Scott Ross, personal interview with author, 7 February 1996.

12.   Simpson, letter to Roachelle, 5.

13.   Charles Simpson, letter to Dick Coleman (*et al.*), 3 April 1975, private holding, 1.

14.   Key, interview, 27 November 1975.

to talk to his wife before he could take such a major step. Mumford recalled, 'It was like putting a wet blanket on the whole thing.'[15] Neverthe-less, for most present, it was a defining moment that solidified their sense of being joined together for God's purposes and deepened their perception of the movement's destiny in declaring the government of God to their generation.

Gathering Clouds

With the earlier concerns over Basham and Prince's emphasis on deliver-ance ministry and questions that surrounded their association with Mum-ford and Simpson, the men were no strangers to controversy. Dennis Bennett had been offended by Bob Mumford's teaching on water baptism by immersion and pictures in *New Wine* of joyful baptisms in the ocean. Given Mumford and *New Wine*'s wide influence in the Charismatic Renewal, Bennett was troubled at what he felt was an affront to the dif-fering traditions regarding the mode of baptism.[16] It is also likely that some Charismatic leaders had lingering suspicions of the four teachers' handling of the Eldon Purvis situation at the HSTM, since Purvis had called or written many of them following his resignation. Now with Sam Phillips in Mobile contacting people with his concerns, many were becoming cau-tious toward Mumford and the other men. Charismatic Presbyterian leader Bob Whitaker reflects this concern in a 1975 letter to Brick Bradford: 'Historically the Ft Lauderdale group has always been coming up with some new emphasis that tends to cause quite a stir.'[17]

The controversy that would soon boil over had been simmering for some time. Simpson was invited by Ralph Wilkerson to teach on discipleship in August 1973 at Melodyland Christian Center in Anaheim, California. After-ward, Wilkerson shared his reservations with Simpson on some of the principles of discipleship. Later, when Simpson returned to Melodyland in August 1974, California evangelist Mario Murillo, at a morning pastors' meeting, openly challenged Simpson regarding his emphasis on disciple-ship.[18] Mumford remembers that the teachings on spiritual authority and

    15. Mumford, interview, 9 February 1996.

    16. Mumford, interview, 9 February 1996.

    17. Bob Whitaker, letter to Brick Bradford and Doug Brewer, 28 July 1975, private holding, 2.

    18. Simpson, interview, 8 February 1996.

submission were like 'iodine on an open wound', with some Charismatics calling the concepts 'bondage'.[19]

Whatever concerns Charismatic leaders may have had before the middle of 1974, they were not openly challenging the concepts the five were teaching. At both the spring 1973 and 1974 Charismatic leaders conferences, leaders amiably discussed the subjects of authority, submission, and shepherding. At the 1974 conference, Simpson made a presentation on 'The Shepherds Responsibility', and Prince taught on 'Authority in the Body of Christ'. Questions were raised, but no opposition was evident in the discussions that followed.[20]

The Montreat national Shepherds conference in May 1974 seemed to be the turning point. After Montreat, it became clear that the five teachers were leading a growing movement, while continuing to travel and teach widely in the broader renewal. They were using *New Wine* as a powerful voice for their distinctive teachings; and as a consequence, many Charismatic leaders began to see the Shepherding movement as a threat to the ecumenical character of the renewal. Historian Vinson Synan said some leaders 'felt threatened...they were afraid that these guys were running away and getting a lockhold on the leadership of the whole Charismatic movement'.[21] In the perception of the five teachers, they were not building a new ecclesiastical system. They were developing committed relationships for accountability and pastoral care that resulted from themes God was speaking to the Charismatic Renewal in particular and to the larger church in general. They saw the positive and negative responses as an indication that they were addressing real issues for the church in a highly individualistic culture.

In late 1974 and early 1975, Mumford and the other four teachers had meetings canceled with the FGBMFI by the organization's leaders because of the teachings on discipleship.[22] In some cases, they canceled the meetings themselves after being told by the FGBMFI leaders that topics on discipleship were off-limits. Simpson wrote to FGBMFI executive board

19. Mumford, interview, 9 February 1996.
20. 'Summary of Discussions at Conference of Charismatic Leaders 30 April–May 1973', minutes of meetings, 1973, David du Plessis Collection, David du Plessis Archive, Fuller Theological Seminary, 1-26; 'Summary of Discussions at Conference of Charismatic Leaders, 5–9 May 1974', minutes of meetings, 1974, David du Plessis Collection, David du Plessis Archive, Fuller Theological Seminary, 1-19.
21. Synan, interview, 14 February 1996.
22. Charles Simpson, letter to Jack Long, 12 December 1974, private holding, 1.

member Tom Ashcraft in August 1974, explaining and defending the concepts of discipleship. Perhaps in defense of accusations by Bayview Baptist pastor Sam Phillips, Simpson told Ashcraft:

> We do not teach people to come out of churches. My family and I are active in our Southern Baptist Church. On occasions I fill the pulpit. We have an excellent relationship with the pastor. We support the church financially. However, some churches are not as tolerant and members have been put out, as you know. We sympathize with those people too and have tried to teach them the importance of being under leadership.
>
> We know that even the best motives do not prevent us from making some mistakes. We are always open to constructive criticism and honest questions. Christians are using many different methods to train new Christians. We trust that He will give us wisdom, love and patience with each other.[23]

In October 1974, Jay Fesperman, Presbyterian Charismatic, contacted Derek Prince about concerns he was hearing from people around the country about the movement's teachings and practices. Fesperman expressed fear that a 'system or organization' was being imposed…from the outside.[24]

Soon after the March 1975 Atlanta meeting, where the leaders had made zealous covenant commitments, the five teachers became aware of serious opposition to their teachings among FGBMFI leaders, including founder Demos Shakarian. Derek Prince, wanting to address the FGBMFI's opposition to their teachings, arranged a talk-it-over meeting with the FGBMFI executive committee in Chicago on 30 April 1975. FGBMFI canceled the meeting and soon came out with a directive banning anyone who taught Shepherding concepts from any sponsored meetings.[25]

The Controversy Breaks

A series of events would soon 'blow the lid off' the simmering controversy.[26] In May 1975, two former employees of Pat Robertson contacted

23. Charles Simpson, letter to Tom Ashcraft, 12 August 1974, private holding, 2.
24. Moore, 'Shepherding' (1999), 148.
25. Whitaker, letter to Bradford and Brewer, 1; Mumford, interview, 9 February 1996; see also Vinson Synan, *Under His Banner: History of Full Gospel Businessmen's Fellowship International* (Costa Mesa, CA: Gift, 1992), 136, 137.
26. A vivid phrase Dennis Bennett used to describe Pat Robertson's role in the controversy becoming more widely known. In a letter to Mumford and the other four, Bennett says that Robertson 'made the rest of us more keenly aware of what was going on'. Dennis Bennett, letter to the Ministry at Ft Lauderdale, 3 November 1975, private holding, 9.

him over problems they had experienced in Ft Lauderdale. The two men, Wayne Fast and Allen McCarty, had moved to Ft Lauderdale to work for WFCB, Channel 45, the television station associated with the movement in Florida. Fast had been hired as the station's chief engineer.[27] Both Fast and McCarty became involved in Good News Fellowship and were pastored by WFCB general manager Tom Monroe, who was one of Bob Mumford's primary leaders in Good News Fellowship. After Fast and McCarty had a falling out with Monroe, they called Robertson and made many accusations about shepherds controlling the lives of their sheep. According to Fast, 'You must take everything to your shepherd from the most intimate parts of your life to any big decisions, such as buying a car or house.'[28]

In addition, they put Robertson in touch with a couple from Ft Lauderdale who had experienced a severe falling out with their pastor in Good New Fellowship, Ray Ostendorf. They had accused Ostendorf of disciplining them, because the wife had gone out of town without Ostendorf's permission. Further, they had alleged that Ray Ostendorf had, 'in a joking manner', asked them to switch cars—their new Oldsmobile for his old Volkswagen.[29] The couple also told Robertson that leaders in Good News Fellowship had told those in cell groups:

> That we had all seen and experienced all of the religious and spiritual things (i.e. manifestations of gifts of the Spirit, prayer, praise, etc.), and we no longer should dwell on these things or look for them but rather we would be involving ourselves in 'relationships' with each other within the cell group. We also were told to consider ourselves on 'spiritual r and r' [rest and relaxation], no prayer, no leading people to salvation or the baptism in the Holy Spirit, no Bible reading. We were encouraged to bare all of our feelings about each other including how we felt about our marriages, families, group members, and anything else we might think of. There was very little talk about the Lord and seldom did we even talk about the Word.[30]

After hearing from the couple in Ft Lauderdale, Robertson decided to warn listeners about the errors in the Shepherding movement on his 700 Club broadcast. Robertson's comments aired first on 13 May 1975. In a con-

---

27. Monroe, interview, 23 February 1996.

28. Wayne Fast, statement by Wayne Fast, 26 June 1975, private holding, 3. This was a common accusation that shepherds were controlling the lives of their followers. Certainly it was true that in all major life decisions such as engagement, marriage, major purchase of a car or house, followers were expected to seek their shepherd's counsel.

29. Moore, 'Shepherding' (1999), 150.

30. Moore, 'Shepherding' (1999), 150.

versation with Judson Cornwall, a guest on the show, Robertson charged the CGM teachers with seeking to control their followers' lives and told people to 'flee' from leaders or groups that used the terms 'discipleship, shepherding, submission, and covering'.

Even before Robertson had learned of the charges from Fast, McCarty, and the Ft Lauderdale couple, the CBN founder had heard of alleged extremes among others who were practicing the movement's teachings. After the accusations from Ft Lauderdale, Robertson felt he had to act decisively. In a 20 May 1975 memo to all CBN area directors and staff, Robertson wrote that the CBN board of directors was 'unalterably opposed to a Charismatic dictatorship where self-appointed elders begin to take unscriptural control of the lives of others...usurping the role of the Holy Spirit'. The memo continued: 'We further feel a new denomination is coming out of this.'[31]

Two days later, Robertson followed this with another memo in which he said, 'The so-called submission-Shepherding cult is vastly worse than anything I could have conceived of.'[32] At risk of 'serious consequences', Robertson emphatically forbade the broadcast of radio or television tapes that featured 'Bob Mumford, Charles Simpson, Derek Prince, Ern Baxter, John Poole, Don Basham, or any of the lesser lights of the discipleship movement'. Robertson ordered, 'all the tapes erased immediately which feature any of these people'.[33] Robertson asked Fast and McCarty to come to Virginia and write out their charges in detail. Fast wrote several lengthy documents, which McCarty signed as a witness.[34] For whatever reason, Robertson never made any attempt to contact Mumford and Prince to hear their side of the story.

In a 23 June 1975 letter, Charles Simpson, aware of the memos and Robertson's on-the-air comments, wrote to Robertson and made 'a simple plea for direct communication between us'.[35] In the letter, Simpson expressed his appreciation for CBN and Robertson and admitted to some mistakes the teachers had made related to their doctrinal emphases.

31. Pat Robertson, memo to Area Directors and all CBN staff, 20 May 1975, private holding, 1.
32. Pat Robertson, memo to John Gillman and Eric AuCoin, 22 May 1975, private holding, 1.
33. Robertson, memo to Gillman and AuCoin, 1.
34. Fast, statement, 1-6. This statement was also signed by McCarty. I have copies of other more detailed statements by Fast; Wayne Fast, telephone interview with author, 25 August 1998.
35. Charles Simpson, letter to Pat Robertson, 23 June 1975, private holding, 1.

On 27 June 1975, Pat Robertson wrote an open letter to Bob Mumford.[36] This letter, copies of which were sent to many prominent Charismatic leaders, made the controversy over the Shepherding movement the critical issue of the Charismatic Renewal.[37] In the letter to Mumford, Robertson said he had received several 'very disturbing reports' from around the nation about their teachings. He wrote out of his 'personal regard for you [Mumford], but also because CBN for a period of some two years has aired in many cities the various teaching programs which we produced for you [Mumford], Derek, Don, and Charles'.[38]

Robertson went on to mention an affidavit signed by Wayne Fast that contained various accusations. Robertson's letter contained a long section contrasting the Shepherding teachings with Scripture and making serious charges of 'another Charismatic heresy in the order of the manifested sons, the latter rain and Jesus only teaching of the former days'.[39] Essentially, Robertson charged that Mumford and the others were controlling the lives of their followers through an overuse of spiritual authority and that 'sheep cannot buy a car, a home, take a trip, a vacation or engage in any other activity…without permission of their shepherd'.[40] Further, they were not allowing their followers to evangelize before they were spiritually mature.[41] The letter ended with a suggestion that 'a counsel of wise brethren', including David du Plessis, Demos Shakarian, Harald Bredesen, and Dennis Bennett, gather to hear and decide the charges of Fast, McCarty, and the others.[42]

36. Pat Robertson, letter to Bob Mumford, 27 June 1975, private holding, 1-8.

37. Robertson's letter to Mumford was not only sent to leaders for their information, but he encouraged leaders to drop the Ft Lauderdale men from scheduled conferences. His opposition to the teaching was forceful. A copy of a letter to Revd Harold Zimmerman is an example. In the letter Robertson asks Zimmerman to drop the Ft Lauderdale men from the Jesus '75 conference. Pat Robertson, letter to Revd Harold Zimmerman, 15 July 1975, private holding, 1. Robertson's letter to Mumford was only sent to eight or nine men. Apparently one or more of these men widely distributed Robertson's letter. Pat Robertson, letter to Bob Mumford, 15 September 1975, private holding, 2.

38. Robertson, letter to Mumford, 27 June 1975, 1.

39. Robertson, letter to Mumford, 3.

40. Robertson, letter to Mumford, 5.

41. Robertson, letter to Mumford, 6-7.

42. Robertson, letter to Mumford, 8.

Florida pastor and journalist Jamie Buckingham contacted Robertson in July 1975 and questioned the public release of the letter to Bob Mumford and other CBN memos regarding the Shepherding movement 'which somehow have become public domain'. Referring to Robertson's directive to erase all of CBN's Mumford tapes and his order to close all broadcast outlets to anyone teaching the Shepherding principles, Buckingham said, 'It seems that we all have a tendency to form denominations and pass down edicts from headquarters to our "sheep", doesn't it?' Buckingham urged Robertson to meet with Mumford for dialogue. Buckingham thought a broader group of leaders was needed beyond those Robertson originally suggested in his letter to Mumford, which was composed entirely of detractors. Buckingham said Robertson's proposal sounded more like a trial before a 'gathering of Sanhedrin'.[43]

Simultaneous with Robertson's actions, the Presbyterian Charismatic Communion (PCC) held a conference on the Holy Spirit at Montreat in May 1975. The PCC board of directors met together at the conference and, in the words of PCC Western Regional Representative Bob Whitaker, 'the principal concern we faced was the growing tension around the country on the discipleship teaching'.[44] From this meeting, the PCC board felt that the best action was to contact Mumford, Prince, and the other men to 'initiate a face-to-face meeting to share our concerns and hear them out'. Derek Prince had also contacted leaders to try and arrange a meeting of some kind to discuss the growing controversy. Prince was pleased to find the denominational Charismatics open and eager to get together.[45]

Afterward, PCC leader Brick Bradford contacted Bob Mumford and Derek Prince to set up a meeting at the Christian Booksellers Convention in Anaheim in July 1975.[46] Leonard LeSourd, a fellow Presbyterian, also called for a July meeting to hear from Mumford and Prince firsthand about their teachings. LeSourd felt there was much confusion and that a dialogue might bring understanding.

At first, Mumford declined to meet because Prince was unable to attend, and he did not want to meet alone. A late-night meeting, however, was

43. Moore, 'Shepherding' (1999), 154, 155.
44. Bob Whitaker, 'Charismatic Leaders Meeting on "Discipleship"', *PCC News-letter* (September/October 1975), 5.
45. Don Basham, letter to John Beckett (*et al.*), 4 September 1975, private holding, 1.
46. Brick Bradford, telephone interview with author, 12 January 1996.

arranged for 23 July in Logos publisher Don Malachuk's hotel suite. The 11.00 p.m. meeting was attended by Mumford, Jamie Buckingham, Charismatic Lutheran Larry Christenson, California pastor Jack Hayford, Leonard LeSourd, Dan Malachuk, and Bob Whitaker.[47] In the meeting, questions were raised to Mumford about translocal authority and whether CGM was becoming another denomination, which he 'vigorously' denied. Jack Hayford believed 'the present stance of Mumford and team compromised their stated commitments to true submission in the body of Christ'.[48] Whitaker added: 'We tried to get Bob to face up to the fact that with this authority structure…chain of command and a financial structure like he has, he has a new church denomination in the making.'[49] The meeting in Malachuk's room continued until 2.30 a.m. Whitaker wrote about the meeting in a letter to Brick Bradford and Doug Brewer:

> Everyone agreed that what is needed is face-to-face dialog between leaders in a spirit of openness and understanding. Just prior to our meeting Derek had sent out a letter to you, Brick, explaining that he could not be there and calling for a larger meeting of leaders to discuss the whole thing and keep the Charismatic movement on a brotherly basis. We all agreed that such a thing was urgent; we took Derek's letter and added some names to make sure that each denominational fellowship would be represented, and Larry Christenson took upon himself the responsibility to contact most of the men and try to get them to Minneapolis on the 9th and 10th of August. It was felt that it must be then because the planners of the Shepherd's conference will all be together then, and this must take place before the Shepherd's conference because a polarization is taking place.[50]

LeSourd later contacted Mumford, thanking him for his vulnerability at the meeting. LeSourd said he intended to contact Pat Robertson and Demos Shakarian, the two most vocal critics, to try to build a bridge of understanding between the different camps. LeSourd also expressed his distress over Robertson's public statements about Mumford and the Shepherding

---

47. Whitaker, letter to Bradford and Brewer, 1.
48. Related to this writer from Jack Hayford by Janet Kemp, Hayford's personal secretary. Janet Kemp, telephone interview with author, 13 April 1996. According to Kemp, Hayford's calendar does not indicate that he attended this meeting, and Hayford does not remember attending. Whitaker contends he was there, and his notes reflect Hayford's presence. Pastor Hayford acknowledges his involvement in a meeting regarding the controversy but remembers it at a different time.
49. Whitaker, letter to Bradford and Brewer, 2.
50. Whitaker, letter to Bradford and Brewer, 2.

teachers. He also stated that John Sherrill had contacted Robertson, urging others to 'a change of attitude and a willingness to sit down and have a dialogue... All of us are convinced that nobody gains from the kind of ruptures that have been taking place recently in the Charismatic body.'[51] All of this set the stage for one of the most dramatic meetings in the history of the Charismatic Renewal.

---

51. Mumford, interview, 31 July 1998.

Chapter 7

The Drama of Controversy

'Shoot-out at the Curtis Hotel'

Since many leaders were already scheduled to attend the annual Minneapolis conference sponsored by the Lutheran Charismatic Renewal Services, Larry Christenson and others arranged for a dialogue about the discipleship controversy to follow the conference. The 'secret summit', as some called it, was to begin at 2.00 p.m. on Saturday 9 August 1975 at the Curtis Hotel in downtown Minneapolis.[1]

Mumford was especially eager to get to the meeting, expecting it to be a time to establish needed dialogue and reconciliation. He and other leaders recognized that the decision not to hold a 1975 spring Charismatic leaders conference had been a significant mistake because an earlier meeting might have prevented the controversy from becoming so public. Nevertheless, the belated dialogue was an attempt to establish an understanding.

The controversy had become focused on Mumford, since he was the most colorful and well-known of the five teachers. In a July 1975 letter to Logos Publications' Dan Malachuk, David du Plessis made disparaging remarks about Bob Mumford that reflected the suspicion prevalent in many leaders. Du Plessis commented that 'Mumford has become known as the Pope in Ft Lauderdale'. He continued: 'I am almost convinced that these brethren are establishing their own kingdom or Church, and that they are definitely anti- other churches.'[2] Additionally, selected written excerpts from tapes by Mumford and Simpson on Shepherding and discipleship that reflected extremes (in the critics' view) were being widely circulated

---

1.   Plowman, 'The Deepening Rift', 54; Logos Report, 'What Really Happened at Minneapolis?', 60.

2.   David du Plessis, letter to Don Malachuk, 10 July 1975, David du Plessis Collection, David du Plessis Archive, Fuller Theological Seminary, 2.

by FGBMFI leaders. Not only Mumford, but many planning to attend the meeting hoped communication would stop the growing controversy.[3]

On the day of the meeting, Mumford was in his room at the Curtis Hotel when Texas Charismatic leader Robert Ewing knocked at the door. After being invited into the room by Mumford, Ewing began to prophesy to Mumford. He warned him that he would soon experience severe trial and pressure as never before. He told Mumford that he 'should surrender to your enemies for they have the power to destroy you'.[4] Mumford was bewildered by Ewing's words.

As Mumford got onto the elevator to go to the 2.00 p.m. meeting, he ran into Pat Robertson and was surprised to see him carrying a large stack of documents that looked to Mumford like legal briefs. Mumford also remembered Robertson's legal training and wondered if Ewing's prophecy was about to be fulfilled.[5]

The meeting convened at 2.00 p.m. in a small, dimly lit, windowless basement room at the Curtis Hotel, with most of the major leaders of the Charismatic Renewal present.[6] The meeting started with 15 minutes of worship led by Catholic Kevin Ranaghan, followed by each participant introducing himself. An immediate problem was the presence of a number of men who were not originally invited to the meeting. Some of these men had been brought by Pat Robertson expressly to bring charges against the Shepherding teachers.[7] Other men had brought tapes and transcripts they wanted presented as evidence.[8] Near chaos was created when Mumford

3.   Bob Whitaker, telephone interview with author, 11 January 1996.

4.   Bob Mumford, telephone interview with author, 23 December 1998.

5.   Mumford, interview, 23 December 1998.

6.   Unless otherwise noted, the following narrative is taken from: Scott Ross, Notes from Minneapolis meeting, 9–10 August 1975, private holding, 1-6; Bob Whitaker, Notes from Minneapolis meeting, 9–10 August 1975, private holding, 1-24; Bob Mumford, Notes from the Minneapolis meeting, 9–10 August 1975, private holding, 1-21. For other accounts of the Minneapolis meeting see: 'What Really Happened at Minneapolis?', 58-63; Bob Slosser, 'Shepherding Storm is Mounting', *National Courier* (7 October 1975), 9; Peter Brock, 'The Secret Summit Reconstructed', *Christianity Today* (4 April 1980), 45; Bob Whitaker, 'Charismatic Leaders Meeting on "Discipleship"', *PCC Newsletter* (September/October 1975), 5-6. The official minutes are brief and not very helpful: Steve Clark, Official Minutes of the 'National Discussion on Shepherding', 9–10 August 1975, private holding, 1.

7.   Fast, interview, 25 August 1998. Robertson brought along Fast and Alan McCarty.

8.   'What Really Happened at Minneapolis?', 61; Charles Simpson, letter to Jim Reid (*et al.*), 15 August 1975, private holding, 1.

and others challenged the presence of those uninvited and what seemed to be the trial-like approach of Robertson and others.[9] The entire room was cleared, and a committee established to decide who would be readmitted.

Committee members: Brick Bradford, Jamie Buckingham, Larry Christenson, Steve Clark, and Derek Prince decided on 29 men to participate in the meetings, which included the committee members and the other four CGM teachers. Also to be readmitted were: Episcopalians Dennis Bennett and Bob Hawn; FGBMFI leaders Don Locke, Tom Ashcraft, and Bob Ashcroft; Presbyterians, Bob Whitaker and Doug Brewer; Dan Malachuk from Logos; Lutherans Don Pfotenhauer and Rodney Lench; Catholic Charismatics Paul DeCelles, Ralph Martin, Kevin Ranaghan, and Bruce Yocum; CBN president Pat Robertson; Argentinean Juan Carlos Ortiz; Independent Charismatics Harald Bredesen, Gerald Derstine, Scott Ross; and Assemblies of God pastor Eupritt Fjordbak. The list was then posted outside the conference door and the meeting reconvened at 4.15 p.m. Simpson recalls: 'Blood pressures were high.'[10] Needless to say, the uninvited guests were unhappy at their exclusion and stayed just outside the conference room, 'hoping to catch bits of the debate and encouraging their friends when they came out for air in between rounds'.[11] This only added to the sense of tension surrounding the meeting.[12]

Detailed notes of the meeting by Presbyterian Bob Whitaker and participant Scott Ross record an emotion-filled meeting. Brick Bradford had been appointed moderator to maintain a sense of order and establish an agenda for the meeting. Whitaker's notes record the following seven agenda items:

1. Authority and submission especially as it relates to dual submissive nature of ecclesiastical and spiritual authority or Charismatic.
2. Concept of extra-local submission—does it go beyond local pastor and elders? Concept of extra-local authority.
3. Financial area—tithing to an extra-local authority.
4. Logistical concern about upcoming Shepherds Conference in Kansas City being a 'Ft Lauderdale thing'.
5. Reaction of those who disagree with any of the four above, i.e. Pat Robertson and FGBMFI.

9.   Basham (*et al.*), letter to Beckett, 2.
10. Simpson, *The Challenge to Care*, 82.
11. 'What Really Happened at Minneapolis?', 61.
12. Simpson, interview, 21 February 1996.

6. Dennis Bennett asked for a sixth point on the possible emergence of a new Charismatic denomination—is teaching of Charismatic Renewal inherently incompatible with denominations and fellowships?

7. Are there factors present which tend toward a new denomination, and if so, how shall we regard it?[13]

The participants agreed that the meeting would be taped and that everyone would have complete control over what 'he himself' said on the tape.[14] No one was to quote any other participant without permission, but would be free to report on the meeting 'as he judged before God to be good'.[15]

Pat Robertson was the first to raise concerns after the agenda was set. He was forceful in expressing his charges and asserted, 'The authority is the Bible not the shepherd; our covering is the blood not man.' Robertson charged the CGM teachers with usurping the role of the Holy Spirit in the life of the believer and demeaning all Christians by calling them 'dumb sheep'.[16] Robertson told the group that the Ft Lauderdale leaders taught one thing publicly and another privately. He said the cell group approach was divisive and exclusive.

Derek Prince responded to Robertson's charges by calling them a 'gross caricature of my teaching'.[17] Prince said much of what was being reported was one-sided exaggeration, and that the real question was, 'who has authority to teach' and to govern teachings? Prince suggested that authority should be vested in a 'group of proven leaders with established ministries and fruit who are submitted to one another without deception'. He then raised the question: 'To whom is Pat answerable to?'[18]

Bennett broke in and said, 'I'm here to get answers that threaten my church.'[19] The discussion about the issues became more heated and went back and forth with Robertson, Bennett, Bredesen, and the FGBMFI men leading the challenge. The Shepherding leaders would, in turn, respond to charges and questions. At one point, Bennett, feeling the Shepherding

13. Whitaker, Notes, 3-4.
14. I have interviewed moderator Brick Bradford and also contacted Michele Buckingham, daughter-in-law to deceased Jamie Buckingham who moderated the second day. Neither had the tape or knew of its whereabouts.
15. Clark, Official Minutes, 1.
16. Whitaker, Notes, 5.
17. Whitaker, Notes, 6.
18. Whitaker, Notes.
19. Whitaker, Notes, 4.

leaders were being evasive, said, 'Pat's questions aren't being answered.' Mumford responded to Bennett by reminding him that Robertson 'mailed out letters before ever talking to [me] personally'.[20] Mumford admitted there had been, in some instances, 'gross misapplication of practice', but that many charges against them were erroneous and overstated. Mumford asked Robertson why he did not come to him personally before publishing his concerns so widely. Harald Bredesen agreed that Robertson should have met with Mumford 'before firing salvos'.[21]

Don Basham, in a September 1975 letter to a few close associates, wrote, 'Some of our antagonists, like Pat Robertson and Dennis Bennett, tried to approach the meeting as if it was a court trial.'[22] In an August 1975 letter Baxter sent to men he pastored, he said, 'We were charged with being heretics, a cult, self-styled apostles, and attempting to take over the Charismatic movement.' Baxter continued:

> These were painful things to hear, since we felt none of them were true... I felt more grieved at the manner in which we were attacked than hurt by the attack itself... I was not prepared for the kind of hostile and prosecutional attitudes demonstrated by some of our opponents.[23]

Both Mumford and Simpson were the focus of 'intense' challenge and strongly reacted to their accusers. Many leaders, including the CGM men, were caught off guard, because they thought the meeting was intended for dialogue and reconciliation among trusted leaders. Mumford remembers Catholic Steve Clark confronting Simpson and himself at the dinner break and telling them, 'You are being too defensive and emotional.'[24] Just five days later Simpson wrote, 'Bob and I were a little too defensive. We "emoted" too quickly.'[25]

After a dinner break, the meeting continued with Bradford struggling to keep it under control. Catholic Steve Clark challenged Robertson: 'You consistently do not recognize the chair.' Clark also told Robertson that he had not responded 'to Bob's point of how you mishandled the whole situation in regard to the letter you sent out'. Later Robertson did apologize.[26] Still, as the evening progressed the tension continued to mount:

20. Whitaker, Notes, 6.
21. Whitaker, Notes, 7.
22. Basham (*et al.*), letter to Beckett, 2.
23. Baxter, letter to Beckett (*et al.*), 2-3.
24. Mumford, interview, 9 February 1996.
25. Simpson, letter to Reid (*et al.*), 1.
26. Ross, Notes, 2.

Participants often grew exasperated that their arguments were not being heard as each man quickly answered accusations with a defensive attitude. On one occasion the CGM men were asked a specific question and they categorically denied this was their teaching—only to be told 'we don't believe you'. On other occasions some of the accusers asked honest questions only to have their right even to ask the question thrown back in their faces.[27]

The meeting was dismissed at midnight with little progress made, and the participants exhausted. Basham called it a 'standoff'.[28]

The next morning, the meeting was moved to the cafeteria of a nearby Catholic school. A few men were unable to participate on this second day of meetings, and Robertson left the meeting early in the morning. Bradford, weary from moderating the Saturday meetings, asked Jamie Buckingham to moderate on Sunday. Before yielding to Buckingham, Bradford summarized the previous day's proceedings, saying that Robertson needed to publicly 'ask forgiveness for his handling of the situation that [contributed to the] controversy'. He called on CGM leaders to 'temper teaching in regard to controversial doctrine'. Bradford asked for a re-establishment of communication and recognition between ministries.[29]

Despite Bradford's appeal and Buckingham's leadership, the meetings, though calmer than on Saturday, were still filled with tension. Dennis Bennett, who had already once walked out of the meeting in disgust, became angry, stood and stormed out, slamming the door behind him. Being unacquainted with the facility, he had unknowingly walked into a janitor's closet. After sounds of banging buckets and brooms, he re-entered the room and sat down; no one found it humorous.[30]

Gradually the morning discussion became less emotional. 'About noon, there was a relaxing of tensions as the men…dropped their defensiveness and heard one another.'[31] The men felt the Holy Spirit had entered the gathering, and a time of praise began. Dan Malachuk asked the men to go directly to each other with problems and concerns and to stop discussing

---

27. 'What Really Happened at Minneapolis?', 61.
28. Basham (*et al.*), letter to Beckett, 2.
29. Whitaker, Notes, 15.
30. Jamie Buckingham, *The Truth Will Set You Free But First It Will Make You Miserable* (Altamonte Springs, FL: Creation House, 1988), 16-17. Buckingham does not give Bennett's name but all those I interviewed who were at the meeting identified the person as Bennett.
31. 'What Really Happened at Minneapolis?', 62.

criticisms publicly.[32] He said that time needed to be given for 'each man to evaluate the course of events and make his own decisions'.[33] Malachuk also called for time to give the CGM leaders opportunity to 'make adjustments'.[34]

Officially, only two decisions were made. First, they agreed to continue the discussion, and the moderator, Brick Bradford, was asked to appoint a committee to plan for the next meeting in the spring of 1976. Second, in view of a question on the agenda about the upcoming National Shepherds Conference in September, the group decided to trust the integrity of the conference planning committee, which included the five CGM men, Christenson, Clark, Martin, and Ranaghan.[35] The meeting then adjourned.

Basham later said the Minneapolis meeting was a time 'of almost total frustration'.[36] Pat Robertson felt the meeting was a farce and said so publicly afterward: 'My concern is for the gross doctrinal error and resulting practice which has been harming the body of Christ nationwide, and yet has been covered up by a cloak of deception of which we saw only part in Minneapolis.'[37] For Robertson, the August meeting was a turning point. He wrote in 1982: 'Ever since that horrible meeting in Minneapolis...I determined that never again would I be a "Charismatic". From that moment, I was an Evangelical.'[38]

Notwithstanding this perception of the Minneapolis meeting, denominational Charismatics believed that it was significant that dialogue had been established and would continue.[39] Some felt that Robertson's public statements violated the spirit of the Minneapolis meeting's conclusion. Robertson, however, was not present when Malachuk called for discretion in public statements.[40] For all involved, 'The Shoot-out at the Curtis Hotel' dramatically revealed the depth and seriousness of the controversy.

32. Whitaker, Notes, 20.
33. 'What Really Happened at Minneapolis?', 62.
34. Whitaker, Notes, 20.
35. Clark, Official Minutes, 1.
36. McDonnell, 'Seven Documents', II, 118.
37. 'What Really Happened at Minneapolis?', 63.
38. Pat Robertson, memo to Ray Harrelson, Bob Slosser, Tucker Yates, Harald Bredesen, D. Roberts, 30 August 1982, private holding, 2. See also David Edwin Harrell, *Pat Robertson* (San Francisco: Harper & Row, 1987), 126-28.
39. Whitaker, Notes, 6.
40. See Slosser, 'Shepherding Storm is Mounting', 9.

The Controversy Continues

The follow-up to the meeting was furious. Basham, Baxter, and Simpson all wrote letters to the men they pastored locally and translocally urging moderation and caution in the application of Shepherding doctrines.[41] They admitted there were 'some realities to the complaints against us'.[42] Simpson realized the difficulty of Gulf Coast Fellowship's dual authority relationships, in which people were committed to a shepherd in a house church, and yet attended a more traditional church as well. He realized this fueled suspicion of proselytizing. He told his leaders, 'we must...have the permission of the pastor before discipling anyone from another church'.[43] By the end of 1975, Gulf Coast Fellowship stopped any practice of dual authority and became a fully autonomous network of local churches.[44] Simpson also wrote to Dennis Bennett and Pat Robertson, urging ongoing direct communication to settle the dispute.[45]

FGBMFI and Robertson continued their very public resistance to the Shepherding movement. FGBMFI executive board member Don Locke, on behalf of Shakarian who was out of the country, contacted all international directors and officers, discussing the Minneapolis meeting and accusing Mumford of being evasive and unwilling to answer Robertson's questions. Locke said he was 'going to stand with Pat Robertson, because he is doing right'. FGBMFI leaders continued to circulate tape transcriptions of the movement's teachings. In early 1976, chapter officers and those interested in forming new FGBMFI chapters were warned against promoting teaching or materials that advocated Shepherding doctrines.[46]

Part of the FGBMFI reaction went beyond doctrinal issues. Since Basham, Mumford, Prince, and Simpson had been so active in the organization, a number of local FGBMFI leaders were submitting to the CGM leaders or their designates; it became an issue of control. To whom did these local leaders listen? Was it their shepherd or FGBMFI? Moreover, FGBMFI

---

41.   Basham (*et al.*), letter to John Beckett, 3-4; Baxter, letter to Bob Beckett (*et al.*), 3-4; Simpson, letter to Reid (*et al.*), 2.
42.   Basham, letter to Beckett (*et al.*), 1.
43.   Basham, letter to Beckett (*et al.*), 2.
44.   Simpson, letter to Coleman, 25 September 1975, 1.
45.   Charles Simpson, letter to Dennis Bennett, 2 September 1975, private holding, 1-2; Charles Simpson, letter to Pat Robertson, 28 August 1975, private holding, 1.
46.   Moore, 'Shepherding' (1999), 171.

leaders who aligned with Shepherding directed the majority of their financial giving to their shepherd and not to FGBMFI.[47]

In West Texas, the Odessa-Midland chapter had its charter revoked because of its continued involvement with Shepherding leaders after being ordered to stop the association.[48] It is likely that FGBMFI leaders feared that some chapter presidents who associated with the Shepherding movement might turn their local chapters into churches. This would be against the FGBMFI stance as a parachurch support group that existed to serve the local churches.[49]

Some within FGBMFI were unhappy with the organization's opposition to Mumford and the other leaders, and questioned its attempt to address doctrinal issues. Houston attorney and FGBMFI member John Heard wrote to Shakarian and encouraged moderation:

> To my understanding the FGBMFI was not organized and has not been operated over the years to 'straighten out' the doctrinal beliefs of people. I recall the 'Jesus only' dispute of some years ago and the final decision of the FGBMFI not to spearhead or even to become involved in any effort to get all of our factions (even within the FGBMFI itself) to agree on that matter doctrinally.
>
> Even today, we in the FGBMFI certainly are not agitating our Catholic brothers or seeking to exclude them from our fellowship or membership (and certainly not castigating them by name from public platforms) even though doctrinally we may be concerned about them praying to Mary or to their patron saints or believing that the Pope is infallible, nor do we deny Lutherans, some Methodists (and Catholics as well) and others our fellowship because they doctrinally believe in infant baptism and baptism by other than immersion. Essentially the situation on shepherding and discipleship is of the same type and character and FGBMFI should not, to my way of thinking, set itself up to judge or even 'referee' any such dispute. We (the FGBMFI) believe, I feel, that 'His Banner Over Us is Love' and we can and should fellowship and love our fellow believers and look to God and His

---

47. Jamie Buckingham, *Daughter of Destiny* (Plainfield, NJ: Logos, 1976), 284-85; Bill Mayne, telephone interview with author, 28 December 1998. FGBMFI always encouraged people to tithe to their local churches. It did, however, encourage local chapters to give 10 to 20 percent of their gross receipt to the central organizational office. In 1974 FGBMFI sent out pledge cards to chapters asking for a commitment to give.

48. Memo to all International Directors, Field Representatives and Chapter Officers, 12 January 1976, private holding, 1.

49. Memo to all International Directors, Field Representatives and Chapter Officers, 12 January 1976, private holding, 1.

Spirit to unify us in our doctrinal beliefs to the extent He alone determines
is necessary...

There are, of course, a few very basic doctrinal beliefs that go to the very
heart of Christianity (and consequently of the FGBMFI) itself (such as, Jesus
being God's only Son, our Savior, etc.) but the shepherding-discipleship
question is simply not in that crucial category.[50]

Despite appeals, Shakarian remained committed to the course of opposition. Letters critical of the movement continued to be circulated, local
chapters warned that charters would be lifted if they allowed Shepherding
teachings, and some in FGBMFI had their memberships revoked for being
sympathetic to the movement. Aware of all of this, Prince again wrote to
Shakarian and appealed for a meeting to work toward 'a resolution of the
differences'. Prince told Shakarian he was concerned that the controversy
had 'polarized' the Charismatic movement. Prince quoted board member
Tom Ashcraft's public comment of the Shepherding movement: 'Don't
touch that group with a ten-foot pole.' In his letter, Prince offered to meet
with Shakarian 'personally and privately', or in a larger group if it would
help. No meeting eventuated and for many more years FGBMFI stood
with Pat Robertson in opposition to the CGM leaders.

After the Minneapolis meeting, Robertson wrote to Derek Prince expressing his appreciation for 'the opportunity to share briefly with you Sunday
morning as I was leaving the meeting...' Robertson wrote that 'God has
revealed to me that you are a man of intellectual and personal integrity, I
want you to know that I trust you, Derek.'[51] Despite these words to Prince,
Robertson continued to oppose the Shepherding movement. Robertson later
recalled: 'I was really angry.' Historian David Harrell quotes him as saying
'that the independent Charismatic group per se never took official action to
condemn this. And they never have!' Consequently, in Robertson's words:
'I blasted them and...it stopped that thing right in its tracks.'[52] This likely
refers to the formation of a Charismatic denomination which Robertson
and others feared.[53]

Bob Mumford decided to answer Robertson's June letter that had made
the controversy so widespread. In a 9 September 1975 letter to Robertson,

50.   John Heard, letter to Demos Shakarian, 30 October 1975, private holding, 1-2.
51.   Pat Robertson, letter to Derek Prince, 13 August 1975, private holding, 1.
52.   Harrell, *Pat Robertson*, 128.
53.   Robertson's fierce opposition seems to be mostly a matter of believing the leaders were teaching heresy. His gracious comments to Prince, clearly a key formulator of
the early teaching, seem surprising. Since I was unable to interview Robertson, I could
not get his clarification on this matter.

copies of which were sent to a large group of Charismatic leaders, Mumford reiterated his hurt that Robertson had never approached him privately before going public with his comments. He went on to answer Robertson's charges one by one. Mumford admitted that 'some of the charges of legalistic control and mismanagement were true and that steps had been taken to rectify and/or apologize where necessary'.[54] In words that would be restated over the years, Mumford wrote:

> These instances, as far as I know, are occasions of immature use and application of spiritual authority. Misuse and abuse are always wrong. However, the principles I understand to be correct and Biblical. I am not embarrassed to say, 'we have not gone this way before', and some mistakes are unavoidable. We have, as well, sought to walk in all candor, openness and adjustment from responsible leadership—charismatic and noncharismatic.[55]

In this letter, he sought to refute some of the exaggerated claims that were circulating among opponents, such as the rumor he had paid taxes on four million dollars from tithes received the previous year. He called the rumor 'gross and unfounded'.[56] Mumford affirmed to Robertson his and the other teachers' commitment to the Reformation principle of *Sola Scriptura*. He responded to Robertson's criticism of their teaching on authority by challenging Robertson's behavior in the controversy. He wrote:

> The question here is, Who exercised spiritual authority? To what degree? And over whom? Let me address these questions to you as director of Christian Broadcasting Network. How much spiritual authority do you exercise when you decide that I am 'in error', that 'Ft Lauderdale is the Seat of Satan', or when you arbitrarily and unilaterally condemn six [referring to Poole with the other five] of the recognized teachers of this nation. On the basis of your decision, you then issued the two enclosed memoranda—in which you assumed the three roles of prosecutor, witness and judge—all by yourself! To me that is spiritual authority and you were exercising it. It would appear that you are a law unto yourself; your interpretation of the Scripture and your leading become the final spiritual authority...
>
> The simple but profound question is who exercises authority? How much and over whom? You have assumed authority in this matter. Were you right? Could you have done it more scripturally? Should you have counseled with others who themselves are in authority before passing your judgment?[57]

---

54.   Bob Mumford, letter to Pat Robertson, 9 September 1975, private holding, 1-2.
55.   Mumford, letter to Robertson, 2.
56.   Mumford, letter to Robertson, 3.
57.   Mumford, letter to Robertson, 3-4.

Mumford further challenged Robertson's behavior in the Minneapolis 'shoot-out':

> When you suggested a meeting of the brothers listed in your letter, I pro-
> ceeded to implement the suggestion. An ad-hoc group met in Los Angeles
> consisting of Dan Malachuk, Jamie Buckingham, Bob Whitaker, David Du
> Plessis, Jack Hayford, Len LeSourd, and Larry Christenson. Those recog-
> nized leaders could in no way be construed to be 'pro-Ft Lauderdale' or
> 'pro-discipleship'. The three-fold purpose for calling the Minneapolis meet-
> ing, to which you were invited, was to establish mutual communication, to
> examine the discipleship teaching and to adjust, if necessary, the thrust and
> emphasis of the National Men's Shepherds Conference. It is my conviction
> that you, particularly, attempted to divert a discussion among brothers into a
> courtroom proceeding with the purpose of attaining judgment of 'heresy'
> against Charles Simpson and myself.[58]

Robertson wrote a reply to Mumford on 15 September 1975. Robertson told Mumford: 'I love you as a brother in Christ, but I hate the doctrine which you are espousing.' In the letter he said the doctrine is 'not only extra-Biblical', but akin to what the Apostle Paul referred to as 'teachings of devils', and said Mumford would do himself 'a great favor to sit back objectively and ask...where the teaching of "submitted body/covenant discipleship" comes from'.[59] This exchange of correspondence, a clash between two of the most dynamic and powerful personalities in the Charismatic Renewal, showed that neither man gave any ground.

In November 1975, Mumford sent a special newsletter to his entire mailing list and all *New Wine* subscribers, defending himself and the movement. According to Mumford: 'The errors or problems, so far, are limited to the area of practice and application, and are not in the basic Biblical concepts that the Lord is bringing to our understanding.'[60]

The controversy continued to grow in intensity in the fall of 1975 when healing evangelist Kathryn Kuhlman spoke out against Shepherding. In a September sermon, Kuhlman said that the new 'doctrine of discipleship and submission must be stopped or it's going to bring absolute destruction to the great Charismatic movement'.[61] Earlier in September, Kuhlman had received material from a FGBMFI official that opposed the Shepherding movement. The material fueled Kuhlman's concerns and contributed to

---

58. Mumford, letter to Robertson, 6.
59. Robertson, letter to Mumford, 15 September 1975, 2.
60. Mumford, *LifeChangers Newsletter*, 1-4.
61. Moore, 'Shepherding' (1999), 178.

her public statements. In addition, a few female supporters had written to Kuhlman and stopped giving their tithes to her after hearing the Shepherding leaders teach against women in leadership roles. This especially angered her.[62]

Kuhlman, along with several Pentecostal and Charismatic leaders, including Bob Mumford, was scheduled to minister at the Second World Conference on the Holy Spirit to be held in Israel in late October.[63] The conference was sponsored by Logos International. Kuhlman called Logos founder Dan Malachuk and told him: 'If Bob Mumford goes to Israel, I shall not go. The man is a heretic...I shall not appear on the same program with him.'[64] Stunned by the ultimatum, Malachuk notified Mumford and then met with the Logos board of directors to decide what to do. Mumford immediately offered to withdraw from the conference. After much prayer and struggle, Malachuk and the board 'chose to accept Bob's offer and submit to Kathryn's demand'.[65]

Bob Mumford wrote to Kuhlman in October and expressed his dismay about her treatment of him.[66] In his letter Mumford asked for a meeting to bring an understanding between the two. No meeting was ever arranged. Kuhlman's biographers have observed that nobody could demand more loyalty or submission 'than [Kuhlman] did of her employees...' and wrote with some wonder about her vigorous opposition to the movement.[67]

Malachuk and Buckingham, at Logos Publications, responded to the crisis with the September/October 1975 issue of *Logos Journal*. The magazine's cover theme was 'Discipleship' and included articles for and against the Shepherding movement. The editorial said, 'Much of the teaching on discipleship seems solid' but cautioned: 'the tendency to place overemphasis on some tangent aspect of Scripture is always with us, it seems'.[68]

Oral Roberts University professor Charles Farah in his article 'The

62. Wayne Warner, *Kathryn Kuhlman* (Ann Arbor, MI: Vine Books, 1993), 227.
63. The following account is drawn from Buckingham, *Daughter of Destiny*, 284-88. The conference dates were 29 October–7 November 1975.
64. Buckingham, *Daughter of Destiny*, 286. Pat Robertson also refused to participate in the Jerusalem conference because he felt Logos International was giving 'platform to the CGM men'. After Mumford was dropped from the program, Robertson participated in the conference. Jamie Buckingham, letter to Frank (no last name on letter), 8 September 1975, private holding, 1.
65. Buckingham, *Daughter of Destiny*, 287.
66. Bob Mumford, letter to Kathryn Kuhlman, 19 October 1975, private holding, 1-2.
67. Buckingham, *Daughter of Destiny*, 284; Warner, *Kathryn Kuhlman*, 210.
68. Dan Malachuk, 'Publisher's Preface', *Logos* (September/October 1975), 5.

Dilemma of Discipleship', said that, despite the teachers' denials, he thought the seeds of a new Charismatic denomination 'have already been planted'.[69] He said this because Mumford and Simpson were leading their own churches and not just teaching to the renewal at large. Farah believed that the movement had certain institutional features that would inevitably lead to a denomination, even if the leaders did not want it. He also said a new denomination would be 'destructive to Charismatic unity'. Farah recalled the early Pentecostal awakening and how its leaders resisted the idea of denominations. Yet, he said, 'The movement very soon crystallized and took on immovable structure.'[70] Because the issue included articles by Mumford and Juan Carlos Ortiz, FGBMFI leaders felt Malachuk was trying to 'straddle the fence'.[71]

The 10 October issue of the Evangelical publication *Christianity Today* carried a cover title: 'The Deepening Rift in the Charismatic Renewal'. The lengthy news report inside told of the controversy, the Minneapolis meeting, and of the growing division among Charismatics over Shepherding principles.[72]

The Tuesday 16 September 1975 edition of the *New York Times* carried the article, 'Charismatic Movement is Facing Internal Discord Over Teaching Called "Discipling"'. The reasonably objective report was widely distributed through the New York Times News Service.[73]

Logos followed up with more articles and commentary on the Shepherding controversy in the November/December 1975 issue. Jack Hayford, pastor of Church On The Way, wrote an article that challenged both sides of the controversy. Hayford criticized the hasty judgment of some toward the five teachers, but also expressed concerns over the movement's failure, in his view, to thoroughly answer critics' charges 'regardless of how groundless' they may be. Hayford said, 'A self-righteously indignant stance which refuses to dignify the charges with a reply only serves to fortify the stance of the accusers.'[74]

69.   Charles Farah Jr, 'The Dilemma of Discipleship', *Logos* (September/October 1975), 6-10 (9).

70.   Farah Jr, 'The Dilemma', 9.

71.   Moore, 'Shepherding' (1999), 180.

72.   Plowman, 'The Deepening Rift', 52-54.

73.   'Charismatic Movement is Facing Internal Discord Over Teaching Called "Discipling"', *New York Times* (16 September 1975), sec. C31, col. 1.

74.   Hayford, 'Conciliation Without Compromise', 29.

The article was based on an 11-page letter Hayford had written in the summer of 1975 to various leaders, responding to the crisis and reflecting the neutral position of his later *Logos* article. Hayford was bothered that 'Charges, claims, and counterclaims have been bouncing around for the past several months...'[75] and that 'unnecessary lines are being drawn now which will stifle the flow of life between us...'[76] He was 'pained' by the division.[77] Hayford thought Mumford and the other men were making a crusade of a 'single subject'.[78] Like many others, Hayford also questioned the practicality of translocal relationships and the distinction made between ecclesiastical and spiritual authority.[79] Hayford ended by calling for dialogue among Charismatic leaders as the only means to resolve the controversy and affirmed his respect and close ties with men on both sides of the debate.[80]

Calls by Hayford and others for caution and dialogue went unheeded by those who felt the Shepherding movement was heretical. Jesus movement leader and Pastor of Calvary Chapel, Chuck Smith, contacted Mumford with a blistering rebuke in response to Mumford's open letter to Robertson. In answer to Mumford's request for 'time and patience to demonstrate the fruit of what are presently new Biblical concepts',[81] Smith emphatically told him there already was more than enough evidence to reject the movement's teachings as Satan's deception.[82] Smith told Mumford he was praying for the Shepherding leaders that God would help them see their error and the awful fruit they were producing in the lives of many followers. He also told Mumford that he would not want to stand before God to give answer for what the movement's teachings were doing destructively to churches around the nation.[83]

Ralph Mahoney of World Missionary Assistance Plan (World MAP) had been a close friend to Mumford for many years and often invited him

---

75.   Jack W. Hayford, letter to Charismatic Leaders, n.d., private holding. While Hayford's letter is not dated, Mumford refers to the letter in his 9 September 1975 letter to Pat Robertson.
76.   Hayford, letter to Charismatic Leaders, 5.
77.   Hayford, letter to Charismatic Leaders, 7-8.
78.   Hayford, letter to Charismatic Leaders, 10-11.
79.   Hayford, letter to Charismatic Leaders, 7-8.
80.   Hayford, letter to Charismatic Leaders, 10-11.
81.   Mumford, letter to Pat Robertson, 2.
82.   Moore, 'Shepherding' (1999), 182-83.
83.   Moore, 'Shepherding' (1999), 183.

to speak at World MAP conferences. He wrote a strong warning to Mumford in the fall of 1975:

> Bob, I believe we are wrestling with far more than doctrinal or intellectual concepts in these problems. (Eph. 6: 'We wrestle against...') There are strong spirits at work in all this. I was told over two years ago by some people who spend much time in prayer that '... the Lord has showed us that Fort Lauderdale is going to split the Charismatic movement and cause worldwide division and strife...'. They felt World MAP's close identification was dangerous and the Lord wanted to warn me...
>
> I mention it Bob—so you will be aware that there is really a desperate need for you brothers down there in Florida to stop, look, and listen. God is trying to get your attention and I believe needs and wants to see some drastic changes in that situation.[84]

Mahoney would become a vocal critic of the Shepherding movement and publish written articles and audiotaped teachings against the movement's emphases.[85]

In October, Dennis Bennett was asked by the Seattle presbytery to present its concerns to the CGM leaders. His contact with the Shepherding leaders echoed the concerns raised at the Minneapolis meeting. For Bennett, the issue of dual authority was especially close to home. An associate pastor in Bennett's St Luke's parish was seeking a discipleship relationship with Mumford. This angered Bennett, who also had not resolved his disagreement with Mumford over water baptism. Bennett believed that the CGM leaders were starting a new denomination and no longer saw value in the historic churches. When he contacted Mumford he questioned whether the movement was giving up on existing churches by starting their own. Bennett feared that the movement was setting up a new hierarchy to be God's government in the last days. Bennett challenged cell groups, translocal authority, tithes paid to individuals, and the exclusion of women from leadership ministry. Bennett told Mumford that he had come away from Minneapolis heavy-hearted because the Shepherding leader had been evasive and had harassed the witnesses Robertson and others had brought to bring charges. Bennett did acknowledge that Mumford was

---

84. Ralph Mahoney, letter to Bob Mumford and Judy Mumford, 26 November 1975, private holding, 2.

85. The letters of Smith and Mahoney are typical of letters I reviewed of the movement's opponents. The CGM men also received many letters of support from friends and others.

justified in feeling Pat Robertson may have been to quick to publicly attack the movement.[86]

In response to Bennett's communication, Bob Mumford arranged to fly to Seattle for a December 5 meeting with the presbytery to discuss the issues from Bennett's letter. In the gathering, Bennett asserted that the 'Ft Lauderdale men' had no authority in Seattle and, as in Minneapolis, Bennett and Mumford clashed over their disagreements. In the end, the larger presbytery seemed satisfied with Mumford's assurances that there was no 'takeover attempt' by the Shepherding leaders.[87]

The five teachers were now being overwhelmed by all the controversy and struggling with a siege mentality. They began to refer to their Fort Lauderdale center as the 'Fort'. 'Attacks and charges increased daily', Mumford wrote in 1975. He publicly lamented that 'rumors and horror stories have grown to unbelievable proportions. There pervades in it all a kind of hysteria, accompanied in some instances with an attitude that is hypercritical, censorious, and rather frightening.'[88] They were becoming desperate to find some means to calm the storm.

The Ann Arbor Meeting

The meeting that was to follow up the Minneapolis 'shoot out' was scheduled for spring 1976.[89] Since the public controversy was continuing unabated, the Minneapolis committee of Jamie Buckingham, Brick Bradford, Steve Clark, Larry Christenson, and Derek Prince thought they should meet sooner and invited a smaller group of leaders together for a 'serious discussion-among-brothers'.[90]

On 16–17 December 1975, in Ann Arbor, Michigan, this follow-up meeting to Minneapolis was held as a kind of study group for a 'theological and

---

86. Moore, 'Shepherding' (1999), 184-85.

87. Bob Mumford, Notes from Meeting with Dennis Bennett, 5 December 1975, private holding, 1-3.

88. Mumford, *LifeChangers Newsletter*, 1.

89. Brick Bradford, letter to Participants in National Discussion on 'Shepherding', 29 August 1975, private holding, 1.

90. Larry Christenson, letter to Charismatic Leaders, 29 September 1975, private holding, 1; Jamie Buckingham, letter to Brick Bradford, 12 November 1975, private holding, 1.

pastoral evaluation' of the Shepherding controversy.[91] Notably absent were the primary antagonists from Minneapolis, Robertson, Bennett, and the FGBMFI representatives who had not been invited. This would prove problematic to resolving the controversy. The 14 present were: Brick Bradford, Jamie Buckingham, Larry Christenson, Steve Clark, David du Plessis, Everett Fullam, Dan Malachuk, Kilian McDonnell, Bob Mumford, Derek Prince, Kevin Ranaghan, Michael Scanlan, Charles Simpson, and J. Rodman Williams. Charismatic theologians Howard Ervin and Charles Farah had been invited, but were unable to attend.

According to participant McDonnell, the Ann Arbor meeting was 'better organized and calmer…[and] went a long way toward creating an atmosphere in which creative dialogue could take place'. The meeting addressed the questions many were raising: authority and submission, tithing to a shepherd, sheep and shepherd relationships, translocal authority, and the possibility of a new denomination. Following the interaction a statement was released that reported:

> After these two days together we have come to the conviction that a considerable measure of the controversy has resulted from misunderstanding and poor communication. The real differences which exist are well within the bounds of 'allowable variety' in the Body of Christ.[92]

The Ann Arbor meeting concluded with three decisions. First, the leaders recommended that *Logos* and *New Wine* publish a joint question and answer forum with the CGM teachers to clarify their teaching to a wider audience. Second, they recommended that the March 1976 Charismatic leaders conference discuss the establishing of a 'grievance committee' to address similar 'controversies should they arise'. Third, the Ann Arbor group affirmed the statement of ethics which had previously been adopted at the first Charismatic leaders conference in 1971.[93] This six-point ethics statement, mentioned in Chapter 4, included a commitment to address any criticism or complaint against a fellow minister, first by approaching the person directly and privately, then following the steps as directed in Mt. 18.15-17.[94] In the light of the events of 1975, this seemed to be an important commitment. Nevertheless, it did little to calm the storm.

---

91.   A Statement of Information, Ann Arbor, 17 December 1975, private holding, 1. (See Appendix 1 for full statement.)

92.   McDonnell, 'Seven Documents', II, 141-42.

93.   McDonnell, 'Seven Documents', II, 142.

94.   McDonnell, 'Seven Documents', II, 142-43.

Oklahoma City, March 1976

The 1976 Charismatic leaders conference met in Oklahoma City on 8–12 March 1976, with 38 representatives from the Renewal. As with Ann Arbor, Pat Robertson, Dennis Bennett and representatives of the FGBMFI were absent, this time by their own choice or because of schedule conflicts.[95]

In the first session, Larry Christenson drew from his Lutheran heritage a Reformation metaphor, 'a wild boar was loose in the Vineyard of the Lord'. Many present took the 'wild boar' to be a reference to the 'rugged Protestant individualism' that was fueling the ongoing controversy over Shepherding.[96]

The meeting continued discussion on the controversy, with Mumford and Simpson expressing their concern and dismay over the way they had been handled by other leaders. This would become a recurring complaint over the years at the annual Glencoe meetings.[97] While the discussions were calm, they were not without tension. In one meeting, David du Plessis insisted that some kind of apology was needed from the Shepherding leaders.[98] Later that evening, the five teachers met to discuss writing an apology. They decided to write a statement of concern and regret. The statement read:

> We realize that controversies and problems have arisen among Christians in various areas as a result of our teaching in relation to subjects such as submission, authority, discipling, shepherding. We deeply regret these problems and, insofar as they are due to fault on our part, we ask forgiveness from our fellow believers whom we have offended.
>
> We realize that our teachings, though we believed them to be essentially sound, have in various places been misapplied or handled in an immature way; and that this has caused problems for our brothers in the ministry. We deeply regret this and ask for forgiveness. Insofar as it lies in our power, we

95. All of these men had been invited to attend. Brick Bradford, Confidential Announcement, 1976 Charismatic Leaders Seminar, Oklahoma City, 30 September 1975, private holding, 1-2.

96. McDonnell, 'Seven Documents', II, 119.

97. Synan, interview, 14 February 1996. Synan was later reluctant to take over leadership of the Glencoe leaders' meetings in 1984 because he had wearied of the continuing Shepherding controversy.

98. Charles Simpson, telephone interview with author, 21 February 1996.

will do our best to correct these situations and to restore any broken relationships.[99]

Mumford wanted to go further in the statement and acknowledge more
fully their own mistakes and extremes, but Simpson disagreed.[100] Simpson
felt that, while there had indeed been problems resulting from their teachings, the five men had a responsibility to their committed followers who
had paid a high price to be associated with them. Simpson did not want to
appease the movement's antagonists and thereby shake their followers'
confidence.[101] Despite this disagreement, the statement by the Shepherding
leaders was well received at the conference and seemed to calm the critics.
David du Plessis said at the time it was 'everything [he] could ask for'.[102]
Subsequently, however, du Plessis continue to struggle with the Shepherding movement.

The March conference also followed the Ann Arbor recommendation
and established a 'Charismatic Concerns Committee to help deal with the
issues and problems that arise in the Charismatic Renewal'.[103] This committee elected Larry Christenson as chairman and held its first meeting on
the last day of the conference. Kevin Ranaghan was elected secretary-trea-
surer. The Charismatic Concerns Committee assumed responsibility for
the continuing scheduling of future Charismatic leaders conferences along
with their task of adjudicating disputes in the renewal.[104] The group
also decided that they would only consider matters submitted for their
review after the offended person had 'personally spoken to the offending
brother'.[105] Over the coming years, the committee would be asked to adjudicate a number of problems over the Shepherding controversy.

After the meetings were concluded, a joint statement was released by
the 1976 Charismatic leaders conference. The statement reported:

> Reconciliation among major segments of the Charismatic renewal resulted
> from a week-long meeting of ministers, teachers, and editors in Oklahoma
> City, March 8-12, 1976. Thirty-eight representatives from the movement

99. McDonnell, 'Seven Documents', II, 145.

100. Mumford, interview, 9 February 1996.

101. Simpson, interview, 21 February 1996.

102. Bob Whitaker, Notes from Oklahoma Meeting, 8–12 March 1975, private
holding, 6.

103. McDonnell, 'Seven Documents', II, 145.

104. Kevin Ranaghan, Minutes of the First Meeting of the Charismatic Concerns
Committee, 12 March 1976, Oklahoma City, private holding, 1-2.

105. Ranaghan, Minutes, 2.

gathered at the Center for Christian Renewal for four days of prayer, sharing, and discussion on the shepherding-discipleship-submission controversy
that has troubled Christians in many parts of the world in the last year.

The consensus of the meeting was that allegations of heresy were
unfounded, that there was no reason to question the integrity of the teachers
involved, and that, while many doctrinal differences remain among the
groups represented, those differences fall within acceptable limits.

The conferees agreed that much of the controversy had grown out of
rumor and misunderstanding, misapplication of certain scriptural principles,
and a lack of communication among leaders of different ministries and
groups.[106]

The statement was released to the press and sent to a number of leaders
who did not attend the meeting, asking for their endorsement.

The conference also made an appeal for an end 'to public attacks and
malicious gossip as a way of dealing with differences within the Christian
community'[107] and, as recommended by the Ann Arbor meeting, reaffirmed
the six-point statement of ethics from the 1971 Seattle meeting. Finally, the
leaders agreed to meet together at least annually, since all recognized that
the failure to hold a Charismatic leaders conference in 1975 had exacerbated the controversy.[108] Several published reports on the March conference generally highlighted the progress toward reconciliation.[109]

After receiving the meeting's statement, some leaders challenged the
decisions of the Ann Arbor and Oklahoma City meetings. Oral Roberts University professors Howard Ervin and Charles Farah felt the statement on
ethics was inadequate. They both believed that Mt. 18.15 was concerned
primarily with ethical problems, not doctrinal issues. According to Farah,
it was a 'category mistake' to add 'doctrinal disagreements' to the ethical
focus of Mt. 18.15.[110] Ervin and Farah thought it was appropriate to discuss doctrinal issues publicly, since the teachings on Shepherding were
being presented publicly.

---

106. Report on the 1976 Charismatic Leaders Conference, 8–12 March 1976,
Oklahoma City. (See Appendix 2 for the full statement.)

107. McDonnell, 'Seven Documents', II, 144.

108. McDonnell, 'Seven Documents', II, 144-45.

109. Vinson Synan, 'Reconciling the Charismatics', *Christianity Today* (9 April
1976), 46. Russell Chandler, 'Charismatics Close Shepherding Gap', *Los Angeles
Times* (20 March 1976), Part 1, 26.

110. Moore, 'Shepherding' (1999), 192. See also Howard M. Ervin, letter to Kevin
Ranaghan, 12 April 1976, Holy Spirit Research Center, Oral Roberts University, Tulsa,
OK, 1.

Jack Hayford wrote to Ranaghan, declining his endorsement of the conference statement because he was concerned that many of the 'principal dissenters' were not present at the March meetings.[111] Harald Bredesen wrote to David du Plessis, saying he could not in good conscience endorse a statement that he believed to be inadequate. Bredesen told du Plessis: 'I could not sign the statement until the Ft Lauderdale group reversed themselves on…their concept of the local shepherd as the door…and so forth.' Bredesen questioned why du Plessis signed the statement.[112]

Dr Ervin wrote to Kevin Ranaghan in April 1976 and challenged the Ann Arbor statement that said the movement's doctrines fell within acceptable limits. Ervin questioned, in some detail, the movement's exegesis of John 10 that presented Jesus as 'the Door' to the sheepfold and the shepherd/pastor as 'a door'. Ervin challenged the exegesis as potentially ascribing to a human shepherd a soteriological dimension of leadership. Ervin said in his letter: 'By extension of the metaphor…each local shepherd (door) becomes a surrogate "Christ" with the prerogative of arrogating to himself arbitrary and frightening powers over the lives of his disciples.'[113] In an open letter to Prince, Ervin further challenged their view of John 10.[114] Derek Prince wrote a response to Ervin, denying any intention by the movement to give a human shepherd any function that can be exercised by Christ alone. To do so, Prince agreed, would be heresy.[115]

In the spring of 1976, both *Logos* and *New Wine* jointly published the forum which the Ann Arbor conference had recommended.[116] This, along with the Oklahoma City conference statements, made some leaders feel that the controversy was beginning to quieten down. The Charismatic Renewal, however, remained polarized. The strongest antagonists, such as Robertson and FGBMFI, were entrenched in their opposition to the Shepherding

111. Jack W. Hayford, letter to Kevin Ranaghan, 27 April 1976, private holding, 1-2.

112. Harald Bredesen, letter to David du Plessis, 9 June 1976, David du Plessis Collection, David du Plessis Archive, Fuller Theological Seminary, 1.

113. Ervin, letter to Ranaghan, 1-2.

114. Howard M. Ervin, letter to Derek Prince, 27 September 1976, private holding, 1-10.

115. Derek Prince, Outline Reply to letter dated 27 September 1976, n.d., private holding, 1-4.

116. The forum was an identical insert in both magazines. See 'Discipleship Forum in Ft Lauderdale', *New Wine* (March 1976), insert. 'Discipleship Forum in Ft Lauderdale', *Logos* (March 1976), insert.

teachings.[117] Materials were proliferating against the movement. In late 1976, the Assemblies of God published a 14-page pamphlet: *The Disciple-ship and Submission Movement*, which openly challenged many of the teachings.[118] Periodical literature over the next eight years would regularly reveal an undercurrent of opposition to the distinctive emphases of the Shepherding movement.

In retrospect, the opposition to the Shepherding movement was mostly among the independent Charismatic ministries and some denominational Pentecostals,[119] with a few exceptions, such as Episcopalian Dennis Bennett and Charismatic theologians Charles Farah and Howard Ervin. For the most part, the denominational Charismatics were less reactionary and often worked as a calming influence behind the scenes and in meetings for dialogue and reconciliation. For example, the Lutheran Charismatic Renewal Services issued a statement urging restraint and a commitment to the 'ethics of disagreement' in which problems and concerns are handled directly and quietly.[120] The Presbyterian Charismatics, notably, Brick Bradford, Leonard LeSourd, and Bob Whitaker, actively sought to establish dialogue and expressed a basic trust in the integrity of the CGM teachers. The Catholic Charismatic leaders from Ann Arbor and South Bend were often advocates for the five teachers, having established an ongoing relationship with the five men.[121] Perhaps the security and heritage of their denominational affiliations made the Shepherding movement less threatening to these mainline Charismatics. It is true that denominational Charismatics did express concerns that the five teachers may have moved too quickly in declaring their unique emphases and were concerned about extremes. Nevertheless, they seemed less concerned than the independent Charismatics about the movement becoming a new denomination.[122]

The controversy among independent Charismatics was, in essence, a kind of 'turf war'. The reaction against the Shepherding movement was, at least

117. Over the next ten years, people who called the 700 Club counselors at CBN to ask about Shepherding were mailed materials that opposed the movement's teachings.

118. *The Discipleship and Submission Movement*, Assemblies of God pamphlet, 1976, 1-14.

119. McDonnell, 'Seven Documents', II, 122.

120. Lutheran Charismatic Renewal Services, public statement, n.d., private holding, 1-2.

121. McDonnell, 'Seven Documents', II, 122.

122. Both Mumford and Simpson say they grew in regard for the denominational Charismatics as a result of the controversy. Simpson, interview, 21 February 1996; and Mumford, interview, 9 February 1996.

in part, a result of the great diversity in the Charismatic Renewal among the independent Charismatics. The lack of a single identifiable leader in the renewal had created a host of individual leaders and ministries. Many of these independent leaders and ministries were all working within a common constituency and saw the Shepherding movement as an attempt to consolidate and assume leadership of a large portion of the independents. While the five teachers denied any plan along this line, many independent Charismatics who did align with the teachers, had been attached to ministries like FGBMFI.[123] While the CGM men consistently denied being a denomination, they were a clearly identifiable movement of churches self-consciously seeking to develop as 'new wineskins'. This fact, along with the concerns about doctrinal and practical extremes, made the Shepherding movement a threat to many independent Charismatic leaders.

Catholic Steve Clark, an ally and friend of the Shepherding leaders, provides an interesting perspective and analysis of the controversy from outside the independent Charismatic sector. In a 1978 letter, Clark observed:

> The controversy was purportedly over the role of authority and submission in the Christian life... In actuality, it was a controversy about the formation of churches. For the most part, the controversy centered in the independent wing of the Charismatic Renewal... The controversy did not affect the Catholic Charismatic Renewal much directly. The denominational Charismatic fellowships worked together to mediate the dispute. In other words, even though some raised the cry that the CGM men were taking members away from [the historic] churches, in fact, they did very little of that. Moreover, the opponents of the CGM men contained many of the groups that I know of whose members left the Catholic Church as a result of contact with them (e.g. Melodyland, FGBMFI). In other words, it was a controversy within the independent wing of the Charismatic Renewal over who was going to be the leader of that wing.[124]

Some leaders, Jack Hayford for one, called on Mumford, Simpson and the other men to simply acknowledge what, in their view, was a practical fact. Hayford believed the Shepherding movement was a functional denomination regardless of its relational, rather than organizational orientation. Hayford hoped that acknowledging what was a functional reality might calm the storm.[125]

---

123. By far the majority of the Shepherding movement's adherents came from the independent Pentecostal/Charismatic sectors of the church.

124. Steve Clark, 'Our Relationship with the "Council"', February 1978, private holding, 3.

125. Jack Hayford, personal interview with author, 30 January 1984.

Part of the reaction to the teachings on submission resulted from its head-on confrontation with North American individualism, characteristic of many independent, entrepreneurally minded Charismatic leaders. Standing outside of the United States, British Charismatic Michael Harper observed that 'some of the strongest opposition came from those who needed most to hear the message of authority'.[126] Certainly the Shepherding movement's leaders saw it that way. Mumford used strong words in a 1975 statement:

> Present reactions and accusations, other than ones due to personal failure, are due to the salt and iodine of Kingdom authority doing its work against the leprosy of man's autonomy as expressed in the ubiquitous expression of religious and secular humanism as well as situational ethics.[127]

The movement's isolated practice of dual authority added fuel to the fire of controversy, particularly for pastors and existing church leaders.[128] Could a person be submitted to their own local church leadership and also be submitted to a shepherd outside the church? For the CGM leaders, this dilemma was addressed, as previously noted, by making a distinction between ecclesiastical authority (the official church leaders) and spiritual authority (the personal pastor or discipler). The Charismatic Catholic communities had agreeably established such a system, with the Catholic concept of spiritual directorship serving as a model. This did not work well outside the Catholic communion. Pastors such as Dennis Bennett were understandably threatened by the idea of a member of their church submitting to outside authority. While this was not a regular practice for the Shepherding movement, it did happen in a few instances and created further suspicion that the movement was subversive.

The Shepherding leaders believed their attackers were acting unscripturally by airing unsubstantiated rumors and allegations and refusing to engage in meaningful dialogue. The movement's teachers were angered, since they felt they were making substantial efforts at healing the rift. Some Charismatic leaders agreed with them.[129] Michael Harper commended the CGM leaders' restraint in the midst of such fierce opposition and their willingness 'at personal inconvenience, to jet halfway across the United States in search of...unity'.[130] This all contributed to a perception among

126. Harper, *Three Sisters*, 95.
127. Mumford, 'Disciple Position Paper', 5.
128. Hayford, 'Conciliation Without Compromise', 29.
129. Brick Bradford, letter to Bob Mumford, 16 March 1976, private holding, 1.
130. Harper, *Three Sisters*, 94-95.

the movement's leaders that they were being persecuted for their God-directed teachings. They also believed that, because these teachings were a part of God's restoration of New Testament Christianity, Satan was resisting them through the controversy.[131] These perceptions in the face of controversy only reinforced their commitment to the teachings of Shepherding, discipleship, and covenant relationship. In many ways, the conduct of their critics, which they perceived as being unethical, may have contributed to an unwillingness to listen to the legitimate concerns of their opponents.

The opposition and controversy were major factors in the consolidation and development of the movement into a more defined and structured association of churches. No longer were the five men simply Bible teachers with independent ministries within the Charismatic Renewal. While they would continue to speak outside their own network, the controversy had helped push them more inward to focus on the growing number of leaders and churches that were joining the burgeoning movement.

By the summer of 1976, the controversy over the Shepherding movement had forever changed the character of the Charismatic Renewal. Its ecumenical ideal and hope had been shattered. Despite the success of the 1977 Kansas City conference on Charismatic Renewal in the churches, the Charismatic movement would never again be as united as it had been before the dispute over discipleship.

---

131. Derek Prince, letter to Dick Zollor, 8 September 1975, private holding, 1.

Chapter 8

The 1975 National Men's Shepherds Conference

As the controversy raged in August and September 1975, the CGM leaders were working with Catholics Steve Clark, Paul DeCelles, Ralph Martin, and Kevin Ranaghan and Lutheran Larry Christenson in preparation for the 1975 National Men's Shepherds Conference to be held in Kansas City. On the Sunday evening of the infamous Minneapolis 'Shoot-out', the men met to make final plans for the upcoming conference just a few weeks away.[1]

The ecumenical group that served as the Shepherds conference planning committee had been meeting for over a year. After the 1974 Montreat Shepherds conference the group decided to meet with regularity to develop unity and dialogue. The men believed it was significant that their group was composed of leaders from the Protestant, Catholic, and independent sectors of the Charismatic Renewal. In their first meeting in September 1974, they had committed 'to care for and serve what God is doing to restore and reunite his people...and as brothers to care for one another'. The group expressed the wish to be mutually related and submitted.[2] This dialogue and accountability group, referred to variously as the General Council, National Council, and later the Ecumenical Council, gathered two or three times a year for over a decade.[3]

It was this ecumenical group that served as the planning committee for the September Shepherds conference that had been a subject of concern at the August Minneapolis Charismatic leaders meeting. In Minneapolis,

1.   Minutes of the Meeting of the Council, 10–12 August 1975, 1.
2.   Minutes of the Meeting of the Council, 8–10 September 1974, private holding, 1.
3.   Don Basham, Minutes of Ecumenical Council, 5 February 1975, private holding, 1. The consistent members were the five CGM teachers, Christenson, Clark, DeCelles, Martin, and Ranaghan. Lutheran Don Pfotenhauer was added in 1977. DeCelles and Ranaghan dropped out in 1981 and Prince in 1984.

The 'national' or 'ecumenical' council as it was called. Standing: Bob Mumford, Steve
Clark, Charles Simpson, Larry Christenson, Ralph Martin, Paul DeCelles. Seated: Don
Basham, Derek Prince, Ern Baxter, Kevin Ranaghan, Don Pfotenhauer.

The ecumenical council in Jerusalem with Cardinal Suenens. The 1977 trip was an
expression of the growing relationship of the group. From the left: Suenens, Ranaghan,
Mumford, Simpson, Prince, Basham, DeCelles, Baxter, Christenson, Clark, Martin.

the Charismatic leaders had agreed to entrust the Shepherds conference outcome to this council, since it included leaders beyond the circle of Ft Lauderdale and Mobile.

The 1975 National Men's Shepherds Conference was held in Kansas City on 23–26 September. Like the previous Shepherds conferences in 1973 and 1974, the conference exceeded the planners' expectations with 4,600 pastors and lay shepherds in attendance.[4] All five Shepherding teachers spoke in the plenary sessions, along with Clark, Martin, Ranaghan, and Christenson who taught on topics that included: 'The Need for Shepherds', 'How to Exercise Authority', 'Covenant Love', and 'How Ministries Relate Beyond the Local Body'.[5]

Larry Christenson welcomed conferees on the first night and, referring to the controversy, quipped that some saw the conference as 'the platform for the unveiling of the plan for Ft Lauderdale to take over the United States'.[6] The comment drew guarded laughter. Christenson went on to acknowledge the reality of the controversy by sharing a vision received by a woman in his church of a log jam in a river, symbolizing the impasse in the Charismatic Renewal. *New Wine* describes what Christenson said:

> The accepted method for dispersing log jams is by blasting them with dynamite, which splinters and destroys many valuable logs. And in the vision, it seemed that perhaps just such an explosion of radical confrontation in the midst of the 'logs' might be necessary to resolve the controversy over discipleship.
>
> But instead of blasting, God's reply and his solution to the question of the log jam came with these words: 'Pray for the level of the river to rise.'
>
> In other words, rather than letting controversy blast us into increased sectarianism, we were to pray for a higher tide of Christian love, that we might make room for one another in the stream of God's purpose for his Church.[7]

Christenson's words expressed the hope of most of the conference's attendees, two-thirds of whom came from the independent sector of the Renewal and were aged 30 or younger. Many of these young men, comprised of lay pastors and cell group leaders, were either already committed

4.   Estimates of attendance ranged from 4,500 to 5,000. This figure is conservative. 'Logos Report: National Men's Shepherds Conference', *Logos* (November/December 1975), 42.

5.   Conference Brochure, 1975 National Men's Shepherds Conference, private holding.

6.   McDonnell, 'Seven Documents', II, 118.

7.   'Echoes of the Spirit', *New Wine* (November 1975), 12-14.

to the Shepherding movement or considering joining it. They were enthusiastic about the conference. In addition, hundreds of denominational Charismatics attended, and a minority of skeptical observers were present.[8]

Bob Mumford was the opening night plenary speaker and declared the conference to be 'historic' in ecumenical significance, because it was not just a CGM meeting, but included leaders from the historic denominations. Mumford forcefully told the conferees: 'I want to declare to you, categorically, that it is not our design, consciously or unconsciously, intentionally or unintentionally to start or form a new denomination.'[9]

Echoing the familiar restorationist themes, he affirmed his conviction that 'moral degeneration…economic instability, confusion of the male and female role, political instability, religious confusion…are the backdrop on which God wants to say something to his church'. 'We are witnessing a breakdown of the technological society', he proclaimed, and lamented the 'unprecedented individualism and anarchy [that] has swept across our nation'. Mumford told the audience that God was establishing his kingdom in the midst of the confusion and darkness and, as the world systems 'shake and collapse…something is revealed in the earth'. Through it all God was establishing his people as a visible witness to the kingdom.[10]

From Mumford's perspective, this was not about starting a new denomination, but a matter of 'God restoring truth to the Church'. He told the conferees that through these new emphases God wanted to unite the church by men coming into relationship across denominational lines. He urged the men present: 'Please, dear brothers, don't walk alone anymore… Get yourself related to some brother who will love you and want to walk with you.'[11] What some observers heard was an invitation to join the movement.

The conference seemed to be extremely successful, and the conference speakers actively sought to explain and defend the emphasis on shepherding, covenant, and community. The conference held afternoon forum sessions to facilitate answers to questions submitted in writing beforehand. Most of the discussion centered on the controversial topics. Generally the tone was positive with some denominational leaders expressing relief at what they heard.

---

8.   'Logos Report: National Men's Shepherds Conference', 42-43; Brick Bradford, newsletter, 12 November 1975, private holding, 1.

9.   Mumford, *God's Purpose with His People Today*, audiocassette.

10.   Mumford, *God's Purpose with His People Today*, audiocassette.

11.   Mumford, *God's Purpose with His People Today*, audiocassette.

At the Wednesday night session, Ranaghan's message on 'Covenant Love' impacted the audience. After the meeting was dismissed, *Logos* reported:

> Afterward, as the men, shoulder to shoulder, edged their way through the lobby, a spirit of praise enveloped them. They began to sing. Four thousand voices proclaiming 'He is Lord, He is Lord, He is risen from the dead and He is Lord.' They poured out onto the sidewalks and down the side streets to their hotels, still singing, their voices floating high above the darkened streets of the city. He is Lord![12]

On the last night of the conference, the time of praise and worship overwhelmed many present. Thousands removed their shoes in response to a prophetic message from the book of Joshua: 'Remove the shoes from your feet, for the place where you are standing is holy.'[13] Some described the worship time as 'without precedent in their Christian experience'.[14] Ern Baxter followed with the message, 'Thy Kingdom Come', which conferees felt was a mighty proclamation of the message of the kingdom.[15] Simpson remembered the last night's session as 'the most powerful meeting I've ever been in, of a large nature'.[16] The success of the Kansas City Shepherds conference was seen as a confirmation that the movement's teachings were receiving God's blessing even in the midst of 'great opposition'.[17]

Christian Broadcasting Network (CBN) had sent an observer, James Murphy, who wrote a detailed 25-page report on the conference. The report said the 'spirit of worship was tremendous', but that the CGM teachers avoided the 'real issues' and their 'defensiveness [was] evident'. Murphy acknowledged the conference leaders made 'a strong appeal to rise above differences and, in esteem and respect for His Body, to accept and move with all of our brothers with the conquering king in the lead'.[18] Murphy

12. This account is somewhat surprising given the *Logos* article's tone is overall quite negative in its assessment of the Shepherds conference. 'Logos Report: National Men's Shepherds Conference', 43.

13. 'Echoes of the Spirit' (November 1975), 14.

14. Ern Baxter, *Thy Kingdom Come* (Ft Lauderdale, FL: Christian Growth Ministries, 1977), 7.

15. The message became very important to the movement's theological self-definition and was distributed widely in tape and book form.

16. Simpson, interview, 21 February 1996.

17. Roachelle, 'Chronology', 8.

18. James O. Murphy, Report on the 1975 National Men's Shepherds Conference,

was critical of the CGM leaders' use of media to propagate their 'unproved principles' and believed their 'paramount error is in the placing of a man (the shepherd) between a man and the Lord Jesus'.[19]

Logos's coverage of the Shepherds conference mirrored the perspective of many critics who had hoped that at the Kansas City meetings the five CGM leaders would significantly retreat in their teachings. Instead, *Logos* believed the leaders were 'skirting controversial issues...'[20] The Logos Report implied that the Shepherds conference was primarily a promotion of CGM. Christenson, Clark, and Ranaghan, all a part of the planning group, objected to this implication and wrote to Malachuk at Logos Publications. They emphatically stated the conference was not 'controlled by CGM'. They told Malachuk that the magazine's portrayal of the Shepherds conference was 'a grave disservice to the Charismatic Renewal in its current state of controversy'.[21]

The Charismatic Catholic publication *New Covenant* carried a very positive article on the conference that stressed its ecumenical character, in apparent contradiction of the assessment from *Logos* and the Murphy CBN report. The article asserted that:

> Participants left the conference with a clearer understanding of the Christian group and leaders need a military level of dedication, discipline, and cooperation in order to help individual Christians, strengthen the churches, and take the offensive against Satan in the world.[22]

The 1977 Kansas City Conference

Because of the ongoing controversy, the Ecumenical Council decided not to hold another national Shepherds conference, and canceled all regional Shepherds conferences, except for one in March 1976 scheduled for Atlanta, Georgia, which was the last joint Shepherds conference sponsored by the group.[23]

23–26 September 1975, Kansas City, MO (Virginia Beach, VA: Christian Broadcasting Network), 22.

19. Murphy, Report on the 1975 National Men's Shepherds Conference, 23.

20. 'Logos Report: National Men's Shepherds Conference', 43.

21. Larry Christenson, Steven B. Clark, and Kevin Ranaghan, letter to Editor of *Logos*, n.d., private holding, 1.

22. 'Recognizing the "Hazards of Walking Alone"', *New Covenant* (December 1975), 22-23.

23. Minutes of the Meeting of the Council, 27 September 1975, private holding, 1.

Bob Mumford speaking in the Friday evening plenary session at the 1977 Conference on Charismatic Renewal in the Christian Churches (CCRCC).

The decision not to hold any more conferences was part of a plan to actively work toward a national 'Three Rivers' conference. Catholic Ralph Martin delivered a pivotal message at the 1974 Montreat Shepherds conference and later at the 1974 International Conference on the Catholic Charismatic Renewal.[24] His message, entitled 'The Mighty Stream of God', presented the concept of three rivers of renewal in the contemporary church: the Classical Pentecostals, the Protestant Charismatics, and the Catholic Charismatics. Together these three rivers were a 'mighty stream' of God's renewing work in his Church. Martin believed that God was indeed working 'on the riverbeds to enable them to flow together, to present a united witness to the Church and to the world'.[25]

In a December 1974 meeting with Basham, Baxter, Christenson, Clark, DeCelles, Martin, Mumford, Poole, Prince, Ranaghan, and Simpson present, the group discussed the viability of holding a large national conference which would bring the three rivers together. Ranaghan agreed to present a proposal to the council.[26] The group continued to discuss the event in a March 1975 meeting, and at the August Minneapolis meeting that followed

24.   An edited text of Martin's message ran in *New Wine* in late 1974. See Ralph Martin, 'The Mighty Stream of God', *New Wine* (November 1974), 14-17.

25.   Martin, 'The Mighty Stream of God', 17.

26.   Minutes of the Meeting of the Council, 15–17 December 1974, Ft Lauderdale, private holding, 2.

the infamous 'shoot-out', they authorized Ranaghan to 'invite representatives of all major national Charismatic groups to meet' to discuss plans for
a 'three rivers' conference.[27] Ranaghan accepted the commission and went
on to be the chairman of the planning committee for the highly successful
Conference on Charismatic Renewal in the Christian Churches (CCRCC).

It was never widely known that the 1977 Kansas City conference origins
were from this group.[28] Perhaps the leaders wanted to avoid bringing unnecessary controversy to the conference since the five Shepherding leaders
were so much a part of the Ecumenical Council. Whatever the reason, the
group seldom commented publicly on their roles in the Kansas City conference. Catholic Steve Clark did acknowledge their roles in a 1978 letter
that was intended to explain Martin and his role in the council. He wrote in
reference to the CCRCC:

> I would consider this the more mature fruit of our cooperation. The actual
> direction of the conference was in the hands of a planning committee made
> up of leaders of denominational charismatic committees and of representa-
> tives of certain nondenominational groups. None of the planning was done
> in the Council meetings, but the Council agreed to support it. Because we
> pledged ourselves to take the financial risks (through CRS, CGM, and
> LCRS) and because we committed ourselves to get people to come, we
> made the conference possible.[29]
>
> The Kansas City Conference was the first major conference in the Charis-
> matic Renewal that was ecumenical (and not nondenominational). It has to
> be understood against the background of the attempt by Melodyland to
> sponsor a similar conference in 1976. At that time, the Catholic Charismatic
> Renewal Service Committee objected to the plans because they did not rest
> upon a leadership group that was properly constituted and would
> understand how to work in an ecumenical way. We were supported at that
> time by the Council and if we had not been, we might have been faced with
> a different sort of conference in 1976. As a result, we had a conference in
> 1977 that fully affirmed differing church commitments and yet was ecu-
> menical. I believe that the relationship in the Council made this possible.[30]

27.   Minutes, 10–12 August 1975, 1.
28.   In interviews, Ranaghan, Clark, Martin, Mumford, and Simpson confirmed to
me that from their council came the idea and impetus for the 1977 conference.
29.   CRS is the Catholic Renewal Service, LCRS is the Lutheran Charismatic
Renewal Service.
30.   Clark, 'Our Relationship', 2.

Ern Baxter and Bob Mumford at one of the daytime 'non-denominational track B'
sessions at the CCRCC.

The Kansas City conference became a major priority of the Shepherding movement's leaders, who were represented on the planning committee by Bob Mumford. The 1977 conference was to be a 'conference of conferences', since each denominational and independent Charismatic group would hold its own meetings in daytime sessions at various sites, and all groups would come together for evening meetings at Arrowhead stadium in Kansas City.[31] Originally, there was to be one nondenominational group co-led by Mumford and California Charismatic, Robert Frost. As the planning for the conference progressed, the continuing tensions over the Shepherding controversy became apparent. Frost wanted a united nondenominational meeting very much, but California leaders Wilkerson and Mahoney were reluctant to share the platform with the CGM men. Pat Robertson withdrew his name from the speakers list.[32]

Charles Simpson wrote to the planning committee chairman, Kevin Ranaghan, expressing his concerns over a single nondenominational meeting given the hostilities between the two camps of independent Charismatics.

31. Vinson Synan, 'Kansas City Conference', in Burgess and McGee (eds.), *Dictionary*, 515; Synan, *Launching the Decade*, 117-22.

32. Notes from the Planning Committee Meeting, 24–25 January 1977, David du Plessis Collection, David du Plessis Archive, Fuller Theological Seminary, 3.

Simpson did not feel Mumford could 'adequately represent…"the Wild West"', referring to the Southern California Charismatics that included Melodyland's Wilkerson, World MAP leader Mahoney, and FGBMFI leaders who would likely not attend the conference if all grouped together.[33] Simpson did not believe he could rally his people to a meeting where their antagonists were on the same program. Simpson asked Ranaghan to allow the Shepherding teachers to hold separate daytime meetings from the other nondenominational group. Such an arrangement he said 'would add a great deal of impetus to our people to want to be there. And, there would be several thousand…who would follow our leadership under God who would attend.'[34]

Ranaghan agreed to establish separate 'nondenominational tracks A and B'. The decision was made after private discussions and never brought formally to the larger planning committee or its executive committee. This disturbed Frost who, despite his disagreements with Mumford and the movement, wanted a single nondenominational group at Kansas City. After the decision, Frost resigned from the committee and wrote to both Ranaghan and Mumford, explaining his reasons.[35] Judson Cornwall replaced Frost on the planning committee.

Simpson and the other four worked hard at getting as many of their people to the summer 1977 conference as possible. Simpson told his people that 'Kansas City offers us the opportunity to testify to other Christians concerning the nature and availability of our fellowship.'[36] A strong showing in Kansas City, they believed, would demonstrate that their distinctives made them able to marshal their resources and gather their followers for a 'noble and significant purpose'. Goals were established and shepherds were charged with the responsibility of motivating people to go to the conerence.[37] Leaders were given a written list that suggested appropriate conduct at the conference and were encouraged to avoid 'problem' words like 'submission and discipleship'.[38] *New Wine* carried much promotion for the conference, featuring something about it in every issue for nine months before the conference.[39]

33. Charles Simpson, letter to Kevin Ranaghan, 13 August 1976, private holding, 1.
34. Simpson, letter to Ranaghan, 2.
35. Moore, 'Shepherding' (1999), 213.
36. Charles Simpson, memo on Kansas City, 10 March 1977, private holding, 1.
37. Simpson, memo on Kansas City.
38. Suggested Conduct for the Kansas City Conference, private holding, 1.
39. Christian Growth Ministries, *New Wine Magazine* (November 1976–July/

All their efforts paid off, and the CCRCC in Kansas City was another success for the Shepherding movement. While the Catholic Charismatics were the largest group, with 25,000 attendees, the nondenominational track B, which was assigned for the Shepherding group, was the second largest, with estimates ranging from 9,000 to 12,000 in attendance at its day meetings.[40] The other nondenominational track A, which included all other nondenominational Charismatics, had approximately 1,500 in its daytime sessions.[41]

One of the conference highlights was Bob Mumford's Friday night address. As the evening's main speaker, Mumford spoke on 'Helps and Hindrances to Holiness'. About midway through his message, Mumford paused and said: 'Hey! How many of you know that if you take a sneak look at the back of the book, Jesus wins?' At those words, the stadium crowd erupted into a 'sustained roar of praise and spiritual song' that lasted for 15 minutes. After the crowd quieted down Mumford told them with a chuckle: 'You just had a Holy Ghost breakdown, that's all.' The stadium 'roared with laughter'.[42] Most accounts of the CCRCC reported this event.[43]

A step was taken toward some healing of the controversy when the two nondenominational tracks met together for a final session on the Sunday morning of the conference.[44] At the combined meeting, Judson Cornwall apologized to Basham, Mumford, Prince, and Simpson (Baxter was not present) for 'degrading' public comments about the men, which he had made in May of 1975 on CBN's 700 Club. The conversation with Pat Robertson had played a role in spreading the controversy. As Cornwall

August 1977). The July/August issue themed the Kansas City conference and carried the cover title 'The King in Kansas City'.

40. The conservative figure came from Simpson and the larger number from *Logos*. Charles Simpson, letter to Terry Parker *et al.*, 4 August 1977; Carey Moore, 'Kansas City Hears Jesus is Lord', *Logos* (September/October 1977), 50-53 (53).

41. Moore, 'Kansas City Hears Jesus is Lord', 52.

42. David Manuel, *Like a Mighty River* (Orleans, MA: Rock Harbor, 1977), 143-44. Strangely, Manuel's story of the CCRCC all but ignores the Shepherding movement's role in the Kansas City conference.

43. For periodical reports on the CCRCC see Moore, 'Kansas City'; 'Separate, But United in Spirit', *National Courier* (19 August 1977), 1-2; Robert H. Hawn, 'Kansas City: Conference Heard "Round the World"', *Charisma* (September/October, 1977), 10-11, 24; 'The Charismatic Renewal After Kansas City', *Sojourners* (September 1977), 11-13.

44. Moore, 'Kansas City', 52.

embraced the men, there 'were shouts of praise and weeping'.[45] Simpson said at a press briefing that followed the conference that Cornwall's actions had 'melted our hearts'. He told the press that 'we will never be the same again'.[46] As before, however, the symbolic but sincere Sunday meeting did little to bridge the divide between the independent Charismatic groups.

In general, the Kansas City CCRCC was a powerful expression of unity among Charismatics. The evening meetings held at Arrowhead Stadium had more than 45,000 in attendance. To public perception, it was the Charismatic Renewal's apex. The October 1977 issue of *New Wine* was dedicated entirely to coverage of the CCRCC. It printed message excerpts, significant prophecies, and reported extensively on the conference.[47] *New Covenant*, the Catholic Charismatic periodical, also gave significant coverage to the conference.[48]

The five Shepherding leaders met with the Ecumenical Council that had birthed the Kansas City conference in August 1977 and spent much of the three-day meeting debriefing and evaluating the conference. They were not surprised to find that the three groups the council represented had the highest percentage of conferees. The Catholic group had 46 percent, the Shepherding group had 25.7 percent, and the Lutherans 5.6 percent. Together their groups comprised 77.3 percent of all registered conferees.[49] They believed that the unity of the Kansas City conference 'grew out of their unity' and considered going more public about their council.[50]

It is beyond the scope of this project to give a fully detailed history of this Ecumenical Council. It was a most important point of contact for the Shepherding leaders who maintained a strong commitment to Charismatic ecumenism. They also believed it demonstrated that they were not isolated from the larger church and were accountable beyond their own circle of five. The entire group traveled together to Belgium and the Holy Land in 1977. Through Clark and Martin, meaningful dialogue was established with Belgium Charismatic Cardinal Joseph Suenens. Simpson met with the cardinal in the United States and corresponded with him for two years.[51]

45.   Robert Nolte and Michael Berry, 'Discipleship Division Disappears into Oneness', *National Courier* (19 August 1977), 3.

46.   Nolte and Berry, 'Discipleship Division', 3.

47.   See *New Wine* (October 1977), 4-47.

48.   See *New Covenant* (October 1977), 4-14.

49.   Minutes of General Council Meeting, 8–10 August 1977, Ann Arbor, private holding, 1-4.

50.   Minutes, 8–10 August 1977, 3.

51.   Minutes of the General Council, held during Pilgrimage, May/June 1977, private

Minutes of the Ecumenical Council indicate the group self-consciously met for accountability and cooperation. Mumford and Simpson, particularly, seem to have viewed the council as a governmental group in which they placed great importance. For DeCelles, Ranaghan, Martin, and Clark, it was an important ecumenical group, but not a truly governmental one.[52] Nevertheless, for a time they did consider merging their collective communities into a more functional union.[53] In the council, the men submitted to one another. Larry Christenson, for example, related to Simpson for personal headship for a number of years.[54] In the early 1980s, tensions developed between the South Bend communities led by Ranaghan and DeCelles and the Ann Arbor communities led by Clark and Martin. Simpson unsuccessfully tried to adjudicate the issues, but Ranaghan and DeCelles dropped off the council.[55] Derek Prince resigned from the council in 1984, and it was dissolved by mutual consent in February 1985.[56]

There was no doubt considerable mutual influence between the Shepherding movement and the Catholic Charismatic communities, particularly Ann Arbor. The Shepherding movement emphasized more the personal authority that came through definite vertical pastoral relationships, or 'joints', as they called them; while the Catholic communities put more emphasis on being joined to the community leadership as a whole versus the one-to-one pastoral relationship.[57] Both groups have acknowledged the mutual appreciation and respect they enjoyed at the time.[58]

Momentum and Growth

Simpson, Mumford, and the Shepherding movement's leaders were exhilarated by the large representation of their people at the Kansas City

holding, 1-5; Charles Simpson, letter to Cardinal Suenens, 10 January 1978, private holding, 1-2.

52. Ralph Martin, telephone interview with author, 8 December 1998; Kevin Ranaghan, telephone interview with author, 30 November 1998; Clark, telephone interview with author, 3 February 1996.

53. Minutes of the Council, 3–7 January 1977, Ft Lauderdale, private holding, 1; Minutes, May/June 1977, 3-4.

54. Minutes, 8–10 August 1977, 7.

55. Don Basham, Minutes of Ecumenical Council Meeting, 25–27 February 1983, private holding, 1.

56. Basham, Minutes, 5 February 1985, 1.

57. Minutes, May/June 1977, 4.

58. Martin, interview, 8 December 1998; Ranaghan, interview, 30 November 1998; Simpson, interview, 3 August 1998; Minutes, May/June 1977.

conference and saw it as continuing confirmation of God's favor. They believed that what they were building was unique, and that their ability to mobilize their people demonstrated the validity of their themes.

After the 1977 CCRCC Simpson wrote a confidential memo to the men he directly pastored. He told the leaders that 'Kansas City made a difference. One out of four at the conference were related to us or attended our meetings.' He continued: 'Enemies were unchanged, but dealt a blow. We are in a new era. More responsibility is headed my way, and yours... We must make our foundations sure for 1978.'[59]

Adding to the momentum following Kansas City, the Shepherding movement held five regional men's conferences around the nation in the fall of 1977. Conferences were held in Jackson, Mississippi; Daytona, Florida; Louisville, Kentucky; Dallas, Texas; and San Francisco, California. These meetings had a combined attendance of more than 7,500 men. The meetings were intended to unite the men and encourage them to be faithful husbands and fathers. They were encouraged to submit to the local shepherds and serve them in whatever ways possible.[60] Bob Mumford's message on 'Fatherpower'[61] challenged men to lead in their homes and confronted feminism and its attempt, he believed, to emasculate men in relation to their proper biblical role.[62]

---

59.   Charles Simpson, confidential letter to Hugo Zelaya (*et al.*), 15 August 1977, private holding, 1.

60.   Don Basham, *Serving and Being Served* (West Coast Men's Conference; Ft Lauderdale: Christian Growth Ministries, 1977), audiocassette.

61.   The message was reprinted in *New Wine*. See Bob Mumford, 'Fatherpower', *New Wine* (April 1978), 4-10.

62.   These men's meetings were remarkably similar to later men's rallies associated with Promise Keepers led by former football coach Bill McCartney. Following the 1997 Promise Keeper Washington DC rally, attended by more than a million men, the *Washington Post* reported: 'The language McCartney uses, critics say, echoes a controversial religious movement that gained prominence in the 1970s and then went underground because of the backlash it created. Called "shepherding/discipleship", the movement set up a strict hierarchy and gave women a submissive role. Promise Keepers denies any link, although McCartney has acknowledged being "discipled" in the 1970s by one of the leaders.' See Gabriel Escobar and Caryle Murphy's 'Promise Keepers Answer the Call', *Washington Post* (5 October 1997), A18; Martin, interview, 8 December 1998. McCartney never had any direct relationship with Mumford or the other four CGM leaders. His reference to being discipled by someone in the movement likely referred to his relationship with an accountability and Bible study group in Ann Arbor, Michigan, where McCartney was an assistant coach in the 1970s. Ralph Martin, the Catholic Charismatic leader close to the Shepherding leaders, was a part of that group.

In the final conference in San Francisco, Mumford told the 1,100 men in attendance that the movement was no longer on trial. He believed that now it was their critics who had been found wanting. He proclaimed to the men:

> I honestly believe, hear me now, we have five of these [men's conferences] in the bank. I'm going to tell you a little secret. I believe we have the ball. That's the truth. I do not know of anything, anywhere that has the kind of answers that God is beginning to share with us. Now if you have the ball you better be careful what you do with it. Now it will be proven whether or not we will be building a new denomination or whether or not we are going to confront…the Church and society with an alternative lifestyle.[63]

The movement's 1977 success in the face of over two years of controversy had helped create the triumphalistic tone which Simpson and Mumford's statements reflect. Many in the movement saw themselves as leading the way for God's purposes in their day. It was a heady time for the Shepherding movement.

The momentum they were experiencing was a continuation of their steady growth and consolidation since the 1974 Montreat conference. As the controversy raged in 1975 and 1976, the Shepherding movement's two centers were changing and growing. While Ft Lauderdale, with Basham, Baxter, Mumford, and Prince living there, continued to be seen as the movement's center by critics and friends, the Mobile area was becoming the true center of the movement. Gulf Coast Fellowship, under Simpson's leadership, had developed into the structural and governmental model for church life.

Fort Lauderdale

The loosely structured house churches of Good News Fellowship, under Mumford and Prince's overall leadership in Ft Lauderdale, had consolidated into separate formal churches by late 1975. In September, CGM administrator Dick Key started Plantation Fellowship in Plantation, Florida, and Ray Ostendorf started South Broward Fellowship in Hollywood, Florida.[64] Both Key and Ostendorf were submitted to Mumford. Derek Prince and pastoral associate Jim Croft were leading a church in Ft Lauderdale called Southport Fellowship.[65] In the fall of 1976, Southport merged with

---

63. Mumford, *How to Bring Forth* (audio).
64. Sutton, interview, 19 January 1996.
65. Croft, interview, 3 January 1996.

Good News Fellowship, along with Don Basham's house church from Pompano Beach.[66] Baxter continued his association with Good News Fellowship.

In 1976, Prince acknowledged the pressure the teachers were feeling, due to the 'fishbowl effect' of so many antagonists watching closely what they were doing in Ft Lauderdale. This made Prince and the others uncomfortable, because they realized that their churches were still in the developmental stage, and Ft Lauderdale was 'a laboratory' for the movement.[67] Critics such as Oral Roberts University professor Charles Farah had encouraged the movement to stop teaching its distinctives publicly until they had built a working, tested model.[68]

In early 1976, Don Basham became the editor of *New Wine* and, under his leadership, the magazine continued to have a great influence among Charismatics and Pentecostals.[69] Basham's editorial and writing skills served to improve the magazine's format and overall quality. In 1976 and for the next three years, *New Wine* would, more than ever, serve as the principal public voice for the Shepherding movement. During this same time, the magazine began to feature articles by key associates of the five teachers. Jim Croft and Dick Key were frequent contributors, along with Robert Grant, Paul Petrie, and others. Consequently, there were fewer articles by teachers outside of the Shepherding movement. This change was another indication that the controversy was pushing the movement inward.

The Mobile Area
In Pascagoula, Gulf Coast Fellowship was progressing more rapidly in growth and definition than the churches in Ft Lauderdale. Simpson and his leadership team were regularly holding training meetings for emerging leaders as well as their regular men's meetings. A June 1975 men's retreat was attended by more than 400 men.[70] The house churches associated with Gulf Coast Fellowship were focused on developing a strong community that went beyond merely spiritual activities. Members worked together to

---

66. Mumford and Prince, *Change of Local Authority*, 575 (audio).
67. Mumford and Prince, *Change of Local Authority*, 380 (audio).
68. Moore, 'Shepherding' (1999), 222.
69. Over the years, in my pastoral and teaching ministry, I was surprised by how many people I encountered who were never directly associated with the movement who nevertheless said *New Wine* was their favorite Christian periodical.
70. Roachelle, 'Chronology', 6.

build houses and complete work projects. The focus of church life continued to be centered in house churches led by shepherds, who were submitted to other leaders, all under Simpson's overall leadership. These groups met weekly, but the focus was not so much on the meetings as it was on the importance of relationships between members outside of the meetings.[71]

In July 1976, Simpson brought all those associated with his leadership together, with more than 2,000 in attendance.[72] In August, he met with the 18 men he was pastoring for three days of meetings. It was during these meetings that an emphasis on spiritual family emerged that would further underscore the movement's relational orientation to church life. A report on the meeting stated:

> While many metaphors are used to describe the people of God, none is more accurate than that of 'family'…no term more denotes the life, structure and dynamics of God's people than that of 'family'. Israel was a family before it was a congregation…right family relationship was required for congregational (church) participation. The family was a kingdom, an army, a race, a nation, etc. Participation in any expression was predicated on family relationship… The constituency of the Gulf Coast Fellowship is a family of people whose relationships are born in the Fatherhood of God and the Lordship of Jesus Christ. Their relationships, therefore, are family in origin, nature, activity, and perpetuity.[73]

This new emphasis on family had a direct effect on the movement. In October 1976, the five teachers met and decided to 'dismantle' any 'headquarters mentality' and keep the focus on family-like relationships.[74] Simpson returned to Pascagoula with a sense that things needed to be dismantled there. He wrote in a 1976 newsletter: 'In the interest of hearing God, we are dismantling our property, offices, or concentration of influence in Pascagoula that might smack of a "headquarters for a new denomination".'[75] Simpson moved to Mobile in December 1976. At the time, Gulf Coast Fellowship had more than 700 members and 20 house churches/ cell groups.[76] Also, in keeping with the desire to decentralize, Bob

71. Longstreth, interview, 29 December 1995.
72. Roachelle, 'Chronology', 10.
73. Charles Simpson, 'Report of Meeting with my Direct Relationships and Local Elders', 26–28 August 1975, private holding, 2.
74. Roachelle, 'Chronology', 10.
75. Charles Simpson, personal newsletter, Christmas 1976, private holding, 1.
76. Charles Simpson, personal newsletter, Fall 1976, private holding, 1.

Mumford announced, with the blessing of the other four teachers and the elders at Good News Fellowship, his plan to move from Ft Lauderdale to the California Bay Area.[77] Bob Mumford's move to California, delayed until the late spring of 1977, was, in part, due to expanding relationships with leaders on the West Coast. Also, Mumford felt that Derek Prince was the real leader of Good News Fellowship and handed the senior leadership over to Prince, who, in turn, made Jim Croft presiding pastor of Good News Fellowship.[78]

Consolidation

From 1975 through 1977, the five teachers were still developing and defining their translocal relationships as more pastors and leaders asked to submit to their leadership.[79] Mumford's move to California was an example of this process. Mumford moved to Cupertino near San Francisco to work with several churches in the area. Just before he arrived in California, he established a relationship with California leader Dennis Peacocke, who was providing leadership to the pastors of several churches in Northern California. When Peacocke submitted to Mumford's leadership, all of his associated churches came into the movement with him.[80] As other leaders and pastors across the nation affiliated with the Shepherding movement, it gained momentum.[81]

The number of pastors wanting to submit to one of the five teachers exceeded their ability to provide personal pastoral care. To manage the growth, a more structured government developed. For example, Bob Mumford selected Dick Key, Robert Grant, and Paul Petrie to pastor 11 other leaders.[82] These 11 men were considered to be submitted 'directly' to

77.   Bob Mumford, 'A Personal Word from Bob Mumford', *New Wine* (November 1976), 11.

78.   Croft, interview, 3 January 1996.

79.   In a letter to Larry Christenson, Simpson said that 'nearly every week, I am asked to assume pastoral care for someone by mail or otherwise'. Charles Simpson, letter to Larry Christenson, 30 November 1976, private holding, 1.

80.   I was one of the pastors under Peacocke's leadership.

81.   San Antonio pastor John Hagee was associated with the movement for a time. Simpson, interview, 5 August 1998, 1. Another well-known personality who joined the movement in 1977 was Graham Kerr, the 'galloping gourmet'. Kerr left the movement disillusioned after disagreements. Mumford, interview, 23 December 1998.

82.   Mumford, interview, 9 February 1995.

Mumford, but were relating to him through Key, Grant, and Petrie, who gave them more personal and regular oversight than Mumford could provide. As already stated, in the Shepherding movement's governing structure, pastors who submitted to the five would pastor other leaders, who, in turn, would pastor others. Many of these relationships were translocal.

Basham and Prince, while pastoring other men, did not have as large or as clear a network of submitted leaders as Mumford and Simpson.[83] Baxter had a large number of men submitted to his leadership but, like Basham and Prince, was looser in his approach.[84] Regardless of some of the differences in leadership style, all five teachers were involved in translocal pastoral relationships within the growing movement.

Frequently, each of the five leaders brought his whole group of leaders together for teaching and fellowship, which could mean a gathering of several hundred men. For example, Mumford brought his leaders to Oklahoma City in September 1979 for several days. Mumford, Simpson, and others taught on spiritual authority, councils and presbyteries, eschatology, and secular humanism. At the conference, Mumford gave each participant R.J. Rushdooney's postmillennially themed booklet *God's Plan for Victory*.[85] Mumford, while not fully embracing Rushdooney's position, nevertheless endorsed the importance of the church's exercising dominion and manifest victory in the last days.[86] He declared that in the face of humanism, communism, and capitalism's dominance in the world, 'There are absolutes; there are answers. God's government [is] the alternative!' Mumford told the men that their movement had the answer, for 'financial and family woes'.[87]

From 1976 through 1979, the Shepherding movement grafted in new churches around the nation, and in some instances started churches. Often a church would be established in response to an invitation by a group of believers who wanted to join the movement. A shepherd would then be sent to pastor the group. It was not unusual for entire groups of people to move with a shepherd to a city or town to start a church.[88] Simpson

83. Croft, interview, 3 January 1995; Leggatt, interview, 1 March 1996.

84. Williams, interview, 28 February 1996.

85. Rousas J. Rushdooney, *God's Plan for Victory: The Meaning of Post-Millennialism* (Fairfax, VA: Thaburn Press, 1977).

86. Bob Mumford, *Concluding Session*, Leaders Conference (n.p.: n.p., September 1979), audiocassette.

87. Bob Mumford, *Concluding Session* (audio).

88. In California, for example, California Shepherding leader, Peacocke sent about

associate Glen Roachelle, along with 150 people, moved to Dallas, Texas, in 1976 and started MetroPlex Fellowship, which grew to more than 800. The movement consolidated by moving some small churches into a larger center. Much of the growth in Mobile from 1976 through 1984 was a result of people moving to the Mobile area from other parts of the nation. For example, a gifted pastor from Pittsburgh, Joseph Garlington, moved to Mobile and became a key leader for Simpson.

In 1978 and 1979, both controversy and consolidation would continue to develop. For Simpson and Gulf Coast Fellowship, 1978 was a year for defining and clarifying 'our government, our beliefs, [and] our lifestyle'.[89] Much of this resulted from the ongoing conflict with Simpson's former pastorate at Bayview Heights Baptist Church. In late 1978, Sam Phillips distributed a pamphlet, *Why We Reject Simpsonism and Mumfordism*, ostensibly written by two California Christian leaders, but adapted by someone at Bayview Heights.[90] The pamphlet was undocumented and admittedly based on hearsay. Nevertheless, it was widely disseminated in Mobile and around the nation.

For several years, Simpson had resisted making creedal statements but, with the ongoing controversy, finally decided it was necessary. In early January 1979, Gulf Coast Fellowship presented to the congregation a series of defining statements regarding the church's beliefs, standards, values, and structure. These statements, along with a financial statement, were distributed to pastors and church leaders in the Mobile area.[91]

For Simpson and his leaders, the Covenant Life Conference in Mobile over the 4 July 1979 weekend was very significant. The conference convened all of Simpson's leaders and their churches from around the nation. More than 8,000 of his leaders and church representatives attended the conference.[92]

Simpson said in 1979 that 'Mobile has, without planning on our part, become a center'.[93] An important factor contributing to this development

75 people from Santa Rosa 100 miles south to Redwood City to start a church. In 1983, he moved an entire South San Francisco church north to Marin County. In these moves people often had to find new employment and sell their homes.

89. Simpson, 'Another Kind of Storm', 27.

90. R.L. Hymers and Kent Philpott, *Why We Reject Simpsonism and Mumfordism* (Mobile, AL: Christian Research Center, n.d.), 1-19.

91. Simpson, 'Another Kind of Storm', 30.

92. Simpson, 'Another Kind of Storm', 31.

93. Simpson, 'Another Kind of Storm', 28.

was *New Wine*'s relocation there in December 1978.[94] Don Basham moved with *New Wine* from Ft Lauderdale and became an elder in Gulf Coast Fellowship.[95] CGM changed its name to Integrity Communications in the fall of 1981. Basham, Baxter, and Simpson also distributed their teaching materials from Mobile. In 1979, and thereafter, many churches in the movement began to include 'Covenant' in their church names, with Simpson's Gulf Coast Fellowship becoming Gulf Coast Covenant Church in December of the year.[96]

Ern Baxter moved from Ft Lauderdale to Southern California in early 1978 to be closer to the men he was leading.[97] While in California, Baxter began teaching at the Morris Cerullo School of Ministry in San Diego, and Cerullo considered joining the movement. Cerullo later decided against doing so and distanced himself from the Shepherding movement.[98] Baxter's move to California lasted for only two years and, after experiencing heart problems, he moved to Mobile in April 1980.[99] Bob Mumford's California move in 1977 was also short-lived and, after just 14 months, he returned to Ft Lauderdale in the summer of 1978.[100]

Again in 1979, an effort was started to decentralize the growing movement. Regional councils and local presbyteries were established around the nation to help provide more localized leadership for associated churches. The long-term goal was to include leaders from outside the movement who shared common values. A distinction was made between 'councils' and 'presbyteries'. A council was comprised of mature senior leaders who exercised translocal authority. A presbytery was a local group of elders who had final authority in administering local church affairs. The councils exercised their authority in areas of national and regional strategy and were also concerned with theological and doctrinal issues. Councils could help mediate disputes in the presbyteries, if asked. In practice, the men on

94. Charles Simpson, letter to Melvin Clark (*et al.*), 10 November 1978, private holding, 3.

95. 'An Important Announcement to Our *New Wine* Family', *New Wine* (February 1979), 24.

96. I have never found any document with a directive to change names. It seems to have been a result of the emphasis on covenant and the example of the Mobile church.

97. Ern Baxter, 'A Personal Word', *New Wine* (March 1978), 16.

98. Charles Simpson, memo to the National Council, 13 August 1979, private holding, 3.

99. Ern Baxter, a personal message from Ern Baxter, n.d., private holding, 1.

100. James Hensley and Beth Hensley, personal interview with author, 30 July 1998.

the councils maintained a submitted relationship to the five or their designee.[101] By late 1982, nine councils were in place, covering most of the United States.[102] In 1981, a broader national and international leadership council was created that included the five teachers and several leaders, all of whom came from the regional councils.[103] In the end, their attempt to decentralize seemed only to lead to more centralized government.

In keeping with their conviction that Christ was Lord over all of life, several task forces were established in public affairs, education, business and economics, publishing, music, and international outreach. The task forces were to help provide leadership and strategy for the movement.[104] The movement's leaders worked behind the scenes to rally their people to vote in the 1980 election. Their conservative orientation meant that Ronald Reagan and others benefited from their efforts.[105]

From 1975 to 1982, estimates of the number of adherents ranged from 50,000 to 100,000. *New Wine* circulation remained strong. In May of 1975, a Spanish edition of *New Wine*, *Vino Nuevo*, had started. It was published under the direction of longtime Simpson associate Hugo Zelaya in Costa Rica. *Vino Nuevo* grew to a circulation of more than 10,000 and was distributed in 38 Spanish-speaking nations.[106] Over the years, CGM, and later Integrity Communications, would publish various newsletters on fatherhood and business issues,[107] and by 1981, would distribute all the teachers' tapes and books, except for Derek Prince, who continued to publish his materials from Ft Lauderdale.

The Shepherding movement placed a strong emphasis on music and worship. In 1977, a well-produced album called *It Filled the Land* was released.[108] Songwriters and worship leaders, Gerrit Gustafson, Pete Sanchez, and Ted Sandquist, put into song many themes of the movement.

101. Charles Simpson, *Councils and Presbyteries* (Leadership Conference; Oklahoma City: n.p., September 1979), audiocassette.

102. List of Regional Councils, 21 November 1982, private holding.

103. Minutes of the Five Teachers' Meeting, 12–14 November 1981, Mobile, AL, private holding, 2.

104. Minutes, 12–14 November 1981, 2-3.

105. Don Basham, *About Being Involved* (Mobile, AL: n.p., December 1980), audiocassette.

106. 'A Report on *Vino Nuevo*', *New Wine* (February 1977), 14-15.

107. *Fathergram* was first published July 1977. *Fathergram* (4 July 1977), 1-2. *BusinessGram* was first announced in 1981. 'Announcing BusinessGram', *New Wine* (November 1981), 28.

108. Pete Sanchez, a musician in the movement, produced the album and wrote many

Notably, the popular worship chorus *I Exalt Thee* was written by Sanchez. In 1985, Integrity Communications started distribution of Hosanna Music worship tapes, which were released six times a year and contained contemporary worship choruses. Hosanna Music proved to be greatly successful and was sold in 1987, becoming Integrity Music, a for-profit corporation that continues today with over 100 employees and 2001 sales of nearly $71 million.[109] Hosanna Music's influence in proliferating contemporary Christian worship music has been far-reaching.

International Relationships

Basham, Baxter, Mumford, Prince, and Simpson traveled extensively and developed relationships with leaders around the world. As the movement consolidated, only a few direct translocal international relationships were established. Ern Baxter was involved with English Charismatic leaders Bryn Jones and Arthur Wallace, but his relationship with these men would not be defined as pastoral or governmental (though some thought it was).[110] Baxter had a pastoral relationship with Australian pastor Howard Carter, who had a number of churches under his leadership. Carter was clearly submitted to Baxter, and his ministry published an Australian version of *New Wine* called *Restore*.

Bob Mumford had a strong relationship with English and Canadian church leader Barney Coombs. For a few years, Mumford pastored Coombs translocally; however, according to Coombs Mumford's leadership was personal and did not directly involve the churches Coombs led in England and Canada.[111]

Generally, the Shepherding movement's international relationships were more in the realm of influence. Nevertheless, the idea of discipling the

---

of its songs. Pete Sanchez, *It Filled the Land* (Texas: Bread of Life and Southeast Texas Fellowship, 1977), album.

109. *Charts* www.integritymusic.com/company/index.html. Mike Coleman, telephone interview with author, 21 February 1996.

110. Andrew Walker's study of the English house church movement takes significant notice of the Shepherding teachers' influence and overstates it. Joyce Thurman also observes their influence on the house churches. See Andrew Walker, *Restoring the Kingdom: The Radical Christianity of the House Church Movement* (London: Hodder & Stoughton, 1985). Joyce Thurman, *New Wineskins: The Study of the House Church* (Frankfurt: Peter Lang, 1982).

111. Barney Coombs, telephone interview with author, 31 January 1996.

nations was a strong theme and motivation within the movement. Mumford often talked of the importance of spiritual preparation because 'nations are opening to us'.[112] A major teaching theme for Ern Baxter was God's purpose to impact the nations with the message of God's government. Baxter's Reformed orientation and his belief in a victorious postmillennial eschatology emphasized the role of the church in extending God's rule on the earth.[113]

Maturation

During the season of growth and consolidation the movement's distinctives had matured and some of its practices had moderated. By 1981, recognizing the ongoing confusion and resistance to the term 'shepherd', the movement replaced its use with the more acceptable term 'pastor'.[114] Gradually the controversial emphasis on providing practical service to leaders was lessened.

Internally, they continued to grapple with their critics' charges. Bob Mumford met with his key leaders in Santa Rosa, California, in 1978 and pointed out a number of problems they needed to address. The group discussed authoritarianism, exclusivism, elitism, neglect of the female role, unbalanced use of metaphors, creation of a jargon, and minimal biblical support for the degree of headship they taught. Mumford acknowledged a deficiency in evangelistic activity among their churches. They discussed the impression outsiders had, that anyone not doing what the movement taught was missing God.[115]

To address the problem, Mumford suggested cultivating a 'greater openness toward all members of the Body of Christ' and a need to recognize any sovereign local presbytery(s) that must not be dictated or controlled. He thought the movement needed to encourage more freedom in relationships, with less emphasis on protocol, and not to 'reduce all relationship to one or two patterns' to which all must be conformed. He concluded that

112. Bob Mumford, *The Shepherd: Part 1* (COM Community Conference; n.p.: n.p., 1979), audiocassette, 456.

113. Ern Baxter, *Thy Kingdom Come* (National Men's Shepherds Conference; n.p.: His Men's Tapes, 1975), audiocassette.

114. I have wondered if they would have been opposed as fiercely if 'pastor' had been used from the beginning of the movement.

115. Bob Mumford, Position Paper, Strategy Meeting, Santa Rosa, California, 3–5 May 1978, private holding, 12-13.

there needed to be a 'new and fresh emphasis on the gifts and operations of the Holy Spirit…'[116]

Significantly, Mumford thought the movement should take great care in application of the principles it held and avoid 'unreasonable and excessive involvement in the lives of people'. He was concerned that, 'due to insensitivity and eagerness, we may fail to wait for the delicate conviction of conscience to absolve or find its own release in the Holy Spirit and Scriptures'. He admitted: 'We may be overly demanding.'[117]

The other leaders shared Mumford's concerns, but they found it difficult to maintain their efforts to produce order, discipline, and maturity and, at the same time, avoid the aforementioned pitfalls.[118] The very things they taught created a propensity toward an abuse of spiritual authority, especially among young immature leaders, or leaders who lacked character and integrity. In the rapid growth and consolidation, many leaders were in place that the five teachers hardly knew. Moreover, the idealism of creating an 'alternate society' necessitated strong exercise of authority that easily could go to the heads of even good men. What is important to establish is that, contrary to the perception of critics, the movement's leaders were aware of the need to correct serious problems as the movement matured.

The ideal of a restoration to New Testament church community remained important in their ethos. Don Basham saw their emphasis on covenant love and loyalty as extremely significant to God's renewing work. He referred to Lesslie Newbigin's classification of three types of Christianity, each of which made important contributions to the universal Church: the Catholic tradition, with its orthodoxy, sacraments, and hierarchy; the Protestant tradition, with emphasis on the authority and proclamation of the Bible; and the Pentecostals, with their central focus on the presence and power of the Holy Spirit.[119] Basham asserted there was now coming a fourth stream, the Covenant stream, with its emphasis on covenant love and loyalty experienced in Christian community.[120]

116. Mumford, Position Paper, 13. Don Basham and Derek Prince, Thoughts from Derek and Don to Share at the 19–23 March Teacher's Meeting in Mobile, 1978, private holding, 1. In the above communication Basham and Prince appeal that the Spirit's gifts 'should not be set aside or neglected'.

117. Mumford, Position Paper, 14.

118. Derek Prince, letter to Charles Simpson, 9 April 1979, private holding, 1-2; Derek Prince, Suggested Course Corrections, n.d., private holding, 1-2.

119. Lesslie Newbigin, *The Household of God* (New York: Friendship Press, 1954).

120. Don Basham, Saturday Morning Session Kemper Arena, Parts 1 and 2; Non-denominational Conference on Charismatic Renewal, 1977.

Basham wrote a description, admittedly an idealistic one, of what a Covenant church ought to be. It was published in *New Wine* and also widely distributed as a lithograph. In part, he wrote:

A Covenant Community

A community of God's redeemed people: bound together in covenant love, submitted to compassionate authority and rulership, and manifesting peace, holiness, and family fidelity expressed through revered fatherhood, cherished woman and motherhood with secure and obedient children. A community where loving correction and instruction produce healthy growth and maturity; where dedication to excellence produces the finest results in arts, crafts, trades and commerce, providing prosperity and abundance for all its members. A community of faith, worship, praise and a selfless ministry, manifesting individually and corporately the gifts and fruit of the Holy Spirit. A community where all life is inspired and directed by the Spirit of Jesus Christ and is lived to His glory as a witness and testimony to the world.[121]

Charles Simpson's influence on the movement's development, self-concept, and ecclesiology became even greater. If Mumford was the movement's prophetic voice, Simpson was its structural architect. In 1980 and 1981, Simpson taught throughout the movement on the theme, 'Internal Integrity, External Integration'.[122] Through the concepts presented in these messages, he subsequently articulated a unique ecclesiological construct for the Shepherding movement. Simpson prepared a series of charts that graphically illustrated the importance of the church in the movement's thinking (see Appendix 3).[123]

Essentially, Simpson taught that God's ultimate goal was the integration of his whole creation, which consisted of the 'complex interrelationships of a myriad of structures'. Because of sin's effect, the various structures of creation—individuals, families, churches, and governments—have lost their integrity or soundness and have been fragmented. Consequently, God's original plan for interdependence has been frustrated.[124]

---

121. Don Basham, 'A Covenant Community', *New Wine* (February 1980), 30.

122. Charles Simpson, *Internal Integrity, External Integration of Structures* (Mobile, AL: Charles Simpson Ministries, 1981), audiocassette.

123. Charles Simpson, *Internal Integrity and External Integration of Structures*, charts, private holding, 1; Charles Simpson, Structure Charts One Through Three, 1981, private holding; Charles Simpson, Larger Christian Leadership Configuration, 1981, private holding.

124. Simpson, *Internal Integrity*, 1.

Simpson believed structures that were 'internally sound and secure [would] naturally seek to harmonize and interrelate with larger structures, because no structure [was] complete within itself'. He taught that 'healthy individuals relate to families, families to churches, churches to the larger church, and the larger church to the Church universal and eternal'. The lack of integration of the structures of creation indicated ill health. As a result, the pastoral goal was to bring soundness and health to each structural part so it would integrate into ever larger structural units.[125]

Ecclesiologically, the aim was to integrate individuals or families into cell groups under a pastor. The cell groups were then to integrate into larger congregational structures, which in turn would integrate into the larger church, and so on.[126] Simpson's Mobile church had always been the primary model, and it reflected his developing ecclesiological concepts. By late 1981, Gulf Coast Covenant Church had 1,200 members and consisted of three separate congregations of 250 to 500 people, each with a number of cell groups. The congregations were led by a pastor who developed his own leadership team, to provide oversight to the group church pastors.[127] The elders from each congregation under Simpson's senior leadership, joined by Basham, Baxter, and Mumford as translocal elders, formed a presbytery that governed the overall church. As with their previous approach, the house churches/cell groups were the primary church structures and met weekly. In this multi-congregational model, each separate congregation of cell groups met on Sunday mornings once a month for worship and teaching. The entire church met every three months in a large rented facility.[128] Simpson appointed key associate John Duke as Gulf Coast Covenant Church's 'presiding pastor' in 1981, and Duke was the day-to-day leader of the Mobile church.[129]

In 1983, they found this approach had not helped accomplish the kind of unity and integration they desired. Simpson believed the infrequent gathering of the whole church caused them to act like 'several churches instead

125. Simpson, *Internal Integrity*.

126. Charles Simpson, Larger Christian Leadership Configuration, 1.

127. Charles Simpson, letter to Melvin Clark (*et al.*), March 1983, private holding, 2-3.

128. Joseph Garlington, telephone interview with author, 23 April 1998. Garlington served as the lead elder for one of the congregations.

129. Charles Simpson, letter to Melvin Clark (*et al.*), 23 October 1982, private holding, 1.

of one'.[130] He proposed a significant modification in their approach by establishing weekly all church Sunday morning worship meetings that would be open to the public. The individual congregations would continue to meet once a month, but on Sunday evening, instead of the morning. Other steps were taken to establish and develop overall church unity without disbanding their innovative structures.[131] In order to explain their uniqueness, the church published a well-designed brochure that discussed their multi-congregational approach, contained statements of faith, standards and values, and information on membership and church discipline.[132] The church purchased 40 acres in 1982 and built four buildings to house the church and their publishing arm, Integrity Communications. The buildings were completed in 1983.

Howard Snyder continued to influence the ecclesiology of the Shepherding movement through his books *The Community of the King*[133] and *The Radical Wesley*[134] which emphasized church structure and the church's mission in manifesting God's kingdom on the earth. Baxter required his men to read *The Community of the King* and told them he so liked the book that he wished he would have written it first. *The Radical Wesley*, with its study of Wesley's ecclesiology (instrumented discipleship in various kinds of small groups, means of grace, etc.) further confirmed and reinforced the movement's own efforts at workable and innovative structures despite internal problems and outside opposition. Leonard Verduin's book *The Reformers and their Stepchildren*, a study on the divide between the Magisterial Reformers and the Radical Reformers,[135] was important to the movement and was widely promoted.[136] The Shepherding movement identified with the Anabaptist emphasis on the visible, believing community, comprised of those whose conduct is distinctly different from that the world. Moreover, they identified with the Radical Reformers' rejection and perse-

130. Charles Simpson, letter to the elders of Gulf Coast Covenant Church, March 1983, private holding, 4.

131. Charles Simpson, letter to the elders of Gulf Coast Covenant Church, 4-8.

132. A Statement of Information, Gulf Coast Covenant Church, n.d., private holding, 1-31.

133. Howard A. Snyder, *The Community of the King* (Downers Grove, IL: Inter Varsity Press, 1977).

134. Snyder, *The Radical Wesley*.

135. Leonard Verduin, *The Reformers and their Stepchildren* (Grand Rapids: Eerdmans, 1964).

136. Joseph Garlington, *Our Covenant Heritage* (Mobile, AL: Integrity Communications, 1979), audiocassette.

cution as heretics for truths they deemed faithful to the New Testament. Verduin's sympathetic treatment seemed to be confirmation that radical groups are often rejected in their own times only later to receive some measure of vindication.

Since so many of the Shepherding movement's leaders were often products of the movement's own practice of discipleship and pastoral care, most were without any formal theological training, including many of those serving in full-time pastoral positions. In an effort to remedy some of its internal problems, and bring some quality control to what it was doing, the movement held an eight-day Pastoral Training Institute in Mobile. The January 1984 Institute was attended by 800 pastors from the movement.[137] Baxter, Basham, Mumford, and Simpson taught on varied subjects, including the life and theology of Paul, pastoral care, preparation and delivery of messages, and spiritual warfare. The Institute was followed by the Prophetic Institute in May 1984 and an Evangelism Institute in May 1985.[138]

Simpson's book *The Challenge to Care* was published in 1986 as both an apologetic to the movement's ecclesiology and manual for its practice. The book reflected a moderated application of the principles that had been so controversial in 1975. Few today would have any dispute with what Simpson presented. By 1986, not only had the movement adjusted significantly, but its distinctives were more acceptable. Sociologist Robert Bellah's 1985 book *Habits of the Heart* had brought attention to the destructive side of North American individualism and the general need for a deeper experience of community.[139] Concepts that had been rejected by modernity's individualist ideal were now finding acceptance with the rise of postmodernity and its embrace of 'connectedness'.[140] The forces that push radical movements toward accommodation were fusing with changes within the larger culture.

Though the opposition never went away entirely, by 1986, the Shepherding movement was no longer a major focus of Charismatic controversy, as other issues had become more important. It was, however, to become newsworthy again for a different and surprising reason.

137. Bob Mumford, *Integrity House Newsletter* (1984), 1.

138. Charles Simpson, *Integrity House Newsletter* (20 December 1984), 2-3.

139. Robert Bellah (ed.), *Habits of the Heart* (Berkeley: University of California Press, 1985).

140. The relationship between ecclesiology and postmodernism is beginning to be addressed. Rodney Clapp's *A Peculiar People* is a helpful study on the church in an increasingly post-modern world. Rodney Clapp, *A Peculiar People* (Downers Grove, IL: InterVarsity Press, 1996).

Chapter 9

STRUGGLE AND SEPARATION

Dispute and Dialogue

Many observers of the Shepherding movement mistakenly believed the
March 1976 Charismatic leaders conference had effectively quieted the controversy over the discipleship question.[1] For the next few years the controversy continued fiercely but it became less public. The debate over the
movement's teachings and its own internal problems was placing significant strain on its five leaders. They spent much time from 1976 through
1983 attempting to quiet opposition through dialogue and reconciliation.
Additionally, they traveled extensively to resolve numerous internal crises
that surfaced in their own movement.

In 1977, in response to the published opposition by the Assemblies of
God, at least two meetings were arranged for dialogue. In April a meeting
was held in Chicago to answer questions that were plaguing 'the minds
of many' in the denomination.[2] Part of the tension with the Pentecostal
denomination's leadership was caused by dual authority relationships that
a few of its ministers had with the five. For example, Assemblies of God
pastor Roy Harthern, whose burgeoning Orlando, Florida, church was the
publisher of the new Charismatic periodical *Charisma* magazine, was submitted directly to Derek Prince.[3] Successful Seattle Assemblies of God
pastor Jim Hamann, who had received permission from his denominational
supervisor, was submitted to Bob Mumford.[4] In December, Mumford,
Prince, and Simpson met in Kansas City with Assemblies of God leaders,
including General Superintendent Thomas Zimmerman, to discuss these

---

1.   McDonnell, 'Seven Documents', II, 120; 'Editorials: "No Deepening Rift
Here"', *Logos* (March/April 1976), 54. See also Harper, *Three Sisters*, 95-96.
2.   Conference with Christian Growth Representatives and Assembly of God Ministers, 25–26 April 1977, private holding, 1-3.
3.   Derek Prince, letter to Roy Harthern, 31 October 1977, private holding, 1.
4.   Mumford, interview, 23 December 1998.

issues. Zimmerman contacted Simpson and told him he felt 'much good has been done for the Kingdom in opening up these meaningful lines of communication among brethren'.[5]

Although these efforts were going on, many, including David du Plessis, who had signed the 1976 Montreat Charismatic Leaders Statement, did not believe the Ft Lauderdale brethren had done anything to improve relations 'and that they were causing more and more trouble…and serious divisions in the churches'. Du Plessis believed their 'covenanting was evil' and was concerned about their influence on the 1977 Kansas City conference.[6]

The criticism of the movement's teachings was still a concern in Southern California. Chuck Smith's Maranatha Evangelical Association magazine ran an article against the teachings on submission and the demon possession of Christians. Using words that reflected Pat Robertson's earlier concerns, the article said teachings on submission, covering, and Shepherding came out of Florida, but 'originated in hell'.[7]

Ralph Mahoney of World MAP published articles and produced audiotapes in opposition to the movement's teachings from 1975 through 1978.[8] Mahoney and Ralph Wilkerson's participation in the 1977 Kansas City conference was subdued by their frustration over the prominence given to Mumford and others in the CCRCC.[9]

Simpson wrote to Mahoney asking for a personal meeting if possible. Mahoney's opposition was especially distressing to both Mumford and Simpson in view of their long-standing friendship and association. Mahoney received many reports and letters from people around the world who told him of the misuse or abuse of spiritual authority, and he felt compelled to challenge the movement openly. He continued to believe that there were demons 'that controlled the Ft Lauderdale and Mobile leaders'. He told Mumford in 1978: 'I see such fantastically good qualities in you, and potential, that it tears me apart to see what has happened.'[10]

5.   Moore, 'Shepherding' (1999), 247.

6.   David du Plessis, note to Kevin Ranaghan on 1977 Charismatic Leaders Conference Registration form, 15 April 1977.

7.   Chuck Smith, 'Submission', *Maranatha Good News* 3.2 (1976), 2-3.

8.   Ralph Mahoney, 'Editorial: Disciple', *World MAP Digest* (November/December 1975), 14-15; Ralph Mahoney, 'Submission and Obedience', *World MAP Digest* (November/December 1975), 4-14; Wayne Butchart, 'Soul Bondage', *World MAP Digest* (December 1978), 5-7; Ralph Mahoney, *What's Wrong With Discipleship?* (n.p.: *World MAP*, 1978), three audiocassettes.

9.   Charles Simpson, letter to Ralph Mahoney, 25 August 1977, private holding, 2.

10.   Ralph Mahoney, letter to Bob Mumford and Judy Mumford, 24 May 1978, private holding, 1-2.

In early 1979, a get-together was arranged with Mahoney, Mumford, and the elders of Elim Fellowship in Lima, New York. At the meeting, Mahoney was allowed to lay out his concerns one by one; and later, Mumford was given time to respond. The tone of the meeting was positive. Mahoney, who had been at the March 1976 Charismatic leaders conference in Oklahoma City, did not feel that he had been given a fair hearing there. At the Elim meeting he presented a file 'four or five inches thick', according to Mumford, and presented evidence that was 'heavy'.[11] Most of Mahoney's points stressed how the movement's teachings were controlling people and hurting families by creating inappropriate allegiance to a shepherd. He also challenged 'the difficulties of a binding life covenant' and what he believed were spirits of bondage and legalism.[12]

Mumford's response was that the problems, where true, were not an 'issue of doctrinal heresy, demonic activity and major principalities', but an issue of 'misapplication and intensity'. Mumford charged that Mahoney's national posture had made him a 'national garbage collector' of stories against the movement.[13] In the post-Watergate and post-Jim Jones era, special care needed to be taken not to suspect the worst of brothers, Mumford believed. Mumford also apologized to Mahoney for offending him in 1973 by calling him an unsubmitted man.[14]

It seems the Elim elders were generally more sympathetic to Mumford. They advised Mahoney not to be predisposed to believe the negative stories and encouraged him to have more direct communication and dialogue with Mumford, perhaps mediated through one of the Elim elders.[15] The meeting did help Mahoney and Mumford reach some understanding, and Mahoney's public opposition was not as strong after the meeting.

Pat Robertson's public opposition to the movement had continued, and in 1980, a particular incident created a new confrontation with the Shepherding leaders. On the 7 January 1980 700 Club broadcast, in an answer to a listener's call-in question about the movement, Robertson said:

> We've had many, many calls coming in from on the air. A couple...uh said, that there's a thing known as submitted body teaching, discipleship...they talk about covering, etc. And this has been primarily an expression among

11.   Bob Mumford, meeting with Ralph Mahoney, n.d., private holding, 1-8.
12.   Mumford, meeting with Ralph Mahoney, 2-6.
13.   Mumford, meeting with Ralph Mahoney, 7.
14.   Mumford, meeting with Ralph Mahoney, 6.
15.   Mumford, meeting with Ralph Mahoney, 8.

the Charismatic Catholics as well as Protestants and it's had central location in Fort Lauderdale, Florida…and other things. And somebody said, 'Is it a cult?' Yes it is! There is very little that Jim Jones did that this discipleship doesn't do. The only thing that they haven't done yet is take cyanide in a mutual…suicide pact. I don't think they are engaged in wife swapping and calling people homosexual, but there is the dominance of one individual over the other. That is not biblical.[16]

Robertson followed this strong condemnation with his interpretation of the Bible and its teachings on 'covering' and the pastoral relationship.

Simpson disciple Glen Roachelle, pastoring in Dallas, spearheaded a response to Robertson's comments. Several Dallas area leaders, some not associated directly with the movement, wrote to Robertson objecting to his statements.[17] Robertson wrote back to the men and remained emphatic in his denunciation of discipleship. He said that 'without question this entire teaching is both unbiblical and satanic', and called it 'the most dangerous heresy that has been presented to the so-called Charismatic movement in its entire history in the United States and overseas'. He concluded: 'It is totally repugnant to me and to any intelligent Christian. It has no redeeming characteristics.'[18] In another 1980 letter, Robertson said that the 'Shepherding movement is the most hateful I have ever encountered'.[19]

Roachelle wrote to Kevin Ranaghan of the Charismatic Concerns Committee and asked them to consider grievances he presented as a result of Robertson's January comments, calling them 'inaccurate…unfair…unwarranted and unscriptural'.[20] Roachelle noted the negative materials sent to those who had written to Robertson, and, specifically, requested efforts be made to 'open private dialogue with Robertson'.[21] Simpson wrote to Robertson in February 1980 requesting a personal meeting.[22]

Robertson's concern that the discipleship teachings 'destroyed many lives' led to the CBN counseling center practice of sending anyone who asked about submission or discipleship a copy of Robertson's 1975 letter

16. Transcription of Pat Robertson's Accusation, 700 Club Broadcast of 7 January 1980, private holding, 1.

17. Glen Roachelle, letter to Pat Robertson, 5 March 1980, private holding, 1-4.

18. Pat Robertson, letter to Glen Roachelle, 25 March 1980, private holding, 1.

19. Pat Robertson, letter to Guy Kump, 20 March 1980, private holding, 1.

20. Glen Roachelle, letter to the Charismatic Concerns Committee: Attention Kevin Ranaghan, 30 April 1980, private holding, 2.

21. Roachelle, letter to the Charismatic Concerns Committee, 2-3.

22. Charles Simpson, letter to Pat Robertson, 13 February 1980, private holding, 1-2.

to Mumford, which outlined his biblically based understanding of the error of their teachings.[23] This practice continued for years.

Friend and mentor Ken Sumrall had stood by Simpson and Shepherding leaders during the height of the controversy in 1975 and 1976. There was a point in 1976 in which he was asked to consider joining the inner circle of leaders that included the five teachers and Poole. Sumrall, whose ministry involved not only pastoring his church in Pennsacola, but overseeing a group of pastors nationally, declined the invitation. In 1977, Simpson and Sumrall had a painful falling out with each other. Sumrall, concerned with what he thought was exclusiveness and extreme practices, taught a message in his church which amounted to 'an open confrontation with the "discipleship move"'.[24] The two men attempted to resolve the breech, but the disagreement effectively severed their friendship for several years. Sumrall participated in the 1977 Kansas City conference with the nondenominational track opposite to the Shepherding group. In 1978, Sumrall joined other Charismatic leaders, including Jim Jackson of Christian Believers United,[25] pastor Houston Miles, and Jamie Buckingham, to form the ecumenically focused National Leadership Conference, as an alternative to the Shepherding group.[26]

The controversy also continued to manifest itself in the publishing world. With the five Shepherding teachers' pictures on the front cover, *Charisma*'s September 1978 issue featured the story, 'The Discipleship Controversy Three Years Later'. The article was reasonably objective, but the inside artist's drawing of the five dressed in shepherd's clothing with staffs in hand was objectionable to the five teachers.[27]

Logos International published Charismatic Bill Ligon's book *Discipleship: The Jesus View* in 1979. It was written as 'an alternative to extremism' and against the Shepherding movement.[28] A more objective book, *Shepherds and Sheep*, by Jerram Barrs, was written in 1983 to give attention and correction to 'hierarchical leadership structures, "coverings" and

23.   Joyce W. Rodford, letter to Duke Benedix, 30 January 1980, private holding, 1.

24.   Ken Sumrall, telephone interview with author, 2 November 1998.

25.   Christian Believers United was the new name for Christian Book Unlimited.

26.   Jim Jackson, telephone interview with author, 26 August 1998; Sumrall, interview, 2 November 1998; Hocken, 'Charismatic Movement', 141.

27.   Strang, 'The Discipleship Controversy', 14-24.

28.   Bill Ligon with Robert Paul Lamb, *Discipleship: The Jesus View* (Plainfield, NJ: Logos, 1979), v.

so-called chain of command' principles which he felt were a distortion of New Testament teachings.[29]

In 1986, Pentecostal Evangelist Jimmy Swaggart wrote critically of the movement in his magazine *The Evangelist*.[30] Simpson wrote to Swaggart, objecting, and arranged a meeting in January 1987. The three-and-a-half hour discussion brought some understanding. Swaggart remained concerned about the movement's teachings, but acknowledged the injury his article had done.[31]

Over the years from 1975 to 1986, many critiques were written and articles published against the Shepherding movement. Some were written by reasonable critics; others were no more than hearsay accounts. Detail and discussion of each is beyond the scope of this project.[32]

The continuing dispute did not stop efforts by some leaders to bring healing and renew the ecumenism so important to the Charismatic Renewal. Aware of not only the Shepherding dispute, but also differences between Classical Pentecostals and Charismatics, and criticism of the 'faith' teachers Kenneth Copeland and Kenneth Hagin, a group of 'ecumenically minded' leaders organized the John 17.21 International Fellowship.[33] This group, led by California Assemblies of God pastor Ron Haus, working closely with David du Plessis, held a Dallas, Texas, 'summit' meeting in February 1980. Basham, Baxter, Mumford, Simpson, and about 20 of their

29.   Jerram Barrs, *Shepherds and Sheep* (Downers Grove, IL: InterVarsity Press, 1983), 10.

30.   Jimmy Swaggart, 'Brother Jimmy Swaggart, Here's My Question: Is the Shepherding Movement a Viable Scriptural Discipleship Effort?', *Evangelist* (November 1986), 11-13.

31.   Charles Simpson, 'Report on Meeting with Jimmy Swaggart', n.d., private holding, 1.

32.   I have on file more than 60 articles and critiques that address the movement of which I will list only those which are easily accessible. Many critiques were privately published and are difficult to locate. Without Mumford and Simpson's help I might not have found them. See Carl Beiser, *The Shepherding Movement* (San Juan Capistrano, CA: Christian Research Institute, 1979); Russell T. Hitt, 'The Soul Watchers', *Eternity* (April 1976), 13-15, 34; Larry Hart, 'Problems of Authority in Pentecostalism', *Review and Expositor* 75 (Spring 1978), 249-66; Ronald Enroth, 'The Power Abusers', *Eternity* (October 1979), 23-27; Elliot Miller, 'The Christian and Authority, Part One', *Forward* (Spring 1985), 8-15 (9-11); Elliot Miller, 'The Christian and Authority, Part Two', *Forward* (Summer 1985), 9-26 (24-26); Gordon MacDonald, 'Disciple Abuse', *Discipleship* (November 1985), 24-28.

33.   'Charismatic Leaders Seeking Faith for their Own Healing', *Christianity Today* (April 1980), 44-45.

leaders attended the meeting, joined by Dennis Bennett, Larry Christenson, Judson Cornwall, Charles Farah, Jr, J. Rodman Williams, Juan Carlos
Ortiz, Kevin Ranaghan, Ralph Martin, and many others.

Du Plessis and Mumford, sharing the platform, 'effected a public
reconciliation'. Du Plessis told the group that he and Mumford had differences of opinion but, 'we don't have to agree on all points in order to have
intimate fellowship with each other'.[34] Mumford affirmed his commitment
to the 'radical' answers they taught that were 'needed to correct the "super-
ficial" state of the Church today'. Mumford also apologized for 'any valid
or real hurt or injury' the movement had caused in its application of its
teachings.[35] Dennis Bennett, who originally warned du Plessis against giving his approval to the Shepherding leaders,[36] reportedly 'had many questions answered' at the summit.[37]

Simpson felt there was 'genuine love between the participants' in the
Dallas meeting. By the Shepherding leaders' participation in the summit,
Simpson hoped to 'make a statement to the rest of the leaders about our
interest in Christian unity'.[38] Apparently, that statement was received positively as Ron Haus subsequently commended the movement's leaders for
their 'virtuous endurance through seasons of accusation, malicious attacks,
and ostracisms'.[39] The Dallas meeting was indeed a step toward reconciliation among Charismatics, but the end result of all the attempts by Mumford, Simpson, and the others to quiet the opposition was mixed.[40] While
some healing was accomplished, the criticism never stopped. Moreover,
the energy expended in the process drained energies needed for their work
on their own internal difficulties.

Internal Struggles

While it was not widely known outside of the movement's higher leadership circles, as early as 1976, the five teachers had seriously considered

34. 'Mumford, du Plessis Reconcile at John 17.21 Fellowship Meeting', *Logos*
(May/June 1980), 12.
    35. 'Mumford, du Plessis Reconcile', 12.
    36. 'Charismatic Leaders Seeking Faith', 44.
    37. Moore, 'Shepherding' (1999), 256.
    38. 'Charismatic Leaders Seeking Faith', 44.
    39. Moore, 'Shepherding' (1999), 257.
    40. For two other accounts of the Dallas summit, see Don Basham, 'A Time To Be
Reconciled', *New Wine* (May 1980), 16-17; 'Lord, Make Us One', *Charisma* (May
1980), 49-54.

dissolving their association. In a December 1976 meeting in Naples, Florida, Mumford and the others actually decided to split up. They gathered again a month later in Naples, and Simpson appealed for a continuing association, feeling that disbanding would hurt too many people who were committed to their leadership. Simpson agreed to be the leader within the group of five at the request of the others.[41] All during their association, the five men, all strong, successful, and independent leaders, had struggled to blend their ministries. At times, they admitted to a territorial and competitive mentality that was sometimes exacerbated by personal, practical, and theological differences. The strain from the outside opposition only complicated their internal difficulties.

In 1978, the five again came close to separating, and Simpson held them together as before.[42] Only months before in the fall of 1977, Derek Prince brought to Simpson and the other three teachers, and later to the Ecumenical Council, his desire to marry Ruth Baker, a divorcee he had only recently met.[43] The group of leaders said there was 'no way they could endorse what [Prince] was intending to do'.[44] Basham was especially cautious about Prince's plans and plainly told him so.[45] Prince, who had agreed to submit to their counsel, decided not to pursue the marriage. He later wrote to Simpson and presented an appeal, based on several reasons which he felt justified the marriage.[46] After a few months, the men realized their counsel had been difficult for Prince to receive and decided to bless his marriage plans.[47] Simpson performed the wedding on 17 October 1978. The whole situation regarding the marriage strained Prince's relationship with the other four.[48]

1980 proved to be a challenging year for the movement. First, Mumford faced severe difficulties with his top men. Problems in the Ft Lauderdale

41. Roachelle, 'Chronology', 10.

42. Minutes of the Five Teachers' Meeting, 21, 23 June 1978, private holding, 2.

43. Prince brought the situation first to Simpson then to his four fellow teachers and to the Council that included the five teachers, Clark, DeCelles, Martin, Ranaghan, Christenson, and Pfotenhauer. Prince and Prince, *God is a Matchmaker*, 43-46; Simpson, interview, 23 February 1996.

44. Simpson, interview, 23 February 1996.

45. Don Basham, letter to Derek Prince, 6 September 1977, private holding, 1-2.

46. Derek Prince, letter to Charles Simpson (with attachments), 18 October 1977, private holding.

47. Ad Hoc Meeting of the General Council, 31 March–1 April 1978, St Louis, Missouri, private holding, 1.

48. Howard, 'A New Beginning', 38-43.

area churches pastored by Mumford's men, Dick Key and Ray Ostendorf, resulted in the closing of the two churches in the spring of 1980.[49] Scott Ross moved to Ft Lauderdale in 1979 to be closer to Mumford and got caught in the turmoil. Another leader Mumford pastored, Neal Kay, had moved to Ft Lauderdale in 1979 from the Philadelphia area with 100 people. Within six months, Kay left the movement after disagreements with Mumford and others in Ft Lauderdale.[50] These situations left many followers in the Ft Lauderdale area hurt and disillusioned.

In the fall of 1980, two of Mumford's primary leaders, Robert Grant and Paul Petrie, expressed their own disillusionment with his leadership in their lives. They had come to believe that Mumford was not able to pastor them effectively. Both Grant and Petrie, with Mumford's blessing, later submitted to Charles Simpson. Mumford described 1980 'as the worst year of my life'.[51] He later said that 1980 taught him that he was not called to pastor. He realized his main ministry gift was as a Bible teacher, and the rapid growth of the movement with its emphases had pushed him into a role he could not fulfill. The end result was that, after 1980, Mumford led only a few men who were willing to accept what limited oversight he felt he could provide. With his 'LifeChangers' ministry struggling financially, and given the problems in Ft Lauderdale, Mumford moved to Mobile in 1981 to join Basham, Baxter, and Simpson.

The struggles Mumford experienced were not unique. As early as 1976, people were starting to leave the movement. Baxter had a falling-out with leaders in California not long after he moved there in 1978.[52] The emphasis on personal pastoral care had created expectations that he could not easily fulfill.

Simpson labeled 1980 'a record bad year'. Much of the year he was ill, probably because of stress.[53] Earlier, in 1979, the Internal Revenue Service (IRS) started an investigation of Gulf Coast Covenant Church, which was instigated when some documents, taken from their offices by a disgruntled employee, were given to the IRS. While Gulf Coast Covenant Church would eventually be exonerated, in 1980 the church was the subject of a full IRS audit that eventually cost $100,000 in attorney fees.[54]

49.   Bob Sutton, telephone interview with author, 26 February 1996.
50.   Scott Ross, telephone interview with author, 19 February 1996.
51.   Mumford, interview, 9 February 1996.
52.   Dick Williams, interview, 28 February 1996.
53.   Simpson, interview, 23 February 1996.
54.   As a result of the IRS audit, an alliance was formed with other religious leaders

The five teachers had always maintained their own independent leadership lines or structures, with each one giving leadership to certain pastors and churches. Using the biblical picture of Israel's tribes, each teacher's following was sometimes called his 'tribe'. 'Baxter's tribe', 'Mumford's tribe', and so on. This created a kind of territorial distinctiveness with each leader having his own men who often found it difficult to be united with the others' men.[55] Simpson wanted to bridge this 'tribal mentality' and, drawing from 1 Pet. 2.9 on the church being a holy nation, Simpson began emphasizing the need for the Shepherding movement to see itself as 'one nation'.[56]

The five teachers thereupon agreed to bring together all the movement's leaders for a Congress of Elders in Louisville, Kentucky, expecting several thousand men. The Congress was to include elders from the Catholic Charismatic community in Ann Arbor and South Bend. Two months before the Congress, Mumford and Prince objected to the plan, feeling it was a move toward becoming a denomination, which Simpson adamantly denied was his intention.[57] As a result of Mumford's and Prince's concern, the Congress was canceled.[58] Simpson was extremely frustrated, feeling that the other two men did not trust him, and he released both Mumford and Prince from their commitments to him.[59]

The five leaders then gathered in July to decide what to do with their disagreement. A joint statement was prepared and released to clarify their association. The statement acknowledged their 1970 joining that 'evolved into close cooperation and some degree of structure for the accomplishment of what we have believed was the will of God'.[60] They continued:

> The inner workings of the structure have been an ongoing process of adjustment and development based on our recognition of current needs and diversities of calling.

to lobby Congress for change in church audit procedures. In 1984, the Church Audit Procedures Act was signed into law, protecting churches from unreasonable IRS audits. Coleman, interview, 21 February 1996.

55. Charles Simpson, letter to Derek Prince, 2 March 1978, private holding, 1-2.
56. Charles Simpson, *Building a Nation* (Mobile, AL: Charles Simpson Ministries, 1980), audiocassette.
57. Bob Mumford, Memorandum to Barney Coombs (*et al.*), 12 May 1980, private holding, 1.
58. Mumford, interview, 9 February 1996.
59. Simpson, interview, 23 February 1996.
60. Don Basham, Ern Baxter, Bob Mumford, Derek Prince, Charles Simpson, Statement of Intent, July 1980, private holding, 1.

> These developments have on occasion given rise to concerns among us,
> and other Christian brothers and sisters, that we may be developing a new
> denomination or some form of sectarianism. We wish to address these
> concerns.
>   It has not been, nor is it now, our intention to become a denomination.
> We desire to give support to and have fellowship with all of our fellow
> Christians. We have no headquarters, nor is one intended in any form. Gulf
> Coast Covenant Church in Mobile, Alabama and Good News Fellowship
> Church in Fort Lauderdale, Florida are churches among many others that
> exercise leadership among us, and give support to evangelism around the
> world.[61]

To accomplish this, the statement said that Mumford and Prince would
relate to a Ft Lauderdale group of elders for government. Basham, Baxter,
and Simpson would do the same in Mobile. The five leaders would continue their own council for 'counsel and ministry'.[62] The problems in Ft
Lauderdale and the adjustments with Mumford's men changed the plan.
By the fall of 1980, both Mumford and Prince had re-established their governmental relationship with Simpson, making Mobile even more a center,
despite the denials.

For most of its followers, who were unaware of the inner struggle among
the five, the Shepherding movement seemed to be in a better place than
ever in the early 1980s. The 1980 meeting in Dallas with Charismatic and
Pentecostal leaders had made progress toward healing the latent polariza-
tion that the controversy had created. In 1983, Simpson was reconciled to
his friend and mentor Ken Sumrall at an Ideas Exchange meeting. Sumrall,
while addressing the group, stopped before everyone present and apologized to Simpson. Later in the meeting, he served Simpson communion.[63]
Unofficial alliances were formed with Bob Weiner's Maranatha Campus
Ministries and Larry Tomczak's People of Destiny. Also a loose alliance
had been established with Christian reconstructionist R.J. Rushdooney.[64]

Both Mumford and Simpson were also actively pursuing other ecumenical relationships at this time. Simpson became a charter member of the
Network of Christian Ministries, a group started to build bridges and unity
among Charismatic leaders and ministries. Despite ministry growth and

61.   Basham *et al.*, Statement of Intent.
62.   Basham *et al.*, Statement of Intent, 2.
63.   Sumrall, interview, 2 November 1998; Charles Simpson, 'Interview: Older…
and Wiser', *Ministries Today* (March/April 1990), 67-71 (69-70).
64.   Erick Schenkel, Proposal for Co-operative Seminars with Rousas Rushdooney,
10 March 1980, private holding, 1-2.

the encouraging steps toward reconciliation, the movement was to be
shaken by a lasting break in the association of the five teachers.

The Break Up

Over the years, at least from 1977 on, Derek Prince had struggled with some
of the movement's teachings.[65] In February 1983 he wrote to Simpson
stating:

> For some time past I have been wrestling with the issue of my relationship
> to our 'discipleship stream'. My problem is that I do not believe in some of
> its basic tenets and the way in which they are applied. I have given much
> thought and prayer to this, and I have come to a place where I feel that my
> personal integrity is at stake…
>   At various times in the past I have sought to give expression to my points
> of disagreement, but that does not seem to have affected the overall course
> that we have followed.[66]

That same month, Prince articulated his basic disagreements. First, he
felt the movement was 'by most generally accepted standards' a denomination. Further, Prince said he did not feel there was an adequate scriptural
basis for the concept that 'every Christian should have a personal human
pastor', or 'the practice of a pastor overseeing another pastor translocally'.[67]
Prince's primary associate at Good News Fellowship in Ft Lauderdale, Jim
Croft, wrote to Simpson expressing similar concerns.[68]

Coincidental to his struggles, Prince's ministry was growing rapidly in
Europe and Israel. In 1983, he decided to live in Israel six months out of
every year. Prince was also now the only one of the five left in Ft Lauderdale. The theological and geographical distance between Prince and the
other four teachers culminated in March 1984 with Prince's formal dis-
association from the Shepherding movement. He said in a confidential
statement to key leaders that he had come to recognize 'my continuing
involvement with [the movement] would hinder me from carrying out…
the special tasks…God has committed me to'. He also stated that his withdrawal did not mean he wanted to be separated from the personal relationships [with the other men] 'I have long enjoyed'.[69] Regardless of his

65. Charles Simpson, letter to Derek Prince, 11 March 1977, private holding, 1-2.
66. Derek Prince, letter to Charles Simpson, 12 February 1983, private holding, 1-2.
67. Derek Prince, doctrinal paper, February 1983, private holding, 1-4.
68. Jim Croft, letter to Charles Simpson, 9 February 1983, private holding, 1-12.
69. Derek Prince, unaddressed confidential letter, 28 March 1984, private holding, 1.

*The four teachers in 1984 after Prince's exit. From the left:
Simpson, Basham (seated), Baxter, Mumford.*

intention, Prince seldom met with the men again. Surprisingly, Prince's exit was hardly mentioned publicly within the movement. Croft and Good News Fellowship soon left the movement as well.

The other four teachers continued their association after Prince's departure. As Mumford remembered, tensions remained in their relationships, and he began to have more serious doubts himself about the movement's practices.[70] Baxter moved to San Diego in 1984 and Mumford to Northern California in 1985 and, despite their moves, both men remained a part of the movement.

Adding to growing strains among the remaining four teachers was a growing exodus from the movement. Mumford and Simpson, in particular, were faced with many situations around the nation where leaders were accused of abusing their spiritual authority. Many other leaders and churches were leaving the movement disillusioned because of what they thought were extreme teachings and practices. Scott Ross left in April 1983,

---

70.   Bob Mumford, personal interview with author, 31 July 1998.

severely disillusioned. He felt that the movement had so emphasized human leadership that it had violated the Holy Spirit's role in its followers' lives. This deeply convicted Ross, who felt he had personally been a party to abuse.[71]

New Wine, always a nonsubscription donation-supported periodical, had maintained strong circulation into 1981, but, thereafter, began to experience decline. By summer 1982, circulation had dropped to 63,000, its lowest in ten years.[72] As a result, an appeal was made to the movement's leaders to work to increase circulation and encourage financial gifts.[73] Circulation increased through 1983, but dropped dramatically in 1984 and, by January 1985, fell to under 50,000.[74] Using the fifteenth anniversary of *New Wine* as a beginning place, a fundraising study was undertaken to generate revenue to help boost circulation.[75] Circulation recovered somewhat near the end of 1985, but remained low. The decision in the summer of 1984 to move to a paid subscription base may have been a contributing factor to the circulation problem.[76] With the March 1986 issue, *New Wine*, for the first time in its history, carried advertising to help generate revenue.[77]

The bottom line was, after showing a small profit in 1983, the magazine lost $186,000 in 1984, $362,000 in 1985, and $333,000 in 1986. The only reason its publishing corporation, Integrity Communications, survived was because the Hosanna Music worship tapes had become so profitable that its income offset *New Wine*'s losses.[78] For months, various alternatives were considered and debated as to the future of the magazine.

New Wine's troubles and the other difficulties within the movement finally became too great to try to hold the association together any

71. Ross, interview, 19 February 1996. For an example of a former insider's critique of the movement see Scott Ross, 'Spiritual POWs', 1995, private holding.

72. Charles Simpson, memo to Don Basham, 4 August 1982, private holding, 1.

73. Charles Simpson, letter to Don Basham, Ern Baxter, Bob Mumford, and Derek Prince, 23 August 1982, private holding, 1-2.

74. Minutes, Integrity Communication Board meeting, 16 January 1985, private holding, 4.

75. William D. Hewitt, 'A Feasibility Study for Launching Fundraising Campaign', January 1985, private holding, 1-47.

76. Charles Simpson, letter to Ern Baxter, 15 February 1985, 2. *New Wine* was still sent free to anyone who wrote in saying they could not afford the subscription price.

77. Charles Simpson, letter to Ern Baxter, Bob Mumford, and Don Basham, 30 December 1985, private holding, 2.

78. Summary of Integrity and *New Wine* Operations—1983 through 1986, private holding, 12.

longer.[79] In April 1986, at a meeting in Chicago, Basham, Baxter, Mumford, and Simpson decided to dissolve their structural and governmental ties together as a movement. Each man would maintain his own separate ministry. In August, the four met in Seattle and decided to end *New Wine* with the December 1986 issue, and the October 1986 issue announced: 'The truth is we believe *New Wine* is a symbol of something God is instructing us to lay down.'[80] They went on to say they had no intention of ending their personal relationships. In the November issue of *New Wine*, the four wrote:

> The four of us remain in good relationship and will continue to address issues together. We simply felt God did not want us to form a denomination or to try to centrally control the great variety of ministries among us. We further felt that God was calling us to cooperate with emerging ministry groups. We believe that decentralization will make room for the release of new ministry and power. The four of us are meeting again this month to discuss these and other matters pertaining to our ongoing fellowship. There is no 'split up' here. We are sincerely seeking to obey the Lord and release our gifts to His Body.[81]

Simpson continued to encourage the other three teachers to hold their relationships together, though now without a governmental dimension. He was concerned that a complete breakup might disillusion many of their followers.[82] With this in mind, Simpson wrote to supporters after the decision to close *New Wine* and acknowledged the movement's problems while appealing for endurance:

> To ignore or deny problems and abuses would be wrong. But a bad marriage doesn't invalidate marriage. Nor does the abuse by pastoral leaders invalidate pastoral leadership. We must be challenged to do a better job of finding, training, and supporting God-called leaders. At the same time, we must better train our people to avoid wrong dependency or control.
> My deep concern and prayer are for those of you who have committed yourselves at great cost to a vision of which I am part. I do not want you to

---

79.   In 1981–82, Bob Mumford and Larry Tomczak were involved in a lawsuit by the author of the book *I'm OK, You're OK* because of an erroneous statement by Mumford and Tomczak that the author had committed suicide. He and Tomczak eventually settled out of court. The ordeal, however, was another strain on Mumford and his associates. Michael Ford, letter to Charles Simpson, 21 October 1982, private holding, 1-2.

80.   'Special Announcement', *New Wine* (October 1986), 46-47 (47).

81.   'Special Announcement', *New Wine* (November 1986), 6-7 (6).

82.   Bob Mumford, Handwritten Notes of Seattle Teachers Meeting, n.d., private holding, 2-3.

feel betrayed. I pledge myself to walk out my vows as God gives me grace, and take responsibility for my decisions.[83]

The four men got together in San Diego as planned in November 1986 and tried to decide a future course. They confronted their suspicions, misunderstandings, and personal conflicts head on. When the difficult meeting ended, no final decision was made as to their continued relationships.[84] The four did schedule another meeting in 1987 in hopes of continuing their communication.[85] The San Diego meeting, however, proved to be the last time the four teachers met together. Despite the statement in *New Wine* that there was no 'split up', they indeed had separated. The Shepherding movement as an expression of the five teachers' association had ended.

Separate Paths

The dissolution of the Shepherding movement did not end its history, in that the five leaders continued their own journeys. Moreover, Simpson assumed leadership over many of those who continued to identify with the distinctive emphases that had defined the movement. Baxter maintained a loose association with Simpson and communicated somewhat regularly with him. Basham, Mumford, and Prince publicly distanced themselves from the group they had worked so hard to build for so many years.

Don Basham

In the fall of 1986, Don Basham moved from Mobile to Cleveland, Ohio, where he based his writing and teaching ministry. He continued his popular *New Wine* column 'The Way I See It' in his own newsletter, *Don Basham's Insights*, published from Ohio. On CBN's 700 Club, in June 1987, Basham affirmed the Shepherding movement's good points and also acknowledged the movement's abuses. He apologized to any who had been hurt by the movement and urged them to write to him personally.[86]

---

83.   Charles Simpson, An Open Pastoral Letter, 2 September 1986, private holding, 2.

84.   Bob Mumford, Handwritten Notes of San Diego Teachers Meeting, n.d., 1-3.

85.   Basham wrote an honest, painful exposition of the San Diego meeting and the struggles the men had in trying to live out their covenant relationship. Don Basham, 'Questions and Answers', *Don Basham's Insights* (January 1987), 4.

86.   Don Basham, *Interview on 700 Club* (Virginia Beach, CA: Christian Broadcast Network, 1987), videocassette, 14.30 min.

Don and Alice Basham in 1985.

The dissolution of the teachers' association and, particularly, the end of publication for *New Wine* were difficult for Basham, who had invested so much of his life in the magazine's ministry. In September 1987, Basham was diagnosed with prostate cancer and, although the prognosis was positive, he took the news hard. His disillusionment over some of the more negative aspects of the Shepherding movement, along with the cancer diagnosis, contributed to a battle with serious depression that eventually required hospitalization.[87] In 1988, he suffered a massive heart attack.[88] Thirteen months later, on 27 March 1989, Basham died after suffering another heart attack.[89]

Ern Baxter
Ern Baxter, living in the San Diego area, had formed Christ Chapel Church in 1985, but the church later suffered problems and went through a difficult

87.   Leggatt, interview, 1 March 1996.
88.   Board of Trustees of *Insights*, 'Update', *Don Basham's Insights* (March/April 1988), 3-4. Basham spoke very honestly about his depression and health problems. See Don Basham, 'Update', *Don Basham's Insights* (July/August 1988), 3-4.
89.   Special Memorial Issue, *Don Basham's Insights* (March/April 1989), 1-4.

Ern Baxter.

split. Afterward, Baxter pulled back from any attempt at pastoral leader-ship, intensely disliking church politics. In 1987, he guardedly became in-volved in a house church. Every six months Baxter met with several leaders from around the nation that still looked to him for leadership.[90] He continued to travel some and write from the San Diego area, maintaining a cautious but certain commitment to the principles of Shepherding care.[91] Ruth Baxter said that to the end of his life her husband would say, 'I still believe the principles of Shepherding to be scripturally correct, although I am saddened that the principles were humanly misused.'[92]

Baxter wrote to Simpson not long after their breakup, telling him 'the size of the disappointments at the seeming future of things we were doing, leaves me little hope for seeing any future fulfillment of the things we taught'.[93] A few months later he wrote to Simpson again:

> I continue to experience some deep distress at the manner in which the whole relational thing that existed seemed so easily to come unglued. We

90. Rich Carlton, telephone interview with author, 12 September 1998.
91. Baxter, *The Chief Shepherd.*
92. Ruth Baxter, letter to the author, 13 May 1996, private holding, 2.
93. Ern Baxter, letter to Charles Simpson, 18 May 1987, private holding, 1.

obviously talked a better product than we produced. It is amazing to me to observe the ease with which many former strong adherents of vigorously stated convictions now unapologetically play a different tune. However, such is the nature of our humanness.[94]

Baxter also started the Timothy Distribution Company to market his tapes and books. Although he struggled to find faith for his future, Baxter regularly welcomed young pastors and leaders that he considered his 'Timothies' into his home for long theological and biblical discussions.[95] Baxter's health declined rapidly into the summer of 1993, and he died on 9 July.

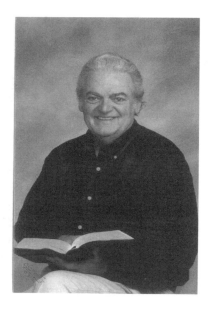

Bob Mumford.

Bob Mumford

After a season he described as 'deep conviction from God' and counseling with leaders, including Jack Hayford, Bob Mumford issued a strong, public statement of apology in November 1989. In his statement, he apologized for his part in what he felt were the extremes of the Shepherding movement.

Mumford's statement was read by Jack Hayford at his annual pastors' conference with more than 1,500 leaders present. Two days later, Mumford

94. Ern Baxter, letter to Charles Simpson, 3 September 1987, private holding, 1.
95. Ruth Baxter, telephone interview with author, 21 February 1996.

read the statement to a leaders conference in Montreat, North Carolina. In this historic statement, Mumford wrote:

> This statement of apology has two known motivations. First, I feel as though I have offended the Lord Himself, resulting in His resistance and conviction. Secondly, I am deeply convinced that only by my stating the truth can those who have been adversely affected be healed and released. The following statement represents my personal convictions, and I do not presume to speak for any other person… Accountability, personal training under the guidance of another and effective pastoral care are needed biblical concepts. True spiritual maturity will require that they be preserved. These biblical realities must carry the limits indicated by the New Testament. However, to my personal pain and chagrin, these particular emphases very easily lent themselves to an unhealthy submission resulting in perverse and unbiblical obedience to human leaders. Many of these abuses occurred within the spheres of my own responsibility. For the injury and shame caused to people, families, and the larger Body of Christ, I repent with sorrow and ask for your forgiveness.[96]

The January/February 1990 issue of *Ministries Today* magazine, a periodical for Charismatic leaders, carried a black cover with these words: '"Discipleship was wrong. I repent. Please forgive me". Bob Mumford'.[97] Charles Simpson and many of the leaders still associated with him were disturbed by the magazine's coverage of Mumford's apology, feeling it bordered on tabloid journalism.[98] At the same time, Mumford received hundreds of letters of support, including a letter from Dennis Bennett, affirming Mumford's courage to make a public apology. Bennett also apologized to Mumford for his own antagonism during the controversy.[99]

A July 1993 letter from Mumford to Pat Robertson and his wife was a poignant footnote to the controversy years. Mumford wrote:

> I felt your initial alarm at the trend and what you perceived as error in the Discipleship–Shepherding movement, was unnecessary. On that occasion I thought you were rather given to theatrics and overkill. Time, however, has a way of clarifying issues and revealing how serious they are. Little did I

---

96.   Bob Mumford, Public Statement Concerning Discipleship, 1 November 1989, private holding, 1.

97.   Jamie Buckingham, 'The End of the Discipleship Era', *Ministries Today* (January/February 1990), 46-51.

98.   Simpson's friend Ken Sumrall wrote a strong letter challenging *Ministries Today*'s handling of Mumford's apology. Ken Sumrall, 'Letter to the Editor', *Ministries Today* (March/April 1990), 15.

99.   Moore, 'Shepherding' (1999), 275.

recognize how prophetic you would prove to be in the ensuing years. Please forgive me for being blind and stubborn. I taught the unity and diversity of ministry, while at the same time closed myself to your warning, advice, and counsel. It is important for me to say that I did feel misunderstood and mishandled. However, I came to understand that due to your voiced and public opposition, both of you already suffered greatly in the months and years that followed. Would you accept my apology for causing and contributing to your pain?[100]

Today, Mumford's ministry, LifeChangers, is based in Raleigh, North Carolina, where he moved in July 1991. Mumford has struggled with health problems for several years, but continues teaching, giving special attention to writing. A particular theme of his ministry is an emphasis on God's *agape* love.

Derek Prince

Derek Prince, who exited the association two years before the other four separated, immediately distanced himself from his Shepherding connection. In March 1984, he taught a series of messages in Ft Lauderdale on *Apostles and Shepherds*.[101] In these meetings he emphasized that Jesus Christ exercised sovereign authority over local presbyteries and apostolic teams and that there were no instances of translocal pastoral care in the New Testament.[102] Prince also affirmed that not every person in the New Testament had a human shepherd, using Peter and Paul as his examples.[103] Finally, he argued that there is no exact pattern for church government in the New Testament and that flexibility is necessary in this regard.[104]

After his departure in 1983–84, Prince seldom referred to his longtime relationship to the Shepherding movement. He publicly wrote in 1995 that he believed the movement was guilty of the Galatian error: 'having begun in the Spirit, we quickly degenerated into the flesh'.[105] Prince made the following observation about the Shepherding movement at the Montreat meeting where Bob Mumford issued his 1989 statement:

100. Bob Mumford, letter to Rev. and Mrs Pat Robertson, 7 July 1993, private holding, 1.

101. Derek Prince, *Apostles and Shepherds* (Charlotte: Derek Prince Ministries, 1984), four audiocassettes.

102. Derek Prince, *Apostles and Shepherds: Verse-by-Verse Outline* (Charlotte: Derek Prince Ministries, 1984), 3-4, 9.

103. Prince, *Apostles and Shepherds*, 6-7.

104. Prince, *Apostles and Shepherds*, 4-10.

105. Prince, *Jubilee 1995 Celebration*, 9.

I don't believe now, looking back, it was ever God's intention to start a movement or to bring forth any kind of institution. I think God wanted us to relate to one another as brothers, and that we could have had a tremendously healing effect on the Body of Christ. We didn't really do that, and I think we all bear a share of the responsibility of failing God and failing the Body of Christ, and I freely acknowledge my own share of responsibility.[106]

Prince's second wife Ruth died on 29 December 1998. Now in his eighties, Derek Prince spends much of his time in Israel and Europe. Derek Prince Ministries International, based in Charlotte, North Carolina, serves as a large and successful platform for the distribution of Prince's teaching materials and for the extension of his popular radio ministry around the world.

Charles Simpson.

Charles Simpson

After the breakup, Simpson remained vitally involved in the leadership of the Mobile church, which changed its name in January 1987 to Covenant Church of Mobile. In late 1986, adjustments were proposed to allow Simpson to be the primary Sunday morning Bible teacher for the church. John Duke, who had left to pastor in Atlanta, was replaced by Billy Duke (his

106. Derek Prince, Derek Prince's Remarks after Bob Mumford's Letter of Repentance, November 1989, private holding, 1.

brother) as presiding pastor, with Simpson remaining the church's senior pastor. A new emphasis was placed on prayer and Bible study.[107]

Simpson also sought to adjust problems in the movement's pastoral structures. He admitted that, while never intended, they had created a kind of pyramidal structure that locked people into relationships. Their long-standing teaching that to be a part of the church one had to be joined personally to a pastor had created a significant problem. If the one-on-one pastoral relationship broke down, then so did the person's relationship to the church. Moreover, if a translocal relationship broke down, a whole church was often cut off from the movement. Simpson was not sure it was biblical for entire groups of people to be dependent on individual relationships.[108] They began to moderate their approach, by encouraging commitment not only to a pastor but also to the church as a whole.

Covenant Church of Mobile sold its buildings and properties to Integrity Music and built a new facility adjacent to its previous location, which was completed in May 1995. The buildings house the congregation's on-campus activities and a Christian day school. A new building was constructed in 1999 for the Ern Baxter Memorial Library and contains the majority of Baxter's extensive theological library, an archive for the movement's history, and will house a theological training school for leaders.[109] The Mobile church continues to require its members to make commitments to a pastoral relationship and to a church 'care group', but maintains more flexibility in administrating its pastoral care.[110] Covenant Church Mobile had a Sunday morning attendance of 350 to 400 when Simpson resigned as senior pastor in 1999.

In January 1987, after *New Wine Magazine* ceased publication, Integrity Communications fulfilled *New Wine*'s prepaid subscriptions with a new magazine, *Christian Conquest*, focused on Simpson's ministry. Integrity Communications changed its name in the summer of 1987 to Charles Simpson Ministries (CSM), which distributes Simpson's books and audiotaped teachings and promotes his national and international ministry. CSM changed the name of its quarterly periodical *Christian Conquest* to *One to*

---

107. The Proposed Plan of Action for Integrity Communications, Gulf Coast Covenant Church, and Charles Simpson Ministries, n.d., private holding, 1-4.

108. Charles Simpson, *The Challenge to Care* (Mobile, AL: Charles Simpson Ministries, 1987), four audiocassettes.

109. Steve Simpson, personal interview with author, 6 August 1998.

110. Steve Simpson, interview, 6 August 1998.

One in the summer of 1998, reflecting a new emphasis in personal evangelism.[111] International Outreach Ministries, a division of CSM, coordinates the world missions outreach of Simpson and his church. The ministry reaches into nations in Latin America, Africa, and Europe.

In March 1987, Charles Simpson founded, 'an association for ministers and churches under his pastoral oversight'.[112] The Fellowship of Covenant Ministers and Churches (FCMC) carried on many of the central themes of the Shepherding movement. Simpson and those still associated with his leadership prefer the name 'Covenant movement', because of the ongoing emphasis on what they see as their central theological tenet: covenant relationship with God and fellow believers.

FCMC, as had the Shepherding movement, emphasized relational or organic unity as opposed to ecclesiastical or organizational unity. The group maintained personal pastoral relationships and convened an annual general conference in Mobile and an 'invitation only' leaders gathering in Atlanta.

Glen Roachelle was asked in 1992 to develop a five-year strategic plan for FCMC. Disagreements with Simpson over the degree of formal organization (Roachelle wanting more) led to Roachelle's withdrawal from FCMC in 1993.[113] Not wanting any semblance of another denominational grouping, Simpson dissolved FCMC at the end of 1993.[114] Today, Simpson maintains a pastoral relationship with a number of men locally, nationally, and internationally, not all of whom are pastors. Some of the men he pastors are themselves leaders of large networks of churches. There is no formal association, grouping, or membership with the men he now pastors translocally.[115] In an October 1995 leaders conference of Simpson's men, they reaffirmed the basic commitment to their distinctives, including discipleship, accountability, covenant, male government, kingdom of God, house groups, and servanthood.[116]

With the aim 'to set forth a systematic presentation of God, His purpose, and activity in history',[117] Simpson published the 416-page *The Covenant*

111. Charles Simpson, A Pastoral Letter from Charles Simpson, July 1998, 1.

112. Charles Simpson, 'Charles Simpson Forms Ministerial Association', press release, 6 March 1987, 1.

113. Glen Roachelle, letter to Charles Simpson, 1 October 1993, private holding, 1.

114. Charles Simpson, telephone interview with author, 12 January 1998.

115. Charles Simpson, telephone interview with author, 18 December 1998.

116. 'What Are the Distinctives of the Covenant Movement?', n.d., private holding, 1.

117. Simpson, *The Covenant and the Kingdom*, 5.

and the Kingdom in 1995. The book was the culmination of several years' work by Simpson and several other leaders of the Covenant movement. The book was designed to serve as a 'comprehensive personal and church Bible resource' and articulates the fully developed and nuanced theology of the movement.

Today, Simpson believes that he and those who continue in association have corrected many of the movement's extremes. He also believes that critics overlook the many people who benefited from the movement, along with those who continue their association with the Covenant movement. Looking back over the years of the Shepherding movement, Simpson expressed his regrets:

> The inability of some to properly live words that we truly believe; the inability in some instances to properly train and care for many sincere and dedicated people; the division between people who loved one another; the carnality that power and resources brought out in some of us; the misuse of leadership by some; and putting people into pastoring who were not called to it—these are some of the things I regret. And personally, I regret any pressure I put on the other teachers to stay in a particular structure. I don't believe some of them were called to it.[118]

118. Simpson, 'Interview: Older...and Wiser', 67.

Chapter 10

A Historical Perspective

Many years have passed since the fires of controversy raged in the Charismatic Renewal in 1975 and 1976. Much has changed and the perspective of time allows for clearer reflection on the Shepherding movement. Several summary observations are suggested by the historical record.[1]

1. The Shepherding movement was a renewal that was driven by a theologically informed, restorationist idealism. Howard Snyder has pointed out that 'renewal movements generally "rediscover" some element or accent in the church or Scripture'.[2] Mumford and the other men saw themselves as a part of a renewal continuum in which God was restoring the vitality and practices of New Testament Christianity. Motivated by their conviction that the church was God's kingdom agent in the earth, they taught on the restoration of biblical church government and the necessity of counter-cultural community. Like other renewal movements in church history they were able to gain and energize a large following with their message.

Like other historical renewal movements they were also perceived as a threat to the status quo, since renewal movements by their nature imply judgment or criticism against existing church structures and institutions. Consequently, controversy and tension were inevitable. The Shepherding movement challenged the pervasive individualism, rampant antinomianism, and extreme independence in the Charismatic Renewal. Many leaders saw this confrontation as a threat that might bring the Renewal back into ecclesiastical bondage.

---

1.   Since the movement continues in various expressions, particularly with leaders associated with Charles Simpson, the observations made in this chapter are in reference to the movement as originally constituted by the five leaders.

2.   Snyder, *Signs of the Spirit*, 269.

The Shepherding movement, like many renewal movements, was at times extreme in its emphases. Even its own leaders have acknowledged this.[3] They self-consciously saw themselves as contending for God's 'now word' but felt they were rewarded with 'charges of heresy'.[4] Without question they were driven to produce mature people in churches that were alternative societies in a deteriorating culture. Their desire for a committed and disciplined constituency led to an often inflexible and overly intense system of pastoral care.

The movement's restorationism was energized by a particular eschatological perspective. They believed God was acting in dark and difficult days to restore his Church.[5]

2. Despite its deep roots in the ecumenical soil of the Charismatic Renewal, the Shepherding movement became a local church-centered movement. This narrative has demonstrated that when Basham, Mumford, Prince, and Simpson joined together in 1970 they never dreamed of starting a network of local churches, having found new freedom outside of traditional church structures. Still, though they relished the vitality and ecumenism of the renewal, they were increasingly disturbed by its problems.

The misconduct of Purvis, their increasing concerns with the lack of character in the renewal, and their perceived sense of God-given prophetic insight, led them to teach on themes that had specific ecclesiological implications and to experiment with practical church structures. From this milieu a church movement was born as they tapped into a leadership vacuum within the Charismatic Renewal. Hundreds of leaders came running to find a pastor. The five teachers believed God had created this response and that their proper course was to steward and build a relationally based network of churches. In the tradition of eighteenth- century Pietism and nineteenth-century Methodism, they saw their church network as a kind of church within the church. Moreover, they saw their churches as a committed spiritual army under delegated authority that could be mobilized to serve the purposes of God. Despite rhetoric that was at times elitist and triumphalistic,

3.   Basham, *True and False Prophets*, 185. Basham says: 'Historically, every movement seeking to implement the revelation it receives suffers its own mistakes and abuses.'

4.   Mumford, *Focusing on Present Issues*, 4.

5.   Mumford wrote in 1981: 'As the shaking continues to increase and the darkness of our society continues to deepen, the light of the gospel will have more and more opportunity to light the way of the world.' Bob Mumford, 'Change in the Wind', *LifeChangers Newsletter* (January/February 1981), 4.

they never saw themselves as anything but a unique expression within the larger Christian church.

3. The Shepherding movement was a house church movement. As previously noted it was called 'the most extensive expression of the house church movement in the United States'.[6] Feeling that contemporary church structures were inadequate and often unbiblical, the movement's leaders developed a house church/cell group model, which of course was also in the spirit of early Pietism and Methodism. In their ecclesiological practice the basic building block of church structure was the house church or cell group led by a pastor.

Their emphasis on house church was an attempt to answer the cry for community that intensified in North America in the 1970s. The changes within culture needed to be addressed with relevant church structures. The house church was the ideal venue for practicing pastoral care, developing covenant relationships, and experiencing true community.

4. The Shepherding movement was a pastoral care movement. Nothing was more central to its ethos than the conviction that personal pastoral care was fundamental and essential to the maturing of the believer. And nothing brought more controversy and opposition. Every Christian and every leader needed a pastor. Believing Jesus and the Twelve served as a model, the movement took seriously the discipleship mandate of Matthew 28. The importance of a relational base for pastoral care and discipleship was always emphasized but often lost in the structural aspects of making the system work.

5. The Shepherding movement emphasized non-professional leadership and non-traditional leadership training. Most of the movement's pastors served part-time in their leadership roles. Generally, these leaders and those who served vocationally as pastors had no formal theological training. They were mentored through a discipleship process that involved personal coaching by their pastor along with regular ministry training events. The importance of personal calling and charismatic gifting were stressed as well.

This approach had its strength and weaknesses. Negatively, many leaders were ill-prepared for the roles they were expected to fill and in ignorance made mistakes. Some willfully misused their authority and injured those they were charged to care. Positively, many leaders were released into

6. Hadaway, Wright and DuBose, *Home Cell Groups*, 30.

ministry and proved to be effective, fruitful leaders, and many became full-time pastors. These leaders may not have had the same opportunity in more traditional settings.

6. The Shepherding movement's exercise of authority was hierarchical.[7] Though the movement was not hierarchical in the sense of the classical system of church government with clergy in formal graded ranks, the Shepherding movement's system of government did involve a top-down approach to the exercise of authority.[8] While freedom of conscience was always taught, followers knew that obedience to one's pastor was very important. Followers were not encouraged to an unquestioning, blind obedience to their shepherd but to an informal trusting obedience that was an outflow of a close caring relationship. The exercise of spiritual authority was well intentioned and seen as a means to bring health and maturity to people. Still, the emphasis on hierarchically oriented submission to God's delegated authorities led to many cases of improper control and abusive authority throughout the movement.[9]

7. The Shepherding movement emphasized the relational organic nature of the church. The church was a covenant community that valued interdependence and mutuality. The church was comprised of a network of 'joints'; people were joined to their leaders and one another in a definite and understood covenant commitment. The irony of this ongoing relational emphasis was that the movement seemed to function as a highly organized and structured oligarchy until its eventual breakup. It is also ironic that the movement's functional consolidation and government was justified at the time because it was seen as a transitional stage and not a formal and lasting institutional arrangement. Somehow the organic nature of their association, given their large following, was especially hard to realize.

---

7.   The movement's leaders would prefer the term 'patriarchal' instead of 'hierarchical'. Nevertheless, the strong emphasis on submission to authority tied to the national network of translocal relationship created a very clear chain of command.

8.   For some support for my observation see Hadaway, Wright and DuBose, *Home Cell Groups*, 200. Both Mumford and Simpson have acknowledged in hindsight the overly authoritarian nature of the movement's pastoral relationships.

9.   It is possible that hierarchical orientation in the exercise of spiritual authority was a consequence of the movement's view of a hierarchy within the Trinity. The movement taught the co-equality, co-essentiality, and co-substantiality of the Godhead but believed the Spirit submitted to the Son who submitted to the Father in function. See Baxter, *The Chief Shepherd*, 64-66.

Historical Lessons

It can be seen that the Shepherding movement's history reveals the inherent tension in renewal movements between the charismatic and institutional dimensions.[10] This account chronicles the movement's striking dichotomy in practice. Its leaders regularly tried to decentralize by rearranging structures, making geographical moves, and publicly disavowing any central government. Just as certainly they maintained many institutional features that are noted in Chapter 5, yet they never became a formalized denomination. Why was this the case? What prevented them from becoming a formalized denomination?

The answer is found in their self-concept. Basham, Baxter, Mumford, Prince, and Simpson affirmed over and over again that their association was a matter of relationship alone. Since they were not planning to build a denomination, whatever developed from their mutual commitments as leaders was to be relationally based as well.

Clearly, all five men did not want to build an institution. They each had experienced their own battles with an institutional Christianity, which they believed had stifled the Holy Spirit's work. Despite the need to organize, manage, and lead their following they continually refused to become a formalized denomination. Leaders such as Jack Hayford for many years urged Simpson and the others to acknowledge their *de facto* denominational characteristics, believing it would not only quiet the controversy but would secure their future as a movement.[11]

Whatever the suspicions and concerns from many Charismatic leaders, about a denomination forming, it was not to be. Becoming a denomination was anathema to the five. They idealistically and emphatically continued to define their movement as an organic association regardless of appearance. They had publicly and repeatedly denied any intent to form a denomination and in the end they were proved correct. Further, the record makes it clear that Mumford, Simpson, and the other three never had any takeover motive or plan to gain control of the Charismatic Renewal.

In retrospect they were forced to confront the inexorable forces that press church renewal movements toward institutionalization: the need for

10. I am using the term 'charismatic' here in a modified Weberian way.

11. Hayford wrote to Simpson in 1985 and acknowledged the difficulty the movement's leaders had in calling themselves a denomination but felt they were in 'deception' to suppose they were not functionally denominational. Jack W. Hayford, letter to Charles Simpson, 28 January 1985, private holding, 3.

order, communication, and survival. These forces pressed their imprint on the movement as seen in its many institutional characteristics. The leaders' resistance to organization eventually proved to be the undoing of the movement which fragmented after they dissolved their association. There were no external, formal structures to hold the movement together after they separated, and many of its former constituents and leaders are now scattered throughout the larger church. Mumford, Simpson, and Prince saw the movement's dissolution as painful but consistent with their conviction that there was not to be a denomination.

Simpson's network and a few other groups are what remains of the influential and highly visible expression of the Charismatic Renewal. Those groups that have taken up the movement's mantle continue to wrestle with the tension between an organic relational emphasis and the need for structure and organization.

Another lesson from the Shepherding movement's history is the tendency of radical renewal movements to moderate and accommodate over time. The historical record reveals that the movement moderated its extremes significantly. Problems and pressures from within and without forced needed adjustments. The need for legitimacy, stability, and survival demanded some measure of cultural accommodation, practical moderation and heeding the counsel of other believers.

The Shepherding story also presents a commentary on the Charismatic Renewal's inability to handle its internal disagreements and disputes. Well-intentioned structures such as the Charismatic leaders conferences and the Charismatic Concerns Committee proved inadequate to adjudicate the controversy. Critics ignored ethical commitments and made outrageous public allegations without much attempt at verification. Seldom were the Shepherding movement leaders contacted personally by its fiercest critics to establish communication. The record indicates the opposite was true for Basham, Baxter, Mumford, Prince, and Simpson who made repeated attempts over the years to meet with their opponents. They maintained regular dialogue with anyone who would meet with them. Some saw this as a ploy to win the endorsement of key leaders. Others, less cynical, saw their efforts at communication as right and well intentioned.[12]

12. Harper, *Three Sisters*, 95; Catholic Kilian McDonnell also acknowledged 'the restraint exercised' by the five teachers 'under severe provocation'. McDonnell seemed to be sympathetic to Mumford and the others during the controversy. Kilian McDonnell, letter to Bob Mumford, 20 February 1979, private holding, 1-2; Brick Bradford

While criticism was deserved, the Shepherding movement was unnecessarily vilified by its opponents. Many failed to recognize its similarities to other renewal movements in church history.[13] They were teaching nothing new. Monasticism, Pietism, and Methodism had carried like themes. Charismatic leaders tolerated the veneration of Mary and papal infallibility among Charismatic Catholics, yet rejected the Shepherding movement's practices. This revealed that the controversy's complexity went beyond doctrinal disagreement; it was also about personality conflicts, control of the Charismatic constituency, and human weakness.

The controversy had a dramatic effect on the Shepherding movement. For a few years, at least from 1976 to 1980, it helped drive the movement inward and fostered an unwillingness among its leaders to listen carefully to the legitimate issues in the critics' charges. Though they were still active in some ecumenical activities, they felt persecuted by many Charismatic leaders and took a 'we will work with our own' attitude. In 1980 Mumford, Simpson, and the others recognized this and intentionally came out of the shell they had created around themselves.

In addition, the controversy closed off a large sector of the Pentecostal and Charismatic movements to the voice and influence of the five teachers.[14] The accusations, once spread, forever affected people's opinion of the men and the movement. Books continue to be written that characterize the five leaders and the movement as heretical.[15] This is unfortunate, because whatever one thinks of the movement's discipleship process and pastoral practice, it clearly was orthodox in the essential doctrines of historic Christianity.

The Shepherding movement, for a number of years, was inflexible, some would say legalistic, in the application of principles of submission and authority in pastoral relationships.[16] This injured a large number of

also commended the five teachers for their conciliation attempts: Brick Bradford, letter to Bob Mumford, 16 March 1976, private holding, 1.

13. See Snyder, *Signs of the Spirit* and *The Radical Wesley*.

14. Jack Hayford wrote to both Mumford and Simpson and lamented what he felt was the loss of influence due to their emphases. Jack Hayford, letter to Charles Simpson, 19 October 1984, private holding, 2. In 1979 Portland pastor Dick Iverson expressed dismay to Mumford that Christendom has 'lost your voice along with the other great men'.

15. For example, Mary Alice Chrnalogar, *Twisted Scripture* (New Kensington, PA: Whitaker House, 1997).

16. Hayford characterized their practices as legalistic in the 1995 outline on the

people and many have publicly recounted their painful stories. Some dis-illusioned followers have been very vocal and insistent in their criticisms. This has reinforced the almost entirely negative perception of the Shep-herding movement. The thousands of people who continue to associate with the Covenant movement and the thousands who left the movement when it dissolved, yet continue to live as strong Christians, must not be overlooked. The perception that all that is left of the movement are hurt and destroyed people is mistaken.

The Shepherding movement had lofty and idealistic goals to build churches that manifested the kingdom of God. Their passion was for redeemed communities that were characterized by disciplined disciples living together in covenant relationships. The five teachers always aimed for enduring covenant relationships among themselves and their followers. Yet this movement that had gained so much attention eventually dissolved. What factors contributed to its inability to realize its dreams? I would suggest eight possible factors:

1. The movement simply grew too fast and exceeded its ability to produce trained and qualified leaders for the task. Finding a mature, able pastor for every ten to twelve households proved impossible. Nevertheless, the movement's idealism insisted on the model and put leaders in place that never should have been given pastoral authority. For whatever reason, it took an extended time to see the problem clearly and by that time many people were injured.

2. The movement's leaders failed to recognize the downside of an authoritarian approach. Many of the young people joining the movement had not been adequately parented and were looking for an authority figure to fill their need. The movement leaders did not understand the co-dependent dynamic in many people. Further, the dictum 'power corrupts and absolute power corrupts absolutely' proved true in many instances. Human carnality got the best of some leaders, who used their authority in self-serving ways without sufficient or timely redress.

3. The movement's ideology forced the five teachers into apostolic and pastoral roles for which they were not called or prepared. Only Simpson was a true pastor; yet all five attempted to fill a pastoral role for long periods. By the time this was realized many of the movement's leaders and

theme of submission. Jack W. Hayford, *The Holy Dynamic of Wholehearted Submission* (Van Nuys: Living Way Ministries, 1995), 1.

pastors were disillusioned. Some recovered and continued, but many left the movement.

4. Their view of covenant limited the options of the five teachers. They believed covenant meant abandoning the option to quit. Consequently they were either going to make it together or not. They were not able to find any middle course in which they could have maintained their relationships without the governmental dimensions and corresponding pressure to lead a movement together. Their emphasis on loyalty also caused them to tolerate problems in key leaders.

5. The enormous pressures of the controversy exacerbated internal and personal struggles. One cannot underestimate the part the fierce opposition played in the movement's eventual dissolution.

6. The movement did not develop an adequate church polity to deal with their Charismatic and institutional tensions.[17] The 'to be or not to be' a denomination struggle was confusing to those both inside and outside the movement. The tension is understandable given the unique background and perspectives of its five leaders. Nevertheless, the constituency was affected by their institutional 'schizophrenia'.

7. The movement's emphasis on authority, submission, and servanthood had a way of silencing dissent. The highly personal, hierarchical, pastoral relationships made it difficult to disagree and challenge one's pastor without appearing disloyal. This was never intended, but it was a practical reality which its leaders have readily acknowledged. As a consequence some problems were perpetuated much longer than necessary.[18]

8. Finally, it simply was impossible to keep five strong, independently successful leaders together. Their ideal was to find a mutual strength out of their unique personalities, diverse backgrounds, and different theological perspectives. In actuality those differences became insurmountable obstacles. Though Simpson was asked by the others and was willing to try and lead their association, it just proved unworkable.

17. Hayford, letter to Simpson, 28 January 1985, 2. Hayford told Simpson his concerns over the movement were not 'doctrinal or ethical' but had to do with their 'church polity'.

18. Since they did not have fully developed ecclesial structures, there was no means to adjudicate grievances or disputes.

Together these factors and others beyond the scope of this project eventually contributed to the Shepherding movement dismantling. The Covenant
movement's leaders have dialogued extensively in recent years and seem to
have 'de-radicalized' the earlier extremes. Dissent is now encouraged and
idealism has given way to a chastened practicality, while the values of relationship, accountability, covenant, and pastoral care are still embraced.

Epilogue

The passage of time has changed many things. In 1975–76, the phrase 'cell
group' was a negative term to many Charismatics who opposed the Shepherding movement, yet today many of the largest Pentecostal–Charismatic
churches around the world are built on a cell church model. This is true
also in the broader Evangelical community, where two of the best-known
churches in America, Willow Creek Community Church in Illinois and
Saddleback Valley Community Church in Southern California, emphasize
and practice small relational groups. There has literally been a 'home cell
group explosion' in recent years.[19]

In addition, there is new exploration of the relationship of the local
church to the kingdom of God, and a call for radical discipleship and 'personal pastoral care'.[20] Seminary professor and church growth specialist
C. Peter Wagner's two most recent books, *The New Apostolic Churches*
and *Churchquake*, analyze and describe new ecclesiological shifts.[21] Wagner discusses churches that are networked together under apostolic leaders.
Those networks, he observes, are organized around personal relationships
and tend to avoid formal organization. There are proposals for innovative
and revolutionary changes in church structure that are readily accepted as
appropriate and viable.[22] Many of these ecclesiological ideas and themes

19. The following are only a sampling of the recent literature on cell churches.
Ralph W. Neighbor, *Where Do We Go From Here?* (Houston, TX: Touch, 1990);
Robert Banks, *The Church Comes Home* (Peabody, MA: Hendrickson, 1998); William
A. Beckham, *The Second Reformation* (Houston, TX: Touch, 1995); Del Birkey, *The
House Church* (Scottsdale, PA: Herald Press, 1988); Joel Comiskey, *Home Cell
Church Explosion* (Houston, TX: Touch, 1998); Larry Stockstill, *The Cell Church*
(Ventura, CA: Regal Books, 1998).

20. Charles Van Engen, *God's Missionary People* (Grand Rapids: Baker Book
House, 1991), 182; Van Engen, a professor at Fuller Theological Seminary, discusses
many ecclesiological issues and themes that the Shepherding movement addressed.

21. Wagner, *The New Apostolic Churches*; *Churchquake*.

22. Carl F. George, *The Coming Church Revolution* (New York: Fleming H. Revell,

are very similar to the Shepherding movement's teachings and practices.[23] As already mentioned, the rhetoric of Promise Keepers echoes some of the values of the Shepherding movement.[24] An extensive research project by German church growth specialist Christian Scharz studied over 1,000 churches in 32 nations. Scharz identified small groups as the most important 'single quality characteristic' for overall church health.[25] He also discussed what he calls a 'third reformation'. After noting that Luther and his companions led a reformation of theology, and the Pietists one of spirituality, he believes that the third reformation is to be an ecclesiocentric one of church structures.[26] Scharz's research indicates that healthy churches have what he calls 'functional structures'. Again, it is worthy of note how Mumford and Simpson and the other three called for small groups and were experimenting with new church structures.

Christian psychotherapist and professor Larry Crabb's two most recent books call for a radical shift in the approach to Christian counseling. Crabb challenges the church to be a healing community and he believes that intimate, open, loving, and supportive relationships are the most basic key to the healing of persons from their brokenness. Rather than the individualistic quest for self-actualization and recovery through psychotherapy, Crabb calls people to 'connect' with fellow Christians in what ought to be the 'safest place on earth', the church as a true biblical community.[27]

These new shifts and emphases are the flowering of many of the seeds of social and religious change to which the Shepherding movement's leaders were responding in a discerning way. Just how much they contributed to all of this is impossible to determine.

1994). Carl F. George, *Preparing Your Church for the Future* (New York: Fleming H. Revell, 1991); Kevin Giles, *What On Earth Is the Church?* (Downers Grove, IL: Inter-Varsity Press, 1995); Brian D. McLaren, *Reinventing Your Church* (Grand Rapids: Zondervan, 1998); Clapp, *A Peculiar People*.

23. Wagner, *Churchquake*, 71-75.

24. See Richard Cimino and Don Luttin, *Shopping for Faith* (San Francisco: Jossey-Bass, 1998), 64.

25. Christian Scharz, *Natural Church Development* (Carol Stream, IL: ChurchSmart Resources, 1996), 33.

26. Christian Scharz, *Paradigm Shift in the Church* (Carol Stream, IL: ChurchSmart Resources, 1999), 82-95. Perhaps Scharz's focus is only on German Pietism because he fails to acknowledge John Wesley's contribution which was very much a renewal of church structures. See Snyder, *The Radical Wesley*.

27. Larry Crabb, *Connecting* (Nashville, TN: Word Books, 1997); Larry Crabb, *The Safest Place on Earth* (Nashville, TN: Word Books, 1999).

Despite signs of a new focus on the importance of ecclesiology, challenges remain as the church today wrestles with the same issues the Shepherding movement sought to address. How does the church disciple in such a way as to form mature and obedient followers of Jesus? How can people be pastored effectively? How much commitment and discipline can be expected of Christians? How can the need for genuine spiritual authority be balanced against the legitimate need for personal freedom? How does the church engage the culture? How can the church practically be salt and light within its unique cultural settings?

In addition to these questions are others that demand ecclesiological answers. Is the church selling out in its quest for cultural relevance?[28] Have pastors and church leaders adequately reflected on the biblical metaphors and mandates for the church? Is the church in the West a cultural dinosaur unwilling to change?

It is clear that the Shepherding movement was at least a harbinger. As well as being a part of a response to larger sociological shifts toward interdependence and community, the movement was an early expression of a new 'ecclesiocentrism' that has marked the last 30 years—particularly the last 10 years in North America. The church is now a 'hot' topic; and, while most of the discussion has tended to focus on church practice,[29] many respected voices have addressed deeper ecclesiological issues.[30]

28. George Barna, *Marketing the Church* (Colorado Springs, CO: Navpress, 1988); Phillip D. Kenneson and James L. Street, *Selling Out the Church* (Nashville, TN: Abingdon Press, 1997); Norman Shawchuck *et al.*, *Marketing for Congregations* (Nashville, TN: Abingdon Press, 1992); Bruce Shelly and Marshall Shelly, *Consumer Church* (Downers Grove, IL: InterVarsity Press, 1992); Douglas D. Webster, *Selling Jesus* (Downers Grove, IL: InterVarsity Press, 1992).

29. Much of the new material on the church has been methodologically oriented or written in testimonial style by successful pastors. E.g., Bill Hybels, *Rediscovering Church* (Grand Rapids: Zondervan, 1995); Rick Warren, *The Purpose Driven Church* (Grand Rapids: Zondervan, 1995).

30. Some scholars are challenging the superficiality and individualism of North American Christianity. University of Southern California philosophy professor Dallas Willard's 1998 book *The Divine Conspiracy* calls for radical discipleship that affects deeply the entire life of the believer. His discipleship theme is connected to a holistic view of the kingdom of God. Willard, like the Shepherding movement, uses the term 'kingdom of God' interchangeably with the 'government' of God and suggests that believers are like Jesus 'bearers' of God's rule on this earth. Dallas Willard, *The Divine Conspiracy* (San Francisco: HarperCollins, 1998), 28.

Pentecostal scholar and exegete Gordon Fee recently confronted the extreme soteriological individualism of the Western church. Fee argues that in Pauline thinking

The ecclesiocentrism is refreshing but more theological dialogue is sorely needed—dialogue that is rooted in biblical texts, and driven by the redemptive mandate to disciple the nations. Ecclesiology has never been a strong point in Evangelical theological study, and this is especially so for Pentecostal-Charismatics. This must change. Instead of simply mimicking the latest successful models and methods for church growth, what is needed is the wedding of ecclesiological orthodoxy and orthopraxis. The Shepherding movement at the least was making an attempt to do this and its story serves the church today as a case study in renewal ecclesiology.

In conclusion, the Shepherding movement, like other renewal movements, blazed a trail, developing church structures that fostered Christian maturity. They seriously grappled with hard issues: the practice of authority and submission in one-on-one Christian discipleship and personal pastoral care. They succeeded and failed in the practice of their principles. While drawing much fire from critics, it seems they may have established a beachhead from which others have advanced. Now over 25 years later concepts called radical in 1975 are much more readily discussed or accepted. They paid a high price for the truths they embraced. The battle over their distinctives, both externally and internally, contributed to their eventual dissolution. Again, it would serve the contemporary church well to examine the Shepherding movement's story and discover what worked and what did not work.

No movement can be adequately judged in its own time. History tells us that people and movements once rejected are sometimes only appreciated generations later. For the Shepherding movement only time will tell. It is hoped this volume will help in that evaluation.

salvation must be perceived corporately and that God is in Christ 'saving a people for his name'. Throughout his book *Paul, the Spirit, and the People of God* ([Peabody, MA: Hendrickson, 1996], 63-64), a book as much about ecclesiology as pneumatology, Fee emphasizes the need for radical and substantive life transformation as God reproduces his life and character in his church. Miroslav Volf addresses issues of individualism, pluralism and institutionalism in Miroslav Volf, *After Our Likeness: The Church as the Image of the Trinity* (Grand Rapids: Eerdmans, 1998).

Some scholars are writing about the ethical implications of being God's covenant community and a renewed emphasis on the Believers' Church. See John Howard Yoder, *The Royal Priesthood* (Grand Rapids: Eerdmans, 1994); Stanley Hauerwas and William H. Willimon, *Resident Aliens* (Nashville: Abingdon Press, 1989). See also the work of the Gospel and Culture network on developing missional churches within North America. George Hunsburger and Craig von Gelder (eds.), *The Church Between Gospel and Culture* (Grand Rapids: Eerdmans, 1996).

Appendix 1

A STATEMENT OF INFORMATION

On 16–17 December 1975, a group of us met in Ann Arbor, Michigan, for theological and pastoral evaluation of the current controversy over 'discipleship' and 'shepherding'. The meeting was called by the planning committee for our scheduled Oklahoma City meeting next March. It was felt that a small study group, meeting in a calm and unhurried setting, could help facilitate further understanding and communication of the issues that are of concern to so many people in the charismatic renewal. We took up the questions that are most frequently raised: the extent of authority and submission, tithing to a shepherd, relationship between 'sheep' and 'shepherd', how extensive the influence of the teachers from Ft Lauderdale, translocal authority, the possibility of a new denomination. We experienced a real measure of understanding. We believe that where there have been abuses and excesses, they can be corrected. After these two days together, we have come to the conviction that a considerable measure of the controversy has resulted from misunderstanding and poor communication. The real differences which exist are well within the bounds of 'allowable variety' in the Body of Christ. We want to encourage all who have been disturbed over this controversy. The Lord was with us in a marked way as we met together. We believe that He will lead all of us to a new and deeper unity in Him. We wanted our brothers and sisters in the Lord to know that we had reached the place which could be best described as a 'committed relationship' to one another. This does not mean that we reached a consensus, but does mean that we no longer believe that we are justified in publicly attacking the motivation, the attitude, the view, the conduct of one another without endeavoring to bring about a reconciliation through the prescribed New Testament procedure as outlined in Matthew 18 in love. It is anticipated that this 'committed relationship' will increase in depth and in numbers among those who have been given responsibility in the charismatic renewal. We arrived at the following specific recommendations to help facilitate greater understanding and communication throughout the Body of Christ: (1) LOGOS and NEW WINE will publish a question and answer forum in which some of the teachers associated with Ft Lauderdale will share with a wider audience some of the information and clarification they shared with us in Ann Arbor. (2) At the meeting in Oklahoma City, we will discuss the possibility of setting up a representative 'grievance committee' which can help handle similar controversies should they arise. (3) We reaffirmed the statement of ethics which was adopted subsequent to the Seattle meeting in 1971, as the basic guideline for the way that we, as leaders, should relate to one another (see below).

Respectfully submitted by

Brick Bradford	Kilian McDonnell
Jamie Buckingham	Bob Mumford
Larry Christenson	Derek Prince
Steve Clark	Kevin Ranaghan
David du Plessis	Michael Scanlan
Everett Fullam	Charles Simpson
Dan Malachuk	J. Rodman Williams

This statement was adopted in a charismatic leaders seminar in Seattle, Washington, in June 1971, and was reaffirmed in the Ann Arbor, Michigan meeting on December 17, 1975.

Ethics for Christian Leaders

1.   We believe that God has set us in position of leadership within the Body of Christ, either as leaders within a local congregation, or as preachers with a ministry to the Body of Christ at large, or in a combination of both these ministries.

2.   So far as we are able, we will seek at all times to keep our lives and ministries sound in respect of ethics, morals, and doctrine.

3.   We will acknowledge and respect all others who have similar ministries and who are willing to make a similar commitment in respect of ethics, morals, and doctrine.

4.   If at any time we have any criticism or complaint against any of our brother ministers within the Body of Christ, we will seek to take the following steps:

First, we will approach our brother directly and privately and seek to establish the true facts.

Second, if thereafter we still find grounds for criticism or complaint, we will seek the counsel and cooperation of at least two other ministers, mutually acceptable to our brother and ourselves in order to make any changes needed to rectify the situation.

Finally, if this does not resolve the criticism or complaint, we will seek to bring the whole matter before a larger group of our fellow ministers, or alternatively, before the local congregation to which our brother belongs.

In following these steps, our motive will be to retain the fellowship of our brother and to arrive at a positive, Scriptural solution which will maintain the Body of Christ.

5.   Until we have done everything possible to follow the steps outlined in Paragraph Four, we will not publicly voice any criticism or complaint against a fellow minister.

6.   In our general conduct toward our fellow ministers and all other believers, we will seek to obey the exhortation of Scripture to 'follow after the things which make for peace and things wherewith one may edify another' (Rom. 14.19).

Reaffirmed in Ann Arbor, 17 December 1975

Appendix 2

REPORT ON THE 1976 CHARISMATIC LEADERS CONFERENCE

Reconciliation among major segments of the charismatic renewal resulted from a week-long meeting of ministers, teachers, and editors in Oklahoma City 8–12 March 1976. Thirty-eight representatives from the movement gathered at the Center for Christian Renewal for four days of prayer, sharing, and discussion on the shepherding-discipleship-submission controversy that has troubled Christians in many parts of the world in the last year.

The consensus of the meeting was that allegations of heresy were unfounded, that there was no reason to question the integrity of the teachers involved, and that, while many doctrinal differences remain among the groups represented, those differences fall within acceptable limits.

The conferees agreed that much of the controversy had grown out of rumor and misunderstanding, misapplication of certain scriptural principles, and a lack of communication among leaders of different ministries and groups.

Leaders associated with Christian Growth Ministries, Ft Lauderdale, Florida, around whom much of the controversy has swirled, said in a statement to the conference that they regretted the abuse and confusion that had resulted from the discipleship teaching. They pledged to correct such abuses and misunderstandings wherever possible.

Other groups represented at the conference—the fifth meeting in a series beginning in Seattle in 1971—were as follows:

American Baptist Charismatic Fellowship, Catholic Charismatic Renewal Service Committee, Church of the Redeemer (Episcopal), Classical Pentecostals, Elim Fellowship, Episcopal Charismatic Fellowship, Logos International Fellowship, Lutheran Charismatic Renewal Service Committee, Mennonite Renewal Services, Presbyterian Charismatic Communion, World Missionary Assistance Plan, Youth With A Mission, and various Christian centers and ministries from every geographical area of the United States and Canada.

Specifically, the conference:

1. Accepted the report from a theological inquiry into the discipleship-shepherding teaching held in Ann Arbor, Michigan, in December 1975.

2. Received and commended a statement of concern and regret issued by the teachers associated with Christian Growth Ministries.

3. Called for an end to public attacks and malicious gossip as a way of dealing with differences within the Christian community.

4. Adopted a statement of ethics for handling differences between ministers, which was drawn up as a result of the meeting in Seattle in 1971.

5. Established a 'Charismatic Concerns Committee' to plan future conferences and to help deal with issues and problems that arise in the charismatic renewal.

6. Agreed to continue to meet together, at least annually, to consider how the charismatic renewal can best serve the renewal of the church.

The Ann Arbor Report

Following are the main elements of the report from the Ann Arbor meeting:

> December 16–17, 1975, a group of us met in Ann Arbor, Michigan, for theological and pastoral evaluation of the current controversy over 'discipleship' and 'shepherding'... We took up the questions which are most frequently raised:
>
> —the extent of authority and submission
> —tithing to a shepherd
> —the relationship between 'sheep' and 'shepherd'—how extensive?
> —the influence of the teachers from Ft Lauderdale
> —trans-local authority, the possibility of a new denomination
>
> We experienced a real measure of understanding. We do not mean that there are not differences which still remain, for there are. But they need not be differences which divide us. In fact, we have come to a great sense of unity in the Spirit. We believe that where there have been excesses and abuses, they can be corrected... We have come to the conviction that a considerable measure of the controversy has resulted from misunderstanding and poor communication. The real differences which exist are well within the bounds of 'allowable variety' in the Body of Christ.
>
> ... We reached the place which could be best described as a 'committed relationship' to one another. This does not mean that we do or will agree with one another in all regards, but it does mean that we are not justified in publicly attacking the motivation, the attitude, the view, the conduct of one another without endeavoring to bring about a reconciliation through the prescribed New Testament procedure as outlined in Matthew 18, in love. It is anticipated that this 'committed relationship' will increase in depth and in numbers among those who have been given responsibility in the charismatic renewal...

Respectfully submitted by:

Brick Bradford	Everett Fullam	Kevin Ranaghan
Jamie Buckingham	Dan Malachuk	Michael Scanlon
Larry Christenson	Kilian McDonnell	Charles Simpson
Steve Clark	Bob Mumford	Rodman Williams
David du Plessis	Derek Prince	

(Note: *Logos Journal* and *New Wine* magazines have published in their March, 1976, issues a Question-and-Answer Forum in which some of the teachers associated with Christian Growth Ministries provided clarification on the discipleship-shepherding issues.)

Statement of Concern and Regret

Following is the statement issued in Oklahoma City by teachers associated with Christian Growth Ministries:

> We realize that controversies and problems have arisen among Christians in various areas as a result of our teaching in relation to subjects such as submission, authority, discipling, shepherding. We deeply regret these problems and, insofar as they are due to fault on our part, we ask forgiveness from our fellow believers whom we have offended.
>
> We realize that our teachings, though we believed them to be essentially sound, have in various places been misapplied or handled in an immature way; and that this has caused problems for our brothers in the ministry. We deeply regret this and ask for forgiveness. Insofar as it lies in our power, we will do our best to correct these situations and to restore any broken relationships.

Don Basham	John Poole
Ern Baxter	Derek Prince
Bob Mumford	Charles Simpson

Response to Statement

The remaining conferees received with gratitude the above statement from the teachers associated with Christian Growth Ministries and thereafter the entire conference made the following response:

We call for an end to the public attacks on those individuals involved in the teaching under question. Public attacks of this kind are a grave disservice to the work of Christ. Also, the multitude of rumors and stories of alleged or actual abuses that are being circulated by members of the Body at large are doing serious harm to His Kingdom.

We appeal to all Christians to live according to the teaching of Scripture which relates to resolving difficulties between members of the Body. In particular, we reaffirm, and invite all Christian leaders to affirm, the following guidelines based on Matthew 18.15-17, as a statement of how we desire to relate to one another when difficult situations arise. These guidelines were originally drawn up after the Seattle meeting in 1971.

> 1. We believe that God has set us in positions of leadership within the Body of Christ, either as leaders within a local congregation, or as preachers with a ministry to the Body of Christ at large, or in a combination of both these ministries.

2. So far as we are able, we will seek at all times to keep our lives and ministries sound in respect to ethics, morals and doctrine.

3. We will acknowledge and respect all others who have similar ministries and who are willing to make a similar commitment in respect to ethics, morals and doctrine.

4. If at any time we have any criticism or complaint against any of our brother ministers within the Body of Christ, we will seek to take the following steps: First, we will approach our brother directly and privately, and seek to establish the true facts. Second, if thereafter we still find grounds for criticism or complaint, we will seek the counsel and cooperation of at least two other ministers mutually acceptable to our brother and ourselves, in order to make any changes needed to rectify the situation. Finally, if this does not resolve the criticism or complaint, we will seek to bring the whole matter before a larger group of our fellow ministers, or alternately before the local congregation to which our brother belongs. In following these steps, our motive will be to retain the fellowship of our brother and to arrive at a positive, scriptural solution which will maintain the unity of the Body of Christ.

5. Until we have done everything possible to follow the steps outlined in paragraph 4, we will not publicly voice any criticism or complaint against a fellow minister.

6. In our general conduct towards our fellow ministers and all other believers, we will seek to obey the exhortation of scripture to 'follow after the things which make for peace, and things wherewith one may edify another' (Rom. 14.19).

Don Basham	Francis MacNutt
Ern Baxter	Ralph Mahoney
Brick Bradford	Ralph Martin
Jack Brombach	Earl Morey
Larry Christenson	Bob Mumford
Steve Clark	Ken Pagard
Dick Coleman	Don Pfotenhauer
Judson Cornwall	John Poole
Loren Cunningham	Derek Prince
David du Plessis	Lester Pritchard
David Edwards	Kevin Ranaghan
Charles Farah	Jeff Schiffmayer
Everett Fullam	Charles Simpson
Joe Garlington	Bob Slosser
James Hamann	Vinson Synan
Bob Hawn	Morris Vaagenes
Rod Lensch	Bob Whitaker
Len LeSourd	Maxwell Whyte
Nelson Litwiller	Bruce Yocum

Appendix 3

INTERNAL INTEGRITY AND EXTERNAL INTEGRATION OF STRUCTURES[*]

PURPOSE OF GOD:
Wholeness of creation.

OBSERVATION:
Creation consists of a complex interrelationship of a myriad of structures.

PROBLEM:
The disintegration of the whole is due to a lack of internal integrity (soundness of substance) within structures (i.e., individuals, families, schools, churches, governments, etc.).

PROPOSAL:
To work toward wholeness of creation by discovering and recognizing those structures that God has ordained; to give ourselves to rebuilding their internal integrity (definition and substance). I propose that we work on the premise that the material, social, and spiritual universes are created in modular fashion and are mutually interdependent.

PRESUPPOSITION:
That structures which are internally sound and secure will naturally seek to harmonize and interrelate with larger structures, because no structure is complete within itself (i.e., healthy individuals relate to families, families to churches, churches to the larger church, and the larger church to the Church universal and eternal).

SYMPTOM:
Failure to integrate into larger structures indicates a tendency toward isolation, and therefore reveals an unhealthy condition or malfunction which expresses itself in sectarianism, fear, doubt, guilt, selfishness, etc. (Cancer cells would be a biological example.)

---

[*] Reproduced by kind permission of Charles Simpson.

CAUTIONS:
(1) Unity is the result of a healthy infrastructure—not the obliteration of infrastructure. 'Statism' or 'Socialism' has sought to be sociological unity at the expense of existing infrastructures. The result has been a temporary unity of coercion—not healthy interdependence of divinely ordered modules.
(2) No divinely ordered unit can be plundered or manipulated for the benefit of another. Each unit is necessary to the effectiveness of the whole social body. Deference and support on the part of each unit for the others is the key to overall health.

COMPONENTS OF HEALTHY STRUCTURE:
(1) A revelation that each individual and module is a product of the will of God—that revelation is personally realized by the participants and not imposed by the larger structure.
(2) Righteousness and equity as a basis for interaction.
(3) Effective and functional joints between the various participating members and modules.
(4) Overview at every level. In other words, the ability of those responsible to attain the view of those over them so that their actions relate to the whole and not merely the benefit of their own sphere.

STRUCTURE CHART—NUMBER ONE*

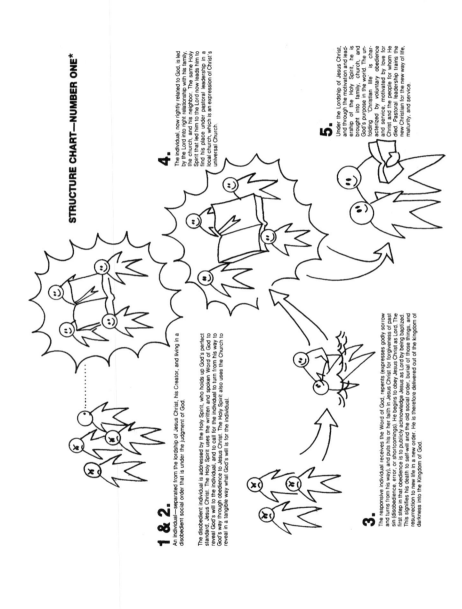

1 & 2.

An individual—separated from the lordship of Jesus Christ, his Creator, and living in a disobedient social order that is under the judgment of God.

The disobedient individual is addressed by the Holy Spirit, who holds up God's perfect standard, Jesus Christ. The Holy Spirit uses the written and spoken Word of God to reveal God's will to the individual, and to call for the individual to turn from his way to God's way through obedience to Jesus Christ. The Holy Spirit also uses the Church to reveal in a tangible way what God's will is for the individual.

3.

The responsive individual receives the Word of God, repents (expresses godly sorrow and turns from his way), and puts his or her faith in Jesus Christ for forgiveness of past sin (disobedience, error, or shortcomings). He begins to obey Jesus Christ as Lord. The first step in that obedience is to publicly acknowledge Jesus as Lord by being baptized. This signifies his death to self-will and the old social order, burial of those things, and resurrection to new life in the new order. He is therefore delivered out of the kingdom of darkness into the Kingdom of God.

4.

The individual, now rightly related to God, is led by the Lord into right relationship with his family, the church, and his neighbor. The same Holy Spirit that led him to the Lord now leads him to find his place under pastoral leadership in a local church, which is an expression of Christ's universal Church.

5.

Under the Lordship of Jesus Christ, and through the motivation and leadership of the Holy Spirit, he is brought into family, church, and God's purpose in the world. The unfolding "Christian life" is characterized by voluntary obedience and service, motivated by love for Christ and the people for whom He died. Pastoral leadership trains the new Christian for the new way of life, maturity, and service.

Growth in personal life, family life and church life through God-ordained leadership

6.
Discipleship under pastoral care.

Individual comes into relationship with God and appointed pastoral care which: 1) upholds and strengthens his relationship to Jesus Christ in the New Covenant; 2) develops his Christian character and spiritual gifts; and 3) helps him to do the will of God. Pastoral leadership is likely to be found among those who helped him come to know Christ. Recognition of the pastor God has chosen for him may come immediately or over several months, but recognizing the pastor as God's appointed servant will be necessary. Upon that recognition and commitment to God's purpose, the pastor gets on with the task of preparing and developing the new Christian for life within the Body of Christ. (When seeking God's leadership for a pastor a new convert should look for a man who demonstrates that his own life is under pastoral care, who is an example, and under whom one would be apprenticed for development.) A pastor is not a substitute for the Holy Spirit or the Lord—but enables the new Christian to know the Lord better by helping him follow the Holy Spirit and understand the Word of God.

7.
Family—God's way.

A. The constant nourishing of family is a basic pastoral priority. B. It is the primary caring unit. C. Proper family life prevents or solves most problems. D. It is the covenantal prototype of the entire church. E. Role models and personal identities are or should be established in the family. F. Families are the first unit of government in God's social order; they are designed to maintain righteousness, peace, and joy in the Holy Spirit. It is where mankind learns to rule well as a steward under God. G. Family life is usually the primary place where one must begin to be a Christian.

8.
The Flock.

A. The flock or cell church is a group of Christians committed to Christ's will, to a common pastoral leadership, and to each other. B. It is made up of families and singles who have been led together through repentance, faith, and baptism into a life of mutual service to Christ and each other. C. The flock or cell church is under the leadership of a pastor or shepherd who is recognized by the larger church leadership. His appointment has come because of God's call, his character, gifts, and recognition by the elders and his flock. D. He demonstrates servanthood to his people, teaches them the Word of God, and how to live together in the New Covenant. E. He receives their honor and service because of his ministry unto the Lord, and in cooperation with the larger church. F. He brings them to the larger Church and it to them. He develops the gifts and resources of his people for God's universal purpose. He guides his flock as unto the Lord and in cooperation with the larger Church. G. He answers for his people to the local church presbytery. H. He knows his people by name and gives account to Jesus Christ, the Chief Shepherd, for his care of them.

STRUCTURE CHART—NUMBER THREE*

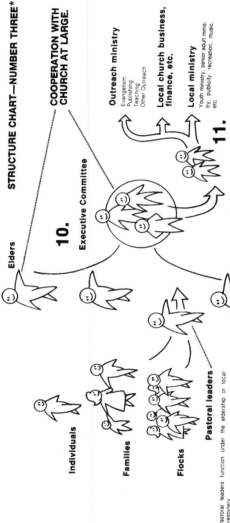

Individuals

Families

Flocks

Pastoral leaders

Pastoral leaders function under the eldership or local presbytery.

Presbytery of Elders

Elders are the men who make up the presbytery. The presbytery is the governing body of the local church. Since the presbytery is the judicial and pastoral leadership body overseeing the entire local church, its members ought to be:

1. God-called pastoral leaders with experience.
2. Men who are mature (generally thirty or over).
3. Men who have proven character and gifts.
4. Men who have developed flocks and pastoral leaders that function successfully.

Presbyteries should meet on a regular basis to pray and seek the Lord, and listen to what God may be saying to them individually and corporately, solve church problems and handle the business of the church.

If a presbytery is large (twelve or more elders) it may choose to have an executive committee to handle interim matters and plan the presbytery agenda.

Elders

9.

10.

Executive Committee

COOPERATION WITH CHURCH AT LARGE.

Outreach ministry
Evangelism
Publishing
Teaching
Other Outreach

Local church business, finance, etc.

Local ministry
Youth ministry, senior adult ministry, publicity, recreation, music, etc.

11.

Administrative matters may be delegated to administrators or deacons to keep the elders free to pray and minister the Word. If there are several such deacons they may function as a council.

They report to the executive committee or presbytery, and serve by appointment.

STEWARDSHIP

Participation at every level of the church is by voluntary commitment to Jesus Christ and the New Covenant. All service is under the oversight of the presbytery. Leadership presupposes that the membership is committed to God's will and to the church government. The church and its members are stewards of creation, under God, who seek to manage and develop resources in a way that honors and pleases God and satisfies His purposes.

Resources

Kingdom Government

Universal Purpose of God

STRUCTURE CHART—NUMBER FOUR*

Translocal Government

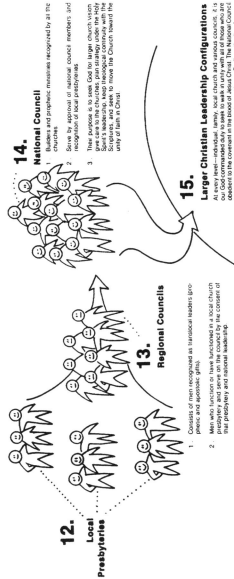

12.
Local Presbyteries

13.
Regional Councils

1. Consists of men recognized as translocal leaders (prophetic and apostolic gifts).

2. Men who function or have functioned in a local church presbytery and serve on the council by the consent of that presbytery and national leadership.

3. These men serve as a consulting and strategic link between local concerns and universal vision.

4. Councils provide government or adjudication only upon request of local presbyteries or in situations that extend beyond the local church.

14.
National Council

1. Builders and prophetic ministries recognized by all the churches.

2. Serve by approval of national council members and recognition of local presbyteries.

3. Their purpose is to seek God for larger church vision give care to the churches, plan strategy under the Holy Spirit's leadership, keep theological continuity with the Scriptures, and seek to move the Church toward the unity of faith in Christ.

15.
Larger Christian Leadership Configurations

At every level—individual, family, local church and various councils, it is our God-commanded duty to seek to walk in unity with all of those who are obedient to the covenant in the blood of Jesus Christ. The National Council has the same obligation to recognize and honor God's authority wherever it is present. Just as the individual, family, and local church must no human instrument is the end of spiritual government, but the Lord is.

THE EXERCISE OF SPIRITUAL AUTHORITY

Authority which exists close to the individual—such as a parent to his or her child—will tend to be more direct in the way it functions. Authority which is removed or distant from the individual—such as a Regional or National Council—will tend to be more advisory. Distant authority must not pre-empt local authority. The direct intensity of how authority operates depends upon its proximity to the person, and the maturity of the person under government.

Spiritual authority more directive

Spiritual authority more advisory

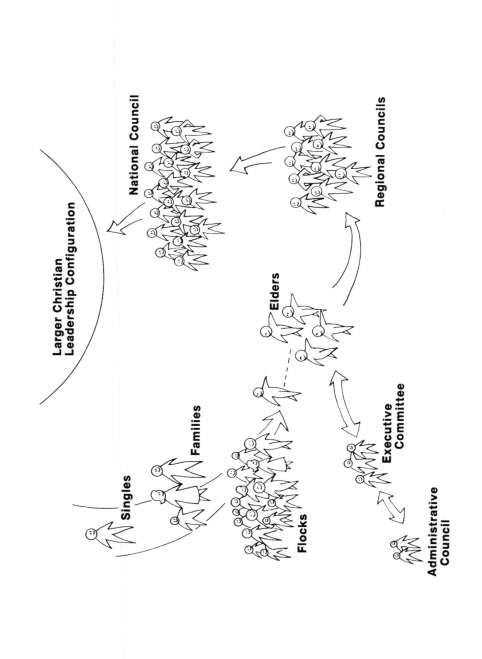

Larger Christian
Leadership Configuration

National Council

Regional Councils

Elders

Executive
Committee

Administrative
Council

Families

Singles

Flocks

REFERENCES AND SOURCES

'An Important Announcement to Our *New Wine Magazine Magazine* Family', *New Wine Magazine* (February 1979), 24.

'Announcing BusinessGram', *New Wine Magazine* (November 1981), 28.

Altizer, Thomas J.J., and William Hamilton, *Radical Theology and the Death of God* (New York: Bobb–Merrill, 1966).

Banks, Robert, *The Church Comes Home* (Peabody, MA: Hendrickson, 1998).

Barna, George, *Marketing the Church* (Colorado Springs, CO: Navpress, 1988).

Barrett, David, *World Christian Encyclopedia* (New York: Oxford University Press, 1982).

Barron, Bruce, *If You Really Want to Follow Jesus...* (Kenmore, NY: Partners', 1981).

—'Shepherding Movement (Discipleship Movement)', in Daniel G. Reid *et al.* (eds.), *Dictionary of Christianity in America* (Downers Grove, IL: InterVarsity Press, 1990).

Barrs, Jerram, *Shepherds and Sheep* (Downers Grove, IL: InterVarsity Press, 1983).

Barzun, Jacques, and Henry F. Graff, *The Modern Researcher* (Boston, MA: Houghton Mifflin, 1995).

Basham, Don, 'Abuse of Authority: Recognizing and Correcting the Problems', *Charisma* (September 1978), 25-30.

—*Beyond Blessing to Obedience* (Ft Lauderdale, FL: Christian Growth Ministries, 1976).

—'Birth of a Mission', *New Wine Magazine* (April 1970), 12-16.

—*Can a Christian Have a Demon?* (Monroeville, PA: Whitaker House, 1971).

—'A Covenant Community', *New Wine Magazine* (February 1980), 30.

—*Deliver Us From Evil* (Old Tappan, NJ: Chosen Books, 1972).

—*Face Up with a Miracle* (Northridge, CA: Voice Christian Publications, 1967).

—'Forum: CGM and New Wine Magazine', *New Wine Magazine* (December 1976), 31.

—'How It All Began', *New Wine Magazine* (June 1984), 10-15.

—'Leadership: A Biblical Look', *New Wine Magazine* (March 1974), 14-17.

—'Questions and Answers', *Don Basham's Insights* (January 1987), 4.

—'A Time To Be Reconciled', *New Wine Magazine* (May 1980), 16-17.

—'Toward Healing the Rift', *New Wine Magazine* (May 1976), 20-22.

—*True and False Prophets* (Grand Rapids: Chosen Books, 1986).

—'Update', *Don Basham's Insights* (July/August 1988), 3-4.

—*The Way I See It* (New York: Fleming H. Revell, 1986).

Baxter, W.J. Ern, *The Beginnings of Church Life* (Greensburg, LA: Manna Christian Outreach, 1974).

—*The Chief Shepherd and His Sheep* (Spring Valley, CA: Timothy Distribution, 1987).

—*God's Agenda for the Church* (Shippensburg, PA: Destiny Image, 1995).

—'*I Almost Died!*' (Mobile, AL: Integrity Communications, 1983).

—*Life on Wings* (Ft Lauderdale, FL: Christian Growth Ministries, 1976).

—'A Personal Word', *New Wine Magazine* (March 1978), 16.

—*Restoring the Balance between the King, the Kingdom, and the Holy Spirit* (Shippensburg, PA: Destiny Image, 1995).

—*Thy Kingdom Come* (Ft Lauderdale, FL: Christian Growth Ministries, 1977).

Beall, James Lee, 'On the Care and Feeding of Sheep', *Logos Journal* (September/October 1975), 19-21.

—'What a Sheep Can Expect From His Shepherd', *New Wine Magazine* (May 1974), 9-11.

—*Your Pastor, Your Shepherd* (Plainfield, NJ: Logos, 1977).

Beckham, William A., *The Second Reformation* (Houston, TX: Touch, 1995).

Beiser, Carl, *The Shepherding Movement* (San Juan Capistrano, CA: Christian Research Institute, 1979).

Bellah, Robert (ed.), *Habits of the Heart* (Berkeley: University of California Press, 1985).

Bennett, Dennis, *St Luke's Newsletter* (13 July 1973).

Birkey, Del, *The House Church* (Scottsdale, PA: Herald Press, 1988).

Bloch, Marc, *The Historian's Craft* (New York: Vintage Books, 1953).

Bloech, Donald G., *The Reform of the Church* (Grand Rapids: Eerdmans, 1970).

Board of Trustees of *Insights*, 'Update', *Don Basham's Insights* (March/April 1988), 3-4.

Bonhoeffer, Dietrich, *Life Together* (New York: Harper & Row, 1954).

Bradley, James, and Richard A. Muller, *Church History: An Introduction to Research, Reference Works, and Methods* (Grand Rapids: Eerdmans, 1995).

Brock, Peter, 'The Secret Summit Reconstructed', *Christianity Today* (4 April 1980), 45.

Bruce, Alexander Balmain, D.D., *The Training of the Twelve* (New Canaan, CT: Keats, 1979).

Buckingham, Jamie, 'Changing Attitudes Among Discipleship Leaders', *Buckingham Report* (20 March 1985), 1-5.

—*Daughter of Destiny* (Plainfield, NJ: Logos, 1976).

—'Discipleship Leaders Break Up', *Buckingham Report* (6 August 1986), 2.

—'The End of the Discipleship Era', *Ministries Today* (January/February 1990), 46-51.

—'*New Wine Magazine* Ceases Publication', *Ministries Today* (November/December 1986), 24.

—*The Truth Will Set You Free But First It Will Make You Miserable* (Altamonte Springs, FL: Creation House, 1988).

Buess, Bob, *Discipleship Pro and Con* (Van, TX: Sweeter Than Honey, 1975).

—*The Pendulum Swings* (Harrison, AR: New Leaf, 1975).

Burgess, Stanley M., and Gary B. McGee (eds.), *The Dictionary of Pentecostal and Charismatic Movements* (Grand Rapids: Zondervan, 1986).

Burks, Ron, and Vicki Burks, *Damaged Disciples: Casualties of Authoritarian Churches and the Shepherding Movement* (Grand Rapids: Zondervan, 1992).

Burrs, J., 'Shepherding Movement', in Sinclair B. Ferguson, David F. Wright and J.I. Packer (eds.), *New Dictionary of Theology* (Downers Grove, IL: InterVarsity Press, 1988), 639-40.

Butchart, Wayne, 'Soul Bondage', *World MAP Digest* (December 1978), 5-7.

Butt, Howard, *The Velvet Covered Brick* (New York: Harper & Row, 1973).

Carter, Howard J., *The Local Assembly* (Hazelbrook, NSW, Australia: Logosprint, 1975).

Chandler, Russell, 'Charismatics Close Shepherding Gap', *Los Angeles Times* (20 March 1976), Part 1, 26.

'Charismatic Leaders Seeking Faith for their Own Healing', *Christianity Today* (April 1980), 44-45.

'Charismatic Movement is Facing Internal Discord Over a Teaching Called "Discipling"', *New York Times* (16 September 1975), sec. C31, col. 1.

'The Charismatic Renewal After Kansas City', *Sojourners* (September 1977), 11-13.

Christian Conquest (Winter 1995), 10-11.
Christenson, Larry, *The Christian Family* (Minneapolis, MN: Bethany Fellowship, 1970).
—*Welcome, Holy Spirit* (Minneapolis, MN: Augsburg, 1987).
'Christian Growth Ministries Report', *New Wine Magazine* (September 1972), 4-9, 22.
'Christian Growth Ministries Report', *New Wine Magazine* (May 1974), 1-31.
'Christian Growth Ministries', *New Wine Magazine* 4.3–13.10 (March 1972–October 1981).
Chrnalogar, Mary Alice, *Twisted Scripture* (New Kensington, PA: Whitaker House, 1997).
Cimino, Richard, and Don Luttin, *Shopping for Faith* (San Francisco: Jossey-Bass, 1998).
Clapp, Rodney, *A Peculiar People* (Downers Grove, IL: InterVarsity Press, 1996).
Clark, Stephen, *Patterns of Christian Community* (Ann Arbor, MI: Servant, 1984).
—*Unordained Elders and Renewal Communities* (New York: Paulist Press, 1976).
Clark, Steve B., 'Where Does Authority Come From?', *New Covenant* (January 1977), 4-7.
Coleman, Robert E., *The Master Plan of Evangelism* (New York: Fleming H. Revell, 1964).
Collins, Robert M., 'Growth of Liberalism in the Sixties', in Farber (ed.), *The Sixties*, 11-44.
Comiskey, Joel, *Home Cell Church Explosion* (Houston, TX: Touch, 1998).
'Contents', *New Wine Magazine* (January 1972), 2.
Cox, Harvey, *Fire from Heaven* (Reading: Addison–Wesley, 1995).
—*The Secular City* (New York: Macmillan, 1965).
Crabb, Larry, *Connecting* (Nashville, TN: Word Books, 1997).
—*The Safest Place on Earth* (Nashville, TN: Word Books, 1999).
Crowe, Terrence Robert, *Pentecostal Unity* (Chicago: Loyola University Press, 1993).
'Derek Prince States Position', *Charisma* (August 1984), 88-90.
Digitale, Robert, 'An Idea Whose Time Is Gone?', *Christianity Today* (19 March 1990), 38-42.
'Discipleship Forum in Ft Lauderdale', *Logos Journal* (March 1976), insert.
'Discipleship Forum in Ft Lauderdale', *New Wine Magazine* (March 1976), insert.
The Discipleship and Submission Movement, Assemblies of God pamphlet (Springfield: Gospel, 1976).
Durnbaugh, Donald, *The Believers' Church* (New York: Macmillan, 1964).
'Echoes of the Spirit', *New Wine Magazine* (July/August 1974), 23.
'Echoes of the Spirit', *New Wine Magazine* (November 1975), 12-14.
'Ecumenical Charismatic Conference Scheduled for 1977', *New Covenant* (July 1976), 24.
'Ecumenical Charismatic Conference Scheduled for 1977', *New Wine Magazine* (November 1975), 12-14.
'Editorials', *Logos Journal* (November/December 1975), 44-47.
'Editorials: A Plea For Unity', *Logos Journal* (May 1975), 54-55.
'Editorials: "No Deepening Rift Here"', *Logos Journal* (March/April 1976), 54-55.
Edwards, Gene, *Letters to a Devastated Christian* (Wheaton, IL: Tyndale, 1984).
—*A Tale of Three Kings* (Goleta, CA: Christian Books, 1980).
Ellwood, Robert S., *One Way: The Jesus Movement and Its Meaning* (Englewood Cliffs, NJ: Prentice–Hall, 1973).
—*The Sixties Spiritual Awakening* (New Brunswick, NJ: Rutgers University Press, 1994).
Enroth, Ronald M., 'Churches on the Fringe', *Eternity* (October 1986), 17-22.
—*Churches That Abuse* (Grand Rapids: Zondervan, 1992).
—*Recovering From Churches That Abuse* (Grand Rapids: Zondervan, 1994).
—'The Power Abusers', *Eternity* (October 1979), 23-27.
'Enter a New Era in Bible Teaching', *New Wine Magazine* (January 1972), 7, 12-13.
Escobar, Gabriel, and Caryle Murphy, 'Promise Keepers Answer the Call', *Washington Post* (5 October 1997), A18.

Farah, Charles, Jr, 'The Dilemma of Discipleship', *Logos Journal* (September/October 1975), 6-10.

Fathergram (4 July 1977), 1-2.

Farber, David, 'The Silent Majority and Talk About Revolution', in *idem* (ed.), *The Sixties*, 291-316.

Farber, David (ed.), *The Sixties... From Memory to History* (Chapel Hill, NC: University of North Carolina Press, 1994).

Fee, Gordon, *Paul, the Spirit, and the People of God* (Peabody, MA: Hendrickson, 1996).

'Forum', *New Wine Magazine* (December 1976), 27-31.

'Forum: Discipleship', *New Wine Magazine* (March 1974), 27-31.

'Forum: God's Government', *New Wine Magazine* (June 1974), 30.

'Forum: Shepherds', *New Wine Magazine* (May 1974), 28-31.

Frank, Neil, 'Editorial', *New Wine Magazine* (June 1969), 2.

—'Editor's Letter', *New Wine Magazine* (November 1970), 2.

—'An Open Letter to the Body of Christ', *New Wine Magazine* (November 1970), 3.

Frost, Robert, 'Editorial', *New Wine Magazine* (June 1969), 2.

—'My Shepherd is the Lord', *New Covenant* (August 1977), 16-19.

George, Carl F., *The Coming Church Revolution* (New York: Fleming H. Revell, 1994).

—*Preparing Your Church for the Future* (New York: Fleming H. Revell, 1991).

Getz, Gene A., *Sharpening the Focus on the Church* (Chicago: Moody Press, 1974).

Ghezzi, Bert, 'Bob Mumford After Discipleship', *Charisma* (August 1987), 20-27.

Giles, Kevin, *What On Earth Is the Church?* (Downers Grove, IL: InterVarsity Press, 1995).

Girard, Robert C., *Brethren Hang Loose* (Grand Rapids: Zondervan, 1972).

Gittlin, Todd, *The Sixties* (New York: Bantam Books, 1993).

Grady, J. Lee, *What Happened to the Fire?* (Grand Rapids: Chosen Books, 1994).

Guder, Darrell L. Guder, *The Missional Church* (Grand Rapids: Eerdmans, 1998).

Hadaway, C. Kirk, Stuart A. Wright, and Francis M. DuBose, *Home Cell Groups and House Churches* (Nashville, TN: Broadman, 1987).

Hamilton, Michael P., *The Charismatic Movement* (Grand Rapids: Eerdmans, 1975).

Hamon, Dr Bill, *The Eternal Church* (Point Washington, FL: Christian International, 1981).

Harper, Michael, *Let My People Grow* (Plainfield, NJ: Logos, 1977).

—*Three Sisters* (Wheaton, IL: Tyndale, 1979).

Harrell, David Edwin, Jr, *All Things Are Possible* (Bloomington: Indiana University Press, 1975).

—*Pat Robertson* (San Francisco: Harper & Row, 1987).

Hart, Larry, 'Problems of Authority in Pentecostalism', *Review and Expositor* 75 (Spring 1978), 249-66.

Hauerwas, Stanley, and William H. Willimon, *Resident Aliens* (Nashville: Abingdon Press, 1989).

Hawn, Robert H., 'Kansas City: Conference Heard "Round the World"', *Charisma* (September/October 1977), 10-11, 24.

Hayford, Jack W., 'Conciliation Without Compromise', *Logos Journal* (November/December 1975), 26-32.

—*The Holy Dynamic of Wholehearted Submission* (Van Nuys: Living Way Ministries, 1995).

—'Reacting To Repentance', *Ministries Today* (January/February 1990), 59-60.

Hitt, Russell T., 'The Soul Watchers', *Eternity* (April 1976), 13-15, 34.

Hocken, Peter, 'The Charismatic Movement', in Burgess and McGee (eds.), *Dictionary*, 130-60.

—*The Glory and the Shame* (Guildford, Surrey: Eagle, 1994).

—'Holy Spirit Teaching Mission', in Burgess and McGee (eds.), *Dictionary*, 444.

'Holy Spirit Teaching Mission', *New Wine Magazine* 1.1–4.2 (June 1969–February 1972).

Holy Spirit Teaching Mission Newsletter, 12 July 1968, 15 November 1968, 29 March 1969, 31 July 1969, 20 September 1969 (Holy Spirit Research Center; Tulsa, OK: Oral Roberts University).

Howard, Linda G., 'Join a Discipleship Group? Not Me!', *Logos Journal* (May 1975), 30-33; (January/February 1990), 59-60.

—'A New Beginning', *Charisma* (April 1984), 38-43.

'An Important Announcement to Our New Wine Magazine Family', *New Wine Magazine* (February 1979), 24.

Hughes, Richard (ed.), *The American Quest for the Primitive Church* (Chicago: University of Illinois Press, 1988).

Hunsberger, George, and Craig von Gelder (eds.), *The Church Between Gospel and Culture* (Grand Rapids: Eerdmans, 1996).

Hunter, H.D., 'Shepherding Movement', in Burgess and McGee (eds.), *Dictionary*.

Hybels, Bill, *Rediscovering Church* (Grand Rapids: Zondervan, 1995).

Hymers, R.L., and Kent Philpott, *Why We Reject Simpsonism and Mumfordism* (Mobile, AL: Christian Research Center, n.d.).

'In Memorium: Don W. Basham', *Don Basham's Insights* (March/April 1989), 2.

Integrity Communications, *New Wine Magazine* 13.11–18.12 (November 1981–December 1986).

'Itineraries 1972', *New Wine Magazine* (February 1972), 31.

Jahr, Mary Ann, 'Christian Growth Ministries: Teaching for the Body of Christ', *New Covenant* (March 1976), 22-24.

Johnson, David, and Jeff van Vonderen, *The Subtle Power of Spiritual Abuse* (Minneapolis: Bethany House, 1991).

Jones, C.E., 'Integrity Communications', in Burgess and McGee (eds.), *Dictionary*, 466.

Jones, E. Stanley, *The Unshakeable Kingdom and the Unchanging Person* (Nashville, TN: Abingdon Press, 1972).

Kelly, Dean M., *Why Conservative Churches Are Growing* (San Francisco: Harper & Row, 1977).

Kenneson, Phillip D., and James L. Street, *Selling Out the Church* (Nashville, TN: Abingdon Press, 1997).

König, A., and H.I. Lederle, *Systematic Theology* (Pretoria, South Africa: University of South Africa Press, 1984).

Lawson, Steven, 'New Wine Magazine Stops Presses', *Charisma* (November 1986), 80-82.

'Leaders Reach Agreement Over Discipleship Controversy', *New Covenant* (June 1976), 24-25.

Lensch, Rodney G., 'Opinion: The Charismatic Army Has Been Fragmented', *Logos Journal* (January/February 1981), 28-30.

LeSourd, Leonard, 'A Wild Boar In Our Midst', *Logos Journal* (May/June 1976), 77-80.

Ligon, Bill with Robert Paul Lamb, *Discipleship: The Jesus View* (Plainfield, NJ: Logos, 1979).

'Logos Report: National Men's Shepherds Conference', *Logos Journal* (November/December 1975), 42-43.

'Logos Report: Kansas City Hears Jesus is Lord', *Logos Journal* (September/October 1977), 53.

'Logos Report: What Really Happened at Minneapolis?', *Logos Journal* (November/December 1975), 58-62.

Longino, Frank S., 'Is It Right To Submit To Men?', *Logos Journal* (May 1975), 64-66.

'Lord, Make Us One', *Charisma* (May 1980), 49-54.

Luker, A. Boyd, Jr, 'A New Testament of Discipling' (unpublished PhD dissertation, Dallas Theological Seminary, 1985).

Luter, A. Boyd, Jr, 'A Theological Evaluation of "Christ Model" Disciple-Making', *Journal of Pastoral Practice* 5.4 (1982), 11-21.

MacDonald, Gordon, 'Disciple Abuse', *Discipleship* (November 1985), 24-28.

Mahoney, Ralph, 'Editorial: Disciple', *World MAP Digest* (November/December 1975), 14-15.

—'Submission and Obedience', *World MAP Digest* (November/December 1975), 4-14.

Mains, David, *Full Circle* (Waco, TX: Word Books, 1971).

Malachuk, Dan, 'Publisher's Preface', *Logos Journal* (September/October 1975), 5.

—'Publisher's Preface', *Logos Journal* (November/December 1975), 3.

Manuel, David, *Like A Mighty River* (Orleans, MA: Rock Harbor, 1977).

Marius, Richard, *A Short Guide to Writing about History* (New York: HarperCollins, 1989).

Martin, Ralph. 'The Mighty Stream of God', *New Wine Magazine* (November 1974), 14-17.

Martin, Ralph, Ken Pagard, and Charles Simpson. 'Christian Community: What Does It Take?', *New Covenant* (August 1977), 4-9.

Maust, John, 'Charismatic Leaders Seeking Faith for Their Own Healing', *Christianity Today* (4 April 1980), 44-46.

McDonnell, Kilian (ed.), 'Seven Documents on the Discipleship Question', in *idem* (ed.), *Presence, Power, Praise: Documents on the Charismatic Renewal* (3 vols.; Collegeville, MN: Liturgical Press, 1980), 116-47.

McGrath, Alister (ed.), *The Blackwell Encyclopedia of Modern Christian Thought* (Cambridge, MA: Basil Blackwell, 1993).

McIntire, C.T., and Ronald A. Wells, *History and Historical Understanding* (Grand Rapids: Eerdmans, 1984).

McLaren, Brian D., *Reinventing Your Church* (Grand Rapids: Zondervan, 1998).

Miller, Elliot, 'The Christian and Authority, Part One', *Forward* (Spring 1985), 8-15.

—'The Christian and Authority, Part Two', *Forward* (Summer 1985), 9-26.

Mills, Watson E., *Charismatic Religion in Modern Research Bibliography* (Macon, GA: Mercer University Press, 1985).

Monroe, Tom, 'Editorial', *New Wine Magazine* (January 1970), 2.

Moore, Carey, 'Kansas City Hears Jesus is Lord', *Logos Journal* (September/October 1977), 50-53.

Moore, S. David, 'The Shepherding Movement in Historical Perspective' (unpublished MA thesis, Oral Roberts University, Tulsa, OK, 1996).

—'The Shepherding Movement: History, Controversy, Ecclesiology' (D.Min. dissertation, Regent University, VA, 1999), 50-51.

Mumford, Bob, 'The Biblical Basis for Discipleship', *Logos Journal* (September/October 1978), 10-11.

—'Change in the Wind', *LifeChangers Newsletter* (January/February 1981), 4.

—*Christ in Session* (Ft Lauderdale, FL: Bob Mumford Ministries, 1973).

—'Editorial', *New Wine Magazine* (August 1970), 2.

—'Fatherpower', *New Wine Magazine* (April 1978), 4-10.

—*Fifteen Steps Out* (Plainfield, NJ: Logos, 1969).

—*Focusing on Present Issues* (Hollywood, FL: LifeChangers, 1979).

—*Forty Years in Ministry 1954–1994* (Raleigh, NC: LifeChangers, 1994).

—*Integrity House Newsletter* (1984).

—*The King and You* (New York: Fleming H. Revell, 1974).

—'Lawlessness', *New Wine Magazine* (September 1972).

—*LifeChangers Newsletter* (Holy Spirit Research Center, Oral Roberts University, Tulsa, OK, November 1975), 1-8.

—'A Most Timely Book', *New Wine Magazine* (May 1972), back page.

—'Mumford: Application, Not Doctrine was Flawed', *Christianity Today* (March 1990), 39.

—'Mumford Explains Why', *Ministries Today* (January/February 1990), 53-58.

—'Mumford's Formal Repentance Statement to the Body of Christ', *Ministries Today* (January/February 1990), 52.

—*The Normal Christian Church Life* (Washington DC: International Students, 1962).

—'Obeying the Last Command', *Logos Journal* (September/October 1975), 14-17.

—'A Personal Word from Bob Mumford', *New Wine Magazine* (November 1976), 11.

—*The Problem of Doing Your Own Thing* (Ft Lauderdale, FL: Christian Growth Ministries, 1973).

—*Spiritual Authority* (New York: Christian Fellowship, 1972).

—*Take Another Look at Guidance* (Raleigh, NC: LifeChangers, 1993).

—'The Vision of the Local Church', *New Wine Magazine* (July/August 1975), 4-8.

—*The Way to Spiritual Strength: In the Face of Temptation* (Altamonte Springs: Creation House, 1987).

—'Would God Submit?', *New Covenant* (January 1977), 8-11.

'Mumford, du Plessis Reconcile at John 17.21 Fellowship Meeting', *Logos Journal* (May/June 1980), 12.

'National Men's Shepherds Conference: Recognizing the Hazards of Walking Alone', *New Covenant* (December 1975), 22-23.

Neighbor, Ralph W., *Where Do We Go From Here?* (Houston, TX: Touch, 1990).

Newbigin, Lesslie, *The Household of God* (New York: Friendship Press, 1954).

'New Adventure in the Spirit', *New Wine Magazine* (July 1972), 20-21.

'New Wine Magazine Forum', *New Wine Magazine* (July/August 1973), 30.

'New Wine Magazine Magazine to Cease Publication', *People of Destiny* (November/December 1986), 26.

Noll, Mark, *A History of the United States and Canada* (Grand Rapids: Eerdmans, 1993).

Nolte, Robert, and Michael Berry, 'Discipleship Division Disappears into Oneness', *National Courier* (19 August 1977), 3.

O'Conner, Edward, *The Pentecostal Movement in the Catholic Church* (Notre Dame, IN: Ave Maria Press, 1971).

O'Malley, J.S., 'Discipleship Movement', in Walter A. Elwell (ed.), *Evangelical Dictionary of Theology* (Grand Rapids: Baker Book House, 1984), 319-20.

Ortiz, Juan Carlos, *Call to Discipleship* (Plainfield, NJ: Logos, 1975).

—*Disciple* (Carol Stream, IL: Creation House, 1975).

—'The Duty of a Servant', *New Covenant* (December 1975), 14-17.

—'The Making of Disciples', *Logos Journal* (September/October 1975), 22-27.

Peterson, Duane, *Jesus People* (Glendale, CA: Regal Books, 1971).

Pethybridge, W.J., 'The Lost Secret of the Early Church', *New Wine Magazine* (April 1970), 1, 5-8.

Petrie, Paul, 'The Privilege of Serving', *New Wine Magazine* (January 1979), 24.

Phillips, Keith, *The Making of a Disciple* (New York: Fleming H. Revell, 1975).

Plowman, Edward E., 'The Deepening Rift in the Charismatic Movement', *Christianity Today* (10 October 1975), 52-54.

—*The Jesus Movement in America* (Elgin, IL: David C. Cook, 1971).

Poloma, Margaret, *The Assemblies of God at the Crossroads* (Knoxville, TN: University of Tennessee Press, 1989).

—*The Charismatic Movement* (Boston, MA: Twayne, 1982).

Poole, John M., 'What a Shepherd Can Expect From His Sheep', *New Wine Magazine* (May 1974), 4-8.

Prince, Derek, 'The Apostle—God's Master Builder', *New Wine Magazine* (February 1972), 18-23.

—*Apostles and Shepherds: Verse-by-Verse Outline* (Charlotte: Derek Prince Ministries, 1984).

—'Can These Dry Bones Live?', *New Wine Magazine* (January 1973), 4-10.

—'The Church of the Seventies', *New Covenant* (September 1974), 10-11.

—*Discipleship, Shepherding, Commitment* (Ft Lauderdale, FL: Derek Prince Ministries, 1976).

—'God's Man on the Move', *New Wine Magazine* (March 1973), 11-15.

—*Jubilee 1995 Celebration: 50th Year in Ministry* (Charlotte, NC: Derek Prince Ministries, 1995).

—'The Local Church: God's View Vs Man's View', *New Wine Magazine* (May 1973), 14-18.

—*Shaping History Through Prayer and Fasting* (New York: Fleming H. Revell, 1973).

Prince, Derek, with Ruth Prince, *God is a Matchmaker* (Grand Rapids, MI: Chosen Books, 1986).

Pulkington, W. Graham, *Gathered for Power* (New York: Morehouse–Barlow, 1972).

Purvis, Eldon, 'The Co-ordinator's Report', *New Wine Magazine* (October 1970), 3.

Purvis, Nancy, 'Hostess for a Home Prayer and Bible Study Meeting', *New Wine Magazine* (April 1970), 25.

Quebedeaux, Richard, *The New Charismatics II* (San Francisco: Harper & Row, 2nd rev. edn, 1983).

Ranaghan, Kevin, 'Basic Training for Contemporary Disciples', *New Covenant* (December 1975), 4-7.

—*Catholic Pentecostals* (New York: Paulist Press, 1969).

'Recognizing the "Hazards of Walking Alone"', *New Covenant* (December 1975), 22-23.

'Reflections on a Lifetime of Discipleship: an Interview with Charles Simpson', *People of Destiny* (March 1985), 9-12.

'Renewal Leaders Move Toward Unity', *New Covenant* (August 1974), 26.

'A Report on *Vino Nuevo*', *New Wine Magazine* (February 1977), 14-15.

Richards, Lawrence O., *A New Face for the Church* (Grand Rapids: Zondervan, 1970).

Ross, Scott, 'The Sheep, Shepherds and the Pasture', *Logos Journal* (May/June 1974), 45-47.

Ross, Scott, with John Sherrill and Elizabeth Sherrill, *Scott Free* (New York: Fleming H. Revell, 1976).

Rushdoony, Rousas J., *God's Plan for Victory: The Meaning of Post-Millennialism* (Fairfax, VA: Thaburn Press, 1977).

Sandeen, Ernest, *The Roots of Fundamentalism* (Chicago: University of Chicago Press, 1970).

Scharz, Christian, *Natural Church Development* (Carol Stream, IL: ChurchSmart Resources, 1996).

—*Paradigm Shift in the Church* (Carol Stream, IL: ChurchSmart Resources, 1999).

'Second National Men's Shepherds Conference', *New Covenant* (February 1975), 27.

'Separate, But United in Spirit', *National Courier* (19 August 1977), 1-2.

Shawchuck, Norman, *et al.*, *Marketing for Congregations* (Nashville, TN: Abingdon Press, 1992).

Shelly, Bruce, and Marshall Shelly, *Consumer Church* (Downers Grove, IL: InterVarsity Press, 1992).

Simpson, Charles, *The Challenge to Care* (Ann Arbor, MI: Servant, 1986).

—*Christian Life Seminar* (Mobile, AL: Integrity, 1977).

—*The Covenant and the Kingdom* (Tonbridge: Kent: Sovereign World, 1995).

—'Covenant Love', *New Wine Magazine* (January 1978), 16-20.
—'Covering of the Lord', *New Wine Magazine* (October 1972), 24-27.
—'Establishing the Kingdom', *New Wine Magazine* (October 1974), 24-27.
—'Faithful in the Natural Things', *New Wine Magazine* (September 1975), 24-29.
—*Integrity House Newsletter* (20 December 1984), 2-3.
—'Interview: Older…and Wiser', *Ministries Today* (March/April 1990), 67-71.
—'A Life On Wings: In Memory of Ern Baxter', *Christian Challenge* (September/October 1993), 3-4.
—'Making Disciples', *New Wine Magazine* (March 1974), 4-8.
—*A New Way to Live* (Greensburg, PA: Manna Christian Outreach, 1975).
—'An Open Letter to Our Readers and Christian Friends', *New Wine Magazine* (June 1984), 17-21.
—'The Salt of the Covenant: Loyalty', *New Wine Magazine* (February 1975), 15-18.
—'What Is the Gospel?', *New Wine Magazine* (June 1974), 4-7.
—'What Must We Do?', *New Wine Magazine* (July/August 1974), 18.
—*Your Home or His?* (Ft Lauderdale: Christian Growth Ministries, 1976).
Slosser, Bob G., 'Little New Light Shed On Shepherding', *National Courier* (1 October 1975), 5.
—'Shepherding Storm is Mounting', *National Courier* (7 October 1975), 9.
Smith, Chuck, *Answers for Today* (Costa Mesa, CA: The Word for Today, 1993).
—'Submission', *Maranatha Good News* 3.2 (1976), 2-3.
Smith, Mont W., *What the Bible Says About Covenant* (Joplin, MO: College Press, 1983).
Snyder, Howard A., 'The Church as God's Agent in Evangelism', in J.D. Douglas (ed.), *Let the Whole Earth Hear His Voice* (Minneapolis, MN: World Wide Publications, 1975), 327-60.
—*The Community of the King* (Downers Grove, IL: InterVarsity Press, 1977).
—*The Problem of Wineskins* (Downers Grove, IL: InterVarsity Press, 1975).
—*The Radical Wesley and Patterns for Church Renewal* (Downers Grove, IL: InterVarsity Press, 1980).
—*Signs of the Spirit* (Grand Rapids: Zondervan, 1989).
'Special Announcement', *New Wine Magazine* (October 1986), 46-47.
'Special Annoucement', *New Wine Magazine* (November 1986), 6-7.
Special Memorial Issue, *Don Basham's Insights* (March/April 1989), 1-4.
Spittler, Russell P., 'Du Plessis, David Johannes', in Burgess and McGee (eds.), *Dictionary*, 250-54.
Stedman, Ray, *Body Life* (Glendale, CA: Regal Books, 1972).
Stockstill, Larry, *The Cell Church* (Ventura, CA: Regal Books, 1998).
Strang, Stephen, 'The Discipleship Controversy Three Years Later', *Charisma* (September 1978), 14-24.
—'Preface: An Open Letter to Derek Prince, Bob Mumford, Don Basham, Charles Simpson, and Ern Baxter', *Charisma* (September 1978), 8.
Sumrall, Ken, 'Letter to the Editor', *Ministries Today* (March/April 1990), 15.
Swaggart, Jimmy, 'Brother Jimmy Swaggart, Here's My Question: Is the Shepherding Movement a Viable Scriptural Discipleship Effort?', *Evangelist* (November 1986), 11-13.
Swindoll, Orville, 'The Dam Overflows In Argentina', *Logos Journal* (July/August 1974), 55-60.
Synan, Vinson, *The Holiness-Pentecostal Movement in the United States* (Grand Rapids: Eerdmans, 1971).
—*The Holiness-Pentecostal Tradition* (Grand Rapids: Eerdmans, 1997).
—'Kansas City Conference', in Burgess and McGee (eds.), *Dictionary*, 515.

—*In the Latter Days* (Ann Arbor, MI: Servant, 1991).

—*Launching the Decade of Evangelization* (South Bend, IN: North American Renewal Service Committee, 1990).

—'Reconciling the Charismatics', *Christianity Today* (9 April 1976), 46.

—*The Twentieth-Century Pentecostal Explosion* (Altamonte Springs, CA: Creation House, 1987).

—*Under His Banner: History of Full Gospel Businessmen's Fellowship International* (Costa Mesa, CA: Gift, 1992).

Thurman, Joyce, *New Wine Magazineskins: The Study of the House Church* (Frankfurt: Peter Lang, 1982).

Tipton, Steven M., *Getting Saved from the Sixties* (Berkeley: University of California Press, 1982).

Trudinger, Ron, *Cells for Life* (Plainfield, NJ: Olive Tree, 1979).

Trueblood, Elton, *The Company of the Committed* (New York: Harper & Row, 1961).

Van Engen, Charles, *God's Missionary People* (Grand Rapids: Baker Book House, 1991).

Verduin, Leonard, *The Reformers and their Stepchildren* (Grand Rapids: Eerdmans, 1964).

'Video Ministry News', *New Wine Magazine* (February 1972), 15.

Volf, Miroslav, *After Our Likeness: The Church as the Image of the Trinity* (Grand Rapids: Eerdmans, 1998).

Wagner, C. Peter, *Churchquake* (Ventura, CA: Regal Books, 1999).

—*The New Apostolic Churches* (Ventura, CA: Regal Books, 1998).

Walker, Andrew, *Restoring the Kingdom: The Radical Christianity of the House Church Movement* (London: Hodder & Stoughton, 1985).

Warner, Wayne, *Kathryn Kuhlman* (Ann Arbor, MI: Vine Books, 1993).

Warren, Rick, *The Purpose Driven Church* (Grand Rapids: Zondervan, 1995).

Waterman, David L., 'The Care and Feeding of Growing Christians', *Eternity* (September 1979), 17-21.

Watson, David, *Called and Committed: World-Changing Discipleship* (Wheaton, IL: Harold Shaw, 1982).

Webster, Douglas D., *Selling Jesus* (Downers Grove, IL: InterVarsity Press, 1992).

'What Really Happened at Minneapolis?', *Logos Journal* (November/December 1975), 58.

'Where Are "The Fort Lauderdale Five"?', *Charisma* (September 1998), 15.

Whitaker, Bob, 'Charismatic Leaders Meeting on "Discipleship"', *PCC Newsletter* (September/ October 1975), 5.

Widmark, Don, 'A Concept Whose Time Has Come', *New Wine Magazine* (January 1972), 24-25.

Willard, Dallas, *The Divine Conspiracy* (San Francisco: HarperCollins, 1998).

Williams, Yvonne, 'Discipleship Today', *Ministries Today* (March/April 1990), 62-67.

Wilson, Carl, *With Christ in the School of Disciple Building* (Grand Rapids: Zondervan, 1977).

Yeakley, Flavil (ed.), *The Discipling Dilemma* (Nashville, TN: Gospel Advocate, 1988).

Yoder, John Howard, *The Royal Priesthood* (Grand Rapids: Eerdmans, 1994).

Other Sources

Audiocassettes

Basham, Don, *About Being Involved* (Mobile, AL: n.p., 1980).

—*How Ministries Relate Beyond the Local Body* (National Men's Shepherds Conference; Kansas City: n.p., 1975).

—*Serving and Being Served* (West Coast Men's Conference; Ft Lauderdale: Christian Growth Ministries, 1977).

Basham, Don *et al.*, *Integrity Update* (Mobile, AL: Integrity Communications, 1984).

—*New Wine Magazine Fifteenth Anniversary* (Mobile, AL: Integrity Communications, 1984).

Baxter, Ern, *The Context of the Kingdom* (West Coast Men's Conference; Ft Lauderdale: Christian Growth Ministries, 1977).

—*Covenant Relationships Part 1* (n.p.: n.p., 1976).

—*Elder Meeting* (Ft Lauderdale: Audio Publications Service, 9 November 1975).

—*Elder Meeting* (Ft Lauderdale: Audio Publications Service, 23 November 1975).

—*Elder Meeting* (Ft Lauderdale: Audio Publications Service, 14 December 1975).

—*Elder Meeting: Part 1* (Ft Lauderdale: Audio Publications Service, 30 November 1975).

—*The Spirit and the Kingdom* (West Coast Men's Conference; Ft Lauderdale: Christian Growth Ministries, 1977).

—*The Structure and Submission in God* (N.p.: n.p., 1976).

—*Thy Kingdom Come* (National Men's Shepherds Conference; n.p.: His Men Tapes, 1975).

Baxter, Ern, and Bob Mumford, *Elders' Meeting* (Ft Lauderdale: Audio Publications Service, 9 November 1975).

—*Elders' Meeting: Part 1* (Ft Lauderdale: Audio Publications Service, 16 November 1975).

—*Elders' Meeting: Part 2* (Ft Lauderdale: Audio Publications Service, 30 November 1975).

Christenson, Larry, *That The World May Know* (National Men's Shepherds Conference; Kansas City, MO: n.p., 1975).

—*Welcome* (National Men's Shepherds Conference; San Pedro, CA: Trinity Tapes, n.d.).

Clark, Steve, *How to Exercise Authority* (National Men's Shepherds Conference; Kansas City, MO: n.p., 1975).

Forum (National Men's Shepherds Conference; Kansas City, MO: n.p., 24 September 1975).

Forum (National Men's Shepherds Conference; Kansas City, MO: n.p., 25 September 1975).

Forum (National Men's Shepherds Conference; Kansas City, MO: n.p., 26 September 1975).

Garlington, Joseph, *Our Covenant Heritage* (Mobile, AL: Integrity Communications, 1979).

Longstreth, Bruce, *Stewardship* (Christian Life Seminar; Mobile, AL: Bread of Life Tapes, n.d.).

Mahoney, Ralph, *What's Wrong With Discipleship?* (3 tapes; n.p.: *World MAP*, 1978).

Martin, Ralph, *The Church: A Counterculture* (National Men's Shepherds Conference; Kansas City, MO: n.p., 1975).

Mumford, Bob, *Christ's Victory in the Human Situation* (Shepherd of a Dark and Cloudy Day Series; Ft Lauderdale, FL: LifeChangers, 1973).

—*Concluding Session* (Leader's Conference; n.p.: n.p., 1979).

—*Decline/Dark Ages/Restoration of the Church, Part 1* (Leader's Meeting; Oklahoma City: n.p., 1977).

—*The Difference between Teaching and Training* (Spring Lake Park, MN: Springs of Living Water Tape Library, n.d.).

—*Fatherpower* (West Coast Men's Conference; Ft Lauderdale, FL: Christian Growth Ministries, 1977).

—*Folds and Flocks* (Sheep and Shepherds Series; Leesburg, FL: Westside Tape Ministry, n.d.).

—*God's Purpose with His People Today* (National Men's Shepherds Conference; Kansas City, MO: His Men Tapes, 1975).

—*God's Will for the Body of Christ* (Ft Lauderdale, FL: LifeChangers, 1975).

—*Grand Rapids Leaders Meeting* (n.p.: n.p., 1975).

—*How to Bring Forth New Leadership* (West Coast Men's Conference; Ft Lauderdale: Christian Growth Ministries, 1977).

—*Knowing Authority and Submission* (Spring Lake Park, MN: Springs of Living Water Tape Library, n.d.).

—*Making a Man of God* (Making Men of God; Albuquerque, NM: Hosanna, 1973).

—*The Nature of Covenant* (Ft Lauderdale, FL: LifeChangers, 1979).

—*Need for Soul Doctors* (Making Men of God; Albuquerque, NM: Hosanna, 1973).

—*Power of an Honest Testimony* (Sheep and Shepherds Series; Leesburg, FL: Westside Tape Ministry, n.d.).

—*Religious Politics* (Shepherd of a Dark and Cloudy Day Series; Ft Lauderdale, FL: Life-Changers, 1973).

—*Safety Factors* (Santa Rosa, CA: Spreading His Name, 1978).

—*Seeing the Body of Christ* (Sheep and Shepherds Series; Leesburg, FL: Westside Tape Ministry, n.d.).

—*Sheep and Shepherds* (Sheep and Shepherds Series; Leesburg, FL: Westside Tape Ministry, n.d.).

—*Shepherd of a Dark and Cloudy Day* (5 tapes; Ft Lauderdale: LifeChangers, n.d.).

—*The Shepherd: Part 1, Part 2* (COM Community Conference; n.p.: n.p., 1979).

—*Spiritual Authority* (Spring Lake Park, MN: Springs of Living Water Tape Library, n.d.).

—*Spiritual Authority: Tape 2* (Shepherds Conference—Montreal; Leesburg, FL: Westside Tape Ministry, 1974).

—*Things I Have Learned* (Raleigh, NC: LifeChangers, 1991).

—*Understanding Discipleship: Part 1, Part 2, Part 3, Part 4* (Raleigh, NC: LifeChangers, n.d.).

—*Walk* (n.p.: n.p., 1975).

—*Wheel in the Middle of the Wheel* (Making Men of God; Albuquerque, NM: Hosanna, 1973).

Mumford, Bob, Ray Ostendorf and Jim Croft, *Men's Meeting* (Raleigh, NC: LifeChangers, 1979).

Mumford, Bob, and Derek Prince, *Change of Local Authority* (n.p.: n.p., 1976).

Murrillo, Mario, *Discipleship* (Los Angeles: n.p., 1975).

Petrie, Paul, *Serving* (n.p.: n.p., n.d.).

Poole, John, *How Shepherds Relate in a Local Body* (National Men's Shepherds Conference; Kansas City, MO: n.p., 1975).

Prince, Derek, *Apostles and Shepherds* (4 tapes; Charlotte, NC: Derek Prince Ministries, 1984).

—*Barriers to Healing* (Montreat: Christian Believers United, 1989).

—*The Chief Shepherd and His Undershepherds (1)* (Apostles and Shepherds; Charlotte, NC: Derek Prince Ministries, n.d.).

—*The Chief Shepherd and His Undershepherds (2)* (Apostles and Shepherds; Charlotte, NC: Derek Prince Ministries, n.d.).

—*Covenant Ligaments* (Mentor: Maranatha Ministries, n.d.).

—*Ligaments* (n.p.: n.p., n.d.).

—*Presbyteries and Apostolic Teams (1)* (Apostles and Shepherds; Charlotte, NC: Derek Prince Ministries, n.d.).

—*Presbyteries and Apostolic Teams (2)* (Apostles and Shepherds; Charlotte, NC: Derek Prince Ministries, n.d.).

—*Relationship of Apostles and Elders to the Local Church* (n.p.: n.p., 1973).

—*Update No. 40.*

—*The Vision of the Completed Body* (National Men's Shepherds Conference; Kansas City, MO: n.p., 1975).

—*What Are Shepherds? Qualifications, Function* (n.p.: n.p., 1973).

Ranaghan, Kevin, *Covenant Love* (National Men's Shepherds Conference; Kansas City, MO: n.p., 1975).

Simpson, Charles, *A 30-Year History of the Covenant Movement: Part 1 and Part 2* (Mobile, AL: Charles Simpson Ministries, 1990).

—*All In The Family* (Mobile, AL: Charles Simpson Ministries, n.d.).

—*The Army of God* (Mobile, AL: Charles Simpson Ministries, n.d.).

—*Baptism, Deliverance and Healing* (Christian Life Seminar; Mobile, AL: Bread of Life Tapes, n.d.).

—*The Blessings of Obedience* (Christian Life Seminar; Mobile, AL: Bread of Life Tapes, n.d.).

—*Building a Model Church* (San Francisco: Antioch Fellowship Tapes, 1982).

—*Building a Nation* (Mobile, AL: Charles Simpson Ministries, 1980).

—*Building a Redeemed Community* (Mobile, AL: Integrity Communications, n.d.).

—*The Challenge to Care* (4 tapes; Mobile, AL: Charles Simpson Ministries, 1987).

—*Challenge of Leadership* (Mobile, AL: Charles Simpson Ministries, n.d.).

—*Councils and Presbyteries* (Leadership Conference; Oklahoma City: n.p., 1979).

—*The Covenant Life Seminar* (10 tapes; Mobile, AL: Charles Simpson Ministries, 1977).

—*Covenant Relationships* (Christian Life Seminar; Mobile, AL: Bread of Life Tapes, n.d.).

—*Discipleship* (Spring Lake Park, MN: Springs of Living Water Tape Library, 1971).

—*Facing Your Options as Disciples* (Practical Discipleship; Mobile, AL: Charles Simpson Ministries, n.d.).

—*Family Relationships* (Christian Life Seminar; Mobile, AL: Bread of Life Tapes, n.d.).

—*Fellowship* (Spring Lake Park, MN: Springs of Living Water Tape Library, 1971).

—*For Those Who Care for You* (Mobile, AL: Charles Simpson Ministries, n.d.).

—*God's Basis for Promotion* (Ft Lauderdale: Recommended Tapes from Bob Mumford, n.d.).

—*The Gospel of the Kingdom Of God* (Christian Life Seminar; Mobile, AL: Bread of Life Tapes, n.d.).

—*How Shepherds Relate to Other Shepherds* (Mobile, AL: Charles Simpson Ministries, 1973).

—*How to Enter into Covenant* (Christian Life Seminar; Mobile, AL: Bread of Life Tapes, n.d.).

—*Instruction to Women* (N.p: n.p., 1977).

—*Internal Integrity, External Integration of Structures* (Mobile, AL: Charles Simpson Ministries, 1981).

—*Jesus, King of Kings* (San Francisco: His Name Ministries, 1978).

—*Kingdom Soil* (West Coast Men's Conference; Ft Lauderdale, FL: Christian Growth Ministries, 1977).

—*Loyalty—The Salt of Covenant* (Mobile, AL: Charles Simpson Ministries, n.d.).

—*My Personal Testimony* (Mobile, AL: Charles Simpson Ministries, n.d.).

—*The Nature and Responsibilities* (Big Spring: Tomy Franklin, 1990).

—*The Need for Shepherds* (National Men's Shepherds Conference; Kansas City, MO: n.p., 1975).

—*Process of Making Disciples: Part 1* (Practical Discipleship; Mobile, AL: Charles Simpson Ministries, n.d.).

—*Process of Making Disciples: Part 2* (Practical Discipleship; Mobile, AL: Charles Simpson Ministries, n.d.).

—*Process of Making Disciples: Part 3* (Practical Discipleship; Mobile, AL: Charles Simpson Ministries, n.d.).

—*Qualifications for Making Disciples* (Practical Discipleship; Mobile, AL: Charles Simpson Ministries, n.d.).

—*Repentance and Faith* (Christian Life Seminar; Mobile, AL: Bread of Life Tapes, n.d.).

—*Results of Discipleship* (Practical Discipleship; Mobile, AL: Charles Simpson Ministries, n.d.).

—*The Rewards and Responsibilities of Leadership* (Mobile, AL: Charles Simpson Ministries, n.d.).
—*Serving and Honoring* (Christian Life Seminar; Mobile, AL: Bread of Life Tapes, n.d.).
—*The Shepherd Principle* (Mobile, AL: Charles Simpson Ministries, 1973).
—*A Southern Baptist Pastor Looks At Pentecost* (Spring Lake Park, MN: Springs of Living Water Tape Library, n.d.).
—*Spiritual Discernment* (West Coast Men's Conference; Ft Lauderdale: Christian Growth Ministries, 1977).
—*Through Many Dangers, Toils and Snares* (Mobile, AL: Charles Simpson Ministries, 1996).
—*What is the Role of a Shepherd?* (Big Spring: Tommy Franklin, 1990).
—*Worship* (Spring Lake Park, MN: Springs of Living Water Tape Library, 1971).

Interviews

Arnold, Hap. Telephone interview with author, 26 February 1996.
Basham, Alice. Telephone interview with author, 14 February 1996.
—Telephone interview with author, 10 September 1998.
Baxter, Ruth. Telephone interview with author, 21 February 1996.
Beckett, John. Telephone interview with author, 14 March 1996.
Bohl, Don. Telephone interview with author, 22 February 1996.
Bradford, Brick. Telephone interview with author, 12 January 1996.
—Telephone interview with author, 23 October 1998.
Bredesen, Harald. Telephone interview with author, 8 December 1998.
—Telephone interview with author, 10 December 1998.
Burks, Ron. Telephone interview with author, 12 January 1996.
Carlton, Rich. Telephone interview with author, 12 September 1998.
Christenson, Larry. Telephone interview with author, 11 January 1996.
—Telephone interview with author, 23 October 1998.
Clark, Steve. Telephone interview with author, 3 February 1996.
Coleman, Mike. Telephone interview with author, 21 February 1996.
Coombs, Barney. Telephone interview with author, 31 January 1996.
Croft, Jim. Telephone interview with author, 3 January 1996.
Duke, John. Telephone interview with author, 14 March 1996.
Fast, Wayne. Telephone interview with author, 25 August 1998.
Frank, Neil. Telephone interview with author, 14 October 1998.
Garlington, Joseph. Telephone interview with author, 23 April 1998.
Grant, Robert. Telephone interview with author, 11 January 1999.
Gustafson, Gerrit. Telephone interview with author, 25 January 1996.
Hayford, Jack. Personal interview with author, 30 January 1984.
Hensley, James, and Beth Hensley. Personal interview with author, 30 July 1998.
Jackson, Jim. Telephone interview with author, 26 August 1998.
Kemp, Janet. Telephone interview with author, 13 April 1996.
Key, Dick. Personal interview with author, 27 November 1995.
—Personal interview with author, 30 December 1995.
Leggatt, Dick. Telephone interview with author, 1 March 1996.
—Telephone interview with author, 10 September 1998.
Longstreth, Bruce. Telephone interview with author, 29 December 1995.
Martin, Ralph. Telephone interview with author, 8 December 1998.
—Telephone interview with author, 23 December 1998.

Mayne, Bill. Telephone interview with author, 28 December 1998.
Monroe, Tom. Telephone interview with author, 23 February 1996.
Mumford, Bob. Telephone interview with author, 7 April 1992.
—Personal interview with author, 1 October 1994.
—Personal interview with author, 2 October 1994.
—Personal interview with author, 9 February 1996.
—Personal interview with author, 10 February 1996.
—Personal interview with author, 30 July 1998.
—Personal interview with author, 31 July 1998.
—Telephone interview with author, 23 December 1998.
Norwood, John. Telephone interview with author, 5 March 1996.
Ortiz, Juan Carlos. Telephone interview with author, 22 February 1996.
Raitt, Ed. Telephone interview with author, 26 February 1996.
Ranaghan, Kevin. Telephone interview with author, 14 March 1996.
—Telephone interview with author, 30 November 1998.
Reed, Mike. Telephone interview with author, 27 March 1996.
Roachelle, Glen. Telephone interview with author, 11 January 1999.
—Telephone interview with author, 12 January 1999.
Ross, Scott. Personal interview with author, 7 February 1996.
—Personal interview with author, 8 February 1996.
—Personal interview with author, 10 October 1998.
—Telephone interview with author, 19 February 1996.
Selby, David. Telephone interview with author, 17 November 1998.
Simpson, Charles. Personal interview with author, 3 August 1998.
—Personal interview with author, 5 August 1998.
—Telephone interview with author, 5 February 1996.
—Telephone interview with author, 8 February 1996.
—Telephone interview with author, 21 February 1996.
—Telephone interview with author, 23 February 1996.
—Telephone interview with author, 26 February 1996.
—Telephone interview with author, 9 April 1996.
—Telephone interview with author, 12 January 1998.
—Telephone interview with author, 18 December 1998.
Simpson, Steve. Personal interview with author, 6 August 1998.
—Telephone interview with author, 18 January 1996.
Sumrall, Ken. Telephone interview with author, 2 November 1998.
Sutton, Bob. Telephone interview with author, 19 January 1996.
—Telephone interview with author, 26 February 1996.
Synan, Vinson. Telephone interview with author, 14 February 1996.
Whitaker, Bob. Telephone interview with author, 11 January 1996.
Williams, Dick. Personal interview with author, 28 February 1996.
Williams, J. Rodman. Telephone interview with author, 8 December 1998.

Record
Sanchez, Pete, *It Filled the Land* (Bread of Life and Southeast Texas Fellowship, 1977). Album.

Unpublished Sources

Ad Hoc Meeting of the General Council. 31 March–1 April 1978. St Louis, MO.

Articles of Incorporation and Bylaws of the Good News Fellowship Church, Inc. July 1974.

Basham, Don (*et al.*), Letter to Derek Prince, 6 September 1977.

—Letter to John Beckett, 4 September 1975.

—Statement of Intent, July 1980.

Basham, Don, and Derek Prince, Thoughts from Derek and Don to Share at the 19–23 March Teacher's Meeting in Mobile, 1978.

Baxter, Ern, Letter to Bob Beckett (*et al.*), 29 August 1975.

—Letter to Charles Simpson, 3 September 1987.

—Letter to Charles Simpson, 18 May 1987.

—A personal message from Ern Baxter, n.d.

—Transcript of 'Thy Kingdom Come' message delivered at the National Men's Shepherds Conference, 1975, Holy Spirit Research Center, Oral Roberts University, Tulsa, OK

Baxter, Ern, and Bob Mumford, Transcript of Elders' Meeting, 16 November 1975.

Baxter, Ruth, Letter to David Moore, 13 May 1996.

Bradford, Brick, Confidential Announcement, 1976 Charismatic Leaders Seminar, Oklahoma City, 30 September 1975.

—Letter to Bob Mumford, 16 March 1976.

—Letter to Participants in National Discussion on 'Shepherding', 29 August 1975.

—Newsletter, 12 November 1975.

Bredesen, Harald, Letter to David du Plessis, 9 June 1976. David du Plessis Collection, David du Plessis Archive. Fuller Theological Seminary.

Christenson, Larry, Letter to Charismatic Leaders, 29 September 1975.

Christenson, Larry, Steven B. Clark and Kevin Ranaghan, Letter to Editor of *Logos Journal*, n.d.

Clark, Steve B., Official Minutes of the 'National Discussion on Shepherding', 9–10 August 1975.

—'Our Relationship with the "Council"', February 1978.

Conference Brochure, 1975 National Men's Shepherds Conference.

Conference with Christian Growth Representatives and Assembly of God Ministers, 25–26 April 1977.

Croft, Jim, Letter to Charles Simpson, 9 February 1983.

du Plessis, David, Letter to Don Malachuk, 10 July 1975. David du Plessis Collection, David du Plessis Archive, Fuller Theological Seminary.

—Note to Kevin Ranaghan on 1977 Charismatic Leaders Conference Registration Form, 15 April 1977.

Ervin, Howard M., Letter to Derek Prince, 27 September 1976.

—Letter to Kevin Ranaghan, 12 April 1976.

Farah, Charles, Jr, 'A Modest Plea for Unity', Holy Spirit Research Center, Oral Roberts University, Tulsa, OK, 1975.

Fast, Wayne, Statement by Wayne Fast, 26 June 1975.

Fundraising case for *New Wine Magazine*, Memorandum 1984 (Mobile, AL: Integrity Communications).

Gulf Coast Covenant Church, 'A Statement of Information', handout, n.d. Gulf Coast Covenant Church, Florida.

Hayford, Jack W., Letter to Charles Simpson, 19 October 1984.

—Letter to Charles Simpson, 28 January 1985.

—Letter to Kevin Ranaghan, 27 April 1976.
Heard, John, Letter to Demos Shakarian, 30 October 1975.
Hewitt, William D., 'A Feasibility Study for Launching Fundraising Campaign', January 1985.
Hymers, R.L., 'The Mumford Cult', handout, n.d.
Hymers, R.L., and Kent Philpott, 'Why We Reject Simpsonism and Mumfordism', pamphlet, n.d., Christian Research Center.
Ivey, George, 'Charismatic Cults', handout, n.d.
List of Regional Councils, 21 November 1982.
Lutheran Charismatic Renewal Services, Public Statement, n.d.
Mahoney, Ralph, Letter to Bob Mumford and Judy Mumford, 24 May 1978.
—Letter to Bob Mumford and Judy Mumford, 26 November 1975.
Matzat, Don, 'A Critique of Cell Group Discipleship', pamphlet, n.d.
McDonnell, Kilian, Letter to Bob Mumford, 20 February 1979.
Memo to all International Directors, Field Representatives and Chapter Officers, 12 January 1976.
Minutes of Ecumenical Council, 5 February 1985.
Minutes of Ecumenical Council Meeting, 25–27 February 1983.
Minutes of the Meeting of the Council, 8–10 September 1974.
Minutes of the Meeting of the Council, 10–12 August 1975.
Minutes of the Meeting of the Council, 15–17 December 1974.
Minutes of the Meeting of the Council, 27 September 1975.
Minutes of the Meeting of the Council, 3–7 January 1977, Ft Lauderdale.
Minutes of General Council Meeting, 8–10 August 1977, Ann Arbor.
Minutes of the General Council, Held during Pilgrimage, May/June 1977.
Minutes of the Five Teachers' Meeting, 21, 23 June 1978.
Minutes of the Five Teachers' Meeting, 12–14 November 1981, Mobile, AL.
Minutes of the Integrity Communication Board Meeting, 16 January 1985.
Mumford, Bob, 'Disciple Position Paper', unpublished paper, 1976.
—Handwritten Notes of San Diego Teachers Meeting, n.d.
—Handwritten Notes of Seattle Teachers Meeting, n.d.
—Letter to Kathryn Kuhlman, 19 October 1975.
—Letter to Lonnie Frisbee, Bob Grant, Dick Key, Mario Murillo, Duane Peterson, Mike Reed, Roy Rempt, Bob Sworde, 21 July 1971.
—Letter to Pat Robertson, 9 September 1975.
—Letter to Rev. and Mrs Pat Robertson, 7 July 1993.
—Meeting with Ralph Mahoney, n.d.
—Memorandum to Barney Coombs (*et al.*), 12 May 1980.
—Notes from Meeting with Dennis Bennett, 5 December 1975.
—Notes from the Minneapolis Meeting, 9–10 August 1975.
—'A Personal Word from Bob Mumford', personal newsletter, 1974, Ft Lauderdale.
—Position Paper, Strategy Meeting, 3–5 May 1978, Santa Rosa.
—'Principles of Relationship', 1975.
—Public Statement Concerning Discipleship, 1 November 1989.
—Special newsletter, Fall 1975.
Murphy, James O., Report on the 1975 National Men's Shepherds Conference, 23–26 September 1975, Kansas City, MO (Virginia Beach, VA: Christian Broadcasting Network).
Notes from the Planning Committee Meeting, 24–25 January 1977. David du Plessis Collection, David du Plessis Archive, Fuller Theological Seminary.

Petrie, Paul, 'Community Architecture', handout, n.d.

Prince, Derek (Ministries), Derek Prince's Remarks after Bob Mumford's Letter of Repentance, November 1989.

Prince, Derek, Doctrinal paper, February 1983.

—Letter to Charles Simpson (with attachments), 18 October 1977.

—Letter to Charles Simpson, 9 April 1979.

—Letter to Charles Simpson, 12 February 1983.

—Letter to Dick Zollor, 8 September 1975.

—Letter to Kevin Ranaghan, 12 April 1976.

—Letter to Roy Harthern, 31 October 1977.

—Outline Reply to Letter Dated 27 September 1976, n.d.

—Suggested Course Corrections, n.d.

—Unaddressed confidential letter, 28 March 1984.

Prince, Derek, and Lydia Prince, A Personal Letter from Derek and Lydia Prince—Joska! Holy Spirit Research Center, Oral Roberts University, Tulsa, OK, March 1968.

—A Personal Letter from Derek and Lydia Prince, Holy Spirit Research Center, Oral Roberts University, Tulsa, OK, January 1969.

The Proposed Plan of Action for Integrity Communications, Gulf Coast Covenant Church, and Charles Simpson Ministries, n.d.

Purvis, Eldon, 'Notice to Members of the Body of Christ in Pompano Beach, Hollywood, and Ft Lauderdale', n.d. Holy Spirit Research Center, Oral Roberts University, Tulsa, OK.

Ranaghan, Kevin, Minutes of the First Meeting of the Charismatic Concerns Committee, 12 March 1976, Oklahoma City.

Report on the 1976 Charismatic Leaders' Conference, 8–12 March 1976, Oklahoma City.

Roachelle, Glen, 'Chronology' (unpublished paper, 1978).

—Letter to the Charismatic Concerns Committee: Attention Kevin Ranaghan, 30 April 1980.

—Letter to Charles Simpson, 1 October 1993.

—Letter to Pat Robertson, 5 March 1980.

Robertson, Pat, Letter to Bob Mumford, 27 June 1975.

—Letter to Bob Mumford, 15 September 1975.

—Letter to Derek Prince, 13 August 1975.

—Letter to Glen Roachelle, 25 March 1980.

—Letter to Guy Kump, 20 March 1980.

—Letter to Harold Zimmerman, 15 July 1975.

—Letter to Pat Robertson, 5 March 1980.

—Memo to Area Directors and all CBN staff, 20 May 1975.

—Memo to John Gillman and Eric AuCoin, 22 May 1975.

—Memo to Ray Harrelson, Bob Slosser, Tucker Yates, Harald Bredesen, D. Roberts, 30 August 1982, Regent University.

Ross, Scott, Notes from Minneapolis Meeting, 9–10 August 1975.

—Personal Conference Notes, 2–4 March 1996.

—'Spiritual POWs' (unpublished paper, 1995).

Saturday Morning Session Kemper Arena, Parts 1 and 2. Non-denominational Conference on Charismatic Renewal 1977.

Schenkel, Erick, Proposal for Co-operative Seminars with Rousas Rushdooney, 10 March 1980.

Simpson, Charles, 'Another Kind of Storm' (unpublished paper, 1979).

—'Charles Simpson Forms Ministerial Association', Press release, 6 March 1987.

—Confidential letter to Hugo Zelaya (*et al.*), 15 August 1977.

—'A Covenant' (unpublished paper, 1980).
—Larger Christian Leadership Configuration, 1981.
—Letter to Cardinal Suenens, 10 January 1978.
—Letter to Carolyn Rodman, 18 September 1974.
—Letter to Chuck Farrah, 8 May 1975.
—Letter to Dan Malachuk, 22 May 1974.
—Letter to Dan Malachuk, 8 January 1975.
—Letter to Dennis Bennett, 2 September 1975.
—Letter to Derek Prince, 11 March 1977.
—Letter to Derek Prince, 2 March 1978.
—Letter to Dick Coleman, 20 July 1972.
—Letter to Dick Coleman, 25 September 1975.
—Letter to Dick Coleman (*et al.*), 3 April 1975.
—Letter to Don Basham, Ern Baxter, Bob Mumford, and Derek Prince, 23 August 1982.
—Letter to the elders of Gulf Coast Covenant Church, March 1983.
—Letter to Ern Baxter, 15 February 1985.
—Letter to Ern Baxter, Bob Mumford, and Don Basham, 30 December 1985.
—Letter to Fellowship Committee of Mobile Baptist Association, 30 October 1967.
—Letter to friends, 29 May 1972.
—Letter to Gary Browning, 2 October 1973.
—Letter to Glen Roachelle (*et al.*), 17 February 1975.
—Letter to Harald Bredesen, 10 January 1975.
—Letter to Harold Alexander, 7 February 1971.
—Letter to Jack Long, 12 December 1974.
—Letter to Jim Reid (*et al.*), 15 August 1975.
—Letter to John Duke, 7 February 1971.
—Letter to John Duke, 29 March 1971.
—Letter to John Duke, 15 June 1971.
—Letter to John Duke, 3 November 1971.
—Letter to Kevin Ranaghan, 13 August 1976.
—Letter to Larry Christenson, 30 November 1976.
—Letter to Melvin Clark (*et al.*), 10 November 1978.
—Letter to Melvin Clark (*et al.*), 23 October 1982.
—Letter to Melvin Clark (*et al.*), March 1983.
—Letter to Merton L. Jannusch, 24 November 1975.
—Letter to Olive Heath and Mary Louise Heath, 28 May 1974.
—Letter to Pat Robertson, 23 June 1975.
—Letter to Pat Robertson, 28 August 1975.
—Letter to Pat Robertson, 13 February 1980.
—Letter to Ralph Mahoney, 25 August 1977.
—Letter to Steve Clark, 17 August 1973.
—Letter to Terry Parker (*et al.*), 4 August 1977.
—Letter to Tom Ashcraft, 12 August 1974.
—Letter to Wayne Myers, 25 August 1975.
—Memo to Don Basham, 4 August 1982.
—Memo on Kansas City, 10 March 1977.
—Memo to the National Council, 13 August 1979.
—An Open Pastoral Letter, 2 September 1986.

—A Pastoral Letter from Charles Simpson, July 1998.
—Personal newsletter, 1972.
—Personal newsletter, Christmas 1972.
—Personal newsletter, 1975.
—Personal newsletter, Fall 1976.
—Personal newsletter, Christmas 1976.
—Report of Meeting with my Direct Relationships and Local Elders, 26–28 August 1975.
—Report on Meeting with Jimmy Swaggart, n.d.
—Statement to Bayview Heights, October 1970.
—Statement Made to Fellowship BVHBC, 3 February 1974.
—Structure Charts One Through Three, 1981.
A Statement of Information, Ann Arbor, 17 December 1975.
A Statement of Information, Gulf Coast Covenant Church, n.d.
Suggested Conduct for the Kansas City Conference, n.d.
'Summary of Discussions at Conference of Charismatic Leaders', Minutes of meeting. April 30–May 1973, David du Plessis Archive, Fuller Theological Seminary.
'Summary of Discussions at Conference of Charismatic Leaders', Minutes of meeting, 5–9 May 1974, David du Plessis Archive, Fuller Theological Seminary.
Summary of Integrity and New Wine Magazine Operations, 1983 through 1986.
Sumrall, Ken, Letter to Charles Simpson, 27 May 1977.
'Tape Excerpts of the Five Teachers', handout, 9–10 August 1975.
Transcription of 'How Ministries Relate Beyond the Local Church'. Message delivered at the National Men's Shepherds Conference, September 1975. Holy Spirit Research Center, Oral Roberts University, Tulsa, OK.
Transcription of Pat Robertson's Accusation, 700 Club Broadcast, 7 January 1980.
'What Are the Distinctives of the Covenant Movement?', n.d.
Whitaker, Bob, Letter to Brick Bradford and Doug Brewer, 28 July 1975.
—Notes from Minneapolis Meeting, 9–10 August 1975.
—Notes from Oklahoma Meeting, 8–12 March 1975.

Videocassettes

Basham, Don, *Interview on 700 Club* (Virginia Beach, CA: Christian Broadcast Network, 1987).
Baxter, Ern, *Charles Simpson Interviews Ern Baxter* (Mobile, AL: Charles Simpson Ministries, 1988).
—*Conversations with Dr Ern Baxter*, Part 1, Part 2, Part 3 and Part 4 (New York: Laseredit East, 1992).
—*Quiet Talks: Tape 1* (Allenwood: Shore Christian Center Church, n.d.).
—*Quiet Talks: Tape 2* (Allenwood: Shore Christian Center Church, n.d.).

INDEX OF NAMES

Altizer, T.J.J. 17
Arnold, H. 51
Ashcraft, T. 92, 101, 108
Ashcroft, B. 101

Baker, R. 161
Banks, R. 188
Barna, G. 190
Barrett, D. 6
Barrs, J. 158, 159
Barzun, J. 7, 8
Basham, A. 33-35, 37, 42, **170**
Basham, D. 1-3, 6, 7, 11, 12, 24-35, **34**,
    40, 41, 45, 47-52, 54, 57, 58, 66, 68,
    71, 75, 79-81, 85, 87, 90, 94, 96,
    101, 103-106, 125, **126**, 131, 135,
    137-40, 143, 145-47, 149-51, 153,
    159-64, **166**, 168-70, **170**, 180, 183,
    184
Baxter, E. 1, 2, 7, 24, **34**, 36, 37, 42, 45,
    64-66, 68-72, 74, 77, 80-82, 84, 85,
    87, 94, 103, 106, **126**, 129, 131,
    133, 135, 139, 140, 143, 145, 147,
    149, 151-53, 159, 162-64, **166**, 168-
    72, **171**, 176, 182-84
Baxter, M. 36
Baxter, R. 36, 37, 171, 172
Beckett, J. 58, 68
Beckham, W.A. 188
Beiser, C. 159
Bellah, R. 153
Bennett, D. 3, 22, 24, 26, 31, 48, 90, 92,
    95, 101-104, 106, 114-17, 121, 123,
    160, 173
Bentson, K. 58
Berry, M. 136
Birkey, D. 188
Bloech, D.G. 86

Bohl, D. 27
Bradford, B. 90, 96, 97, 101-105, 115-17,
    121, 123, 128, 184, 185
Bradley, J. 8
Branham, W. 36
Bredesen, H. 3, 26, 34, 48, 89, 95, 101-
    103, 120
Brewer, D. 97, 101
Brock, P. 100
Buckingham, J. 33, 96, 97, 101, 102, 104,
    107, 110, 111, 115, 116, 158, 173
Burks, R. 11, 46
Burks, V. 11, 46
Butchard, W. 155

Carlton, R. 171
Carter, H. 147
Carter, J. 20, 105
Cerullo, M. 145
Chandler, R. 119
Christenson, L. 86, 97, 99, 101, 105, 110,
    115-18, 125-27, **126**, 130, 131, 137,
    160, 161
Chrnalogar, M.A. 185
Cimino, R. 189
Clapp, R. 153, 189
Clark, S.B. 24, 63, 64, 100-103, 105, 115,
    116, 122, 125-27, **126**, 130-32, 136,
    137, 161
Coleman, D. 61, 62
Coleman, M. 147, 163
Coleman, R.E. 73
Collins, R.M. 17
Comiskey, J. 188
Coombs, B. 147
Copeland, K. 159
Cornwall, J. 94, 134, 135, 160
Cox, H. 17

Crabb, L. 189
Croft, J. 68, 139, 140, 142, 143, 165, 166

DeCelles, P. 101, 125, **126**, 131, 137, 161
Derstine, G. 101
Digitale, R. 6
Duke, B. 175
Duke, J. 59, 151, 175
DuBose, F.M. 4, 11, 20, 21, 181, 182
Du Plessis, D. 26, 31, 32, 38, 48, 49, 95,
     99, 110, 116-18, 120, 155, 159, 160
Durnbaugh, D. 71

Ellwood, R.S. 19, 20
Enroth, R. 159
Ervin, H.M. 116, 119-21
Escobar, G. 138
Ewing, R. 100

Farah, C. 111, 112, 116, 119, 121, 140,
     160
Farber, D. 16, 17
Fast, W. 93-95, 100
Fee, G. 190, 191
Fesperman, J. 92
Fjordbak, E. 101
Ford, M. 168
Frank, N. 26-29, 31, 54
Frisbee, L. 50, **51**
Frost, R. 133, 134
Fullam, E. 116

Gallup, G. 20
Garlington, J. 144, 151, 152
Gelder, C. von 191
George, C.F. 188, 189
Getz, G.A. 86
Ghezzi, B. 37, 38, 50
Giles, K. 189
Girard, R.C. 86
Gittlin, T. 17
Gothard, B. 86
Graff, H.F. 7, 8
Graham, B. 65
Grant, R. 50, **51**, 140, 142, 143, 162
Gustafson, G. 50, 53, 59, 146

Hadaway, K. 4, 11, 20, 21, 181, 182

Hagee, J. 142
Hagin, K. 159
Hamann, J. 154
Hamilton, W. 17
Harper, M. 3, 7, 47, 48, 123, 154, 184
Harrell, D.E. 23, 39, 105, 108
Hart, L. 159
Harthern, R. 154
Hauerwas, S. 191
Haus, R. 159, 160
Hawn, R.H. 101, 135
Hayford, J.W. 23, 97, 110, 112, 113, 120,
     122, 123, 172, 183, 185-87
Haythorne-Thwaite, B. 54
Heard, J. 107, 108
Hensley, B. 145
Hensley, J. 145
Hewitt, W.D. 167
Hitt, R.T. 159
Hocken, P. 22, 24, 48, 158
Howard, L. 40, 161
Hughes, R. 83
Hunsburger, G. 191
Hybels, B. 190
Hymers, R.L. 144

Iverson, D. 185

Jackson, J. 158
Jahr, M.A. 42
Johnson, L. 16
Jones, B. 147
Jones, E.S. 69
Jones, J. 156, 157

Kay, N. 162
Kelly, D.M. 19
Kemp, J. 97
Kennedy, J. 16
Kennedy, J.F. 18
Kennedy, R. 16
Kenneson, P.D. 190
Kerr, G. 142
Key, D. 50, **51**, 54, 58, 59, 89, 139, 140,
     142, 143, 162
King, M.L. 16, 82
Kuhlman, K. 110, 111

Ladd, G.E. 81
Lamb, R.P. 158
Leggatt, D. 35, 143, 170
Lench, R. 101
LeSourd, L. 96, 97, 110, 121
Ligon, N. 158
Locke, D. 101, 106
Longstreth, B. 53, 141
Luttin, D. 189

MacDonald, G. 159
MacNutt, F. 64
Mahoney, R. 9, 24, 113, 114, 133, 134,
    155, 156
Mains, D. 86
Malachuk, D. 3, 24, 89, 97, 99, 101, 104,
    105, 110-12, 116, 130
Manuel, D. 135
Marius, R. 9
Martin, R. 24, 63, 64, 101, 105, 125-27,
    126, 131, 132, 136-38, 160, 161
Mayne, B. 107
McCartney, B. 138
McCarty, A. 93-95, 100
McDonnell, K. 2, 3, 10, 37, 79, 80, 116-
    19, 121, 127, 154, 184
McGrath, A. 7
McLaren, B.D. 189
Miles, H. 158
Miller, E. 159
Monroe, T. 27, 31, 46, 93
Moore, C. 135
Moore, S.D. 10, 31, 47, 89, 92, 93, 96,
    106, 110, 112, 113, 115, 119, 134,
    140, 155, 160, 173
Muller, R.A. 8
Mumford, B. 1, 2, 7, 10, 13, 14, 24, 27-
    32, **34**, 35, 37-45, 47, 48, 50-58, **51**,
    61-63, 65, 66, 68-87, 89-100, 103,
    106-118, 121-23, **126**, 128, 131-35,
    131, **133**, 137-40, 142, 143, 145,
    147-51, 153-56, 158-64, **166**, 168,
    169, 172-74, **172**, 179, 180, 182-85,
    189
Mumford, J. 38
Munsey, G. 25
Murillo, M. 50, 90
Murphy, C. 138

Murphy, J.O. 129, 130

Nee, W. 55, 58
Neighbor, R.W. 188
Newbigin, L. 149
Nixon, R. 16, 18, 20
Noll, M. 16, 18, 20
Nolte, R. 136

O'Conner, E. 22
Ortiz, J.C. 58, 85, 101, 112, 160
Ostendorf, R. 93, 139, 162

Paloma, M. 2, 9, 19, 84
Parker, T. 59
Peacocke, D. 142, 143
Peterson, D. 20, 50
Pethybridge, W.J. 52
Petrie, P. 50, **51**, 140, 142, 143, 162
Pfotenhauer, D. 101, 125, **126**, 161
Phillips, S. 52, 60, 61, 88, 90, 92, 144
Philpott, K. 144
Plowman, E.E. 3, 19, 20, 99, 112
Poole, J. 64, 65, 94, 131, 158
Prince, D. 1, 2, 7, 23, 24, 27-32, **34**, 35,
    37, 39-42, 45, 47, 49, 51, 53-58, 62,
    63, 66, 68, 69, 71, 76, 77, 80, 81,
    83, 84, 87, 89-92, 94, 96, 101, 102,
    106, 108, 115, 116, 120, 124, 125,
    126, 131, 135, 137, 139, 140, 142,
    143, 146, 147, 149, 150, 154, 161,
    163-66, 169, 174, 175, 180, 183,
    184
Prince, L. 39, 40, 161
Prince, R. 39, 40, 48, 175
Pulkington, W.G. 86
Purvis, E. 11, 25, 26-29, 31, 32, 38, 42,
    47, 51, 90, 180
Purvis, N. 25

Quebedeaux, R. 2, 17-19, 22, 23, 43, 47,
    48

Raitt, E. 52
Ranaghan, K. 22, 24, 100, 101, 105, 116,
    118, 120, 125-27, **126**, 129-34, 137,
    157, 160, 161
Reagan, R. 20, 146

Reed, M. 50, **51**
Rempt, R. 50, **51**
Richards, L.O. 85
Roachelle, G. 12, 31, 59, 63, 88, 129, 140, 141, 144, 157, 161, 177
Robertson, P. 3, 9, 24, 49, 89, 92-98, 100-106, 108-11, 113-17, 120, 133, 135, 155-57, 173
Rodford, J.W. 158
Ross, S. 80, 89, 100, 101, 103, 162, 166, 167
Rushdooney, R.J. 143, 164

Sanchez, P. 146, 147
Sandeen, E. 19
Sandquist, T. 146
Scanlan, M. 16
Scharz, C. 189
Schenkel, E. 164
Schroeder, W. 21
Selby, D. 24, 40
Shakarian, D. 32, 49, 92, 95, 97, 106-108
Shawchuck, N. 190
Shelley, M. 190
Shelly, B. 190
Sherrill, J. 26, 98
Simpson, Carolyn 41
Simpson, Charles 1-3, 6, 7, 10, 12-14, 24, 27-35, **34**, 37, 40-48, 51-66, 68, 69, 71, 73, 76-78, 80, 81, 84, 85, 87-92, 94, 99-101, 103, 106, 110, 112, 116-18, 121, 122, **126**, 129, 131-41, 143-47, 150-55, 157-69, **166**, 171, 173, 175-80, **175**, 182-87, 189
Simpson, S. 176
Slosser, B. 100, 105
Smith, C. 6, 113, 114, 155
Snyder, H.A. 4, 84, 85, 152, 179, 185, 189
Spittler, R.P. 49
Stedman, R. 86
Stockstill, L. 188
Strang, S. 38, 158
Street, J.L. 190
Suenens, J. **126**, 136

Sumrall, K. 41, 47, 158, 164, 173
Sumrall, L. 27
Sutton, B. 54, 58, 59, 139, 162
Swaggart, J. 159
Swindol, O. 58
Swindoll, B. 50, **51**
Synan, V. 6, 7, 19, 22, 38, 39, 48, 91, 92, 117, 119, 133

Thurman, J. 147
Tipton, S.M. 19
Tomczak, L. 164, 168

Van Engen, C. 188
Verduin, L. 152, 153
Vinzant, D. 10
Volf, M. 191

Wagner, C.P. 5, 188, 189
Walker, A. 147
Wallace, A. 147
Warner, W. 111
Warren, R. 190
Webster, D.D. 190
Weiner, B. 164
Wesley, J. 4, 82, 152, 189
Whitaker, B. 90, 92, 96, 97, 100-105, 110, 118, 121
Whitefield, G. 4
Widmark, D. 46
Wilkerson, R. 9, 23, 32, 89, 90, 133, 134, 155
Willard, D. 190
Williams, D. 37, 143, 162
Williams, J.R. 24, 116, 160
Willimon, W.H. 191
Wright, S.A. 4, 11, 20, 21, 181, 182

Yeakley, F. 10
Yocum, B. 101
Yoder, J.H. 191

Zelaya, H. 146
Zimmerman, H. 95
Zimmermann, T. 154, 155